Local Elections in Britain

Local elections in Britain are frequently a source of confusion for the general public, journalists and academics alike. From the complexities of the electoral system through to the election results themselves there is much that is unknown and much that is misunderstood.

Exploring the historical context, the structure and method of operation, *Local Elections in Britain* clearly addresses the key issues and confusions that surround the local election system including:

- the nature and extent of electoral participation including the crucial issue of low turnout
- the candidates, and the growing proportion of women challenging for council seats
- the performance of political parties, now a central feature of local elections
- the dangers of viewing local elections as national opinion polls

Drawing on the results of more than 100,000 local elections dating back over three decades the book is the most comprehensive study of local elections in Britain. It will provide the reader with detailed information unavailable elsewhere about the local electoral system as well as confronting the main issues facing a system whose ability to provide democratic and accountable local government has come increasingly into question.

Colin Rallings is a Reader in Electoral Politics. **Michael Thrasher** is a Reader in Public Policy. Both are at the Local Government Chronicle Elections Centre, University of Plymouth.

Local Elections in Britain

Colin Rallings and Michael Thrasher

London and New York

First published 1997
by Routledge
11 New Fetter Lane, London EC4P 4EE

Simultaneously published in the USA and Canada
by Routledge
29 West 35th Street, New York, NY 10001

Typeset in Times by LaserScript, Mitcham, Surrey
Printed and bound in Great Britain by
Creative Print and Design (Wales), Ebbw Vale

British Library Cataloguing in Publication Data
A catalogue record for this book is available from the British Library

Library of Congress Cataloging in Publication Data
Rallings, Colin,
    Local elections in Britain/Colin Rallings & Michael Thrasher.
    p.   cm.
    Includes bibliographical references.
    1. Local elections – Great Britain.   I. Thrasher, Michael.
    II. Title.
    JS3215.R35   1997
    324.941'085—dc21   96–36978

ISBN 0–415–05953–4

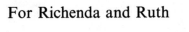
For Richenda and Ruth

Contents

Figures

Tables

x *Tables*

Acknowledgements

When we first planned this book a decade ago the simple truth was that it could not be written. Information about local government elections was both sparse and widely dispersed. Our first task therefore was to compile a data set which would allow the analysis of trends throughout the period from local government reorganisation in the early 1970s to the ever-moving present day. With financial support from the *Local Government Chronicle* we began in 1985 to produce an annual Local Elections Handbook detailing the results of each year's set of local elections. Grants from the Economic and Social Research Council (grants nos. E/00/23/2117 and Y304253002) enabled us to extend this process back to 1973. The data collection bore initial fruit in 1993 with the publication of *Local Elections in Britain: a Statistical Digest* (Plymouth: Local Government Chronicle Elections Centre). This volume sets out the electoral history of each local authority in Great Britain on one easy-to-read page, and was produced with the aid of a further grant from the Arthur McDougall Trust. The raw material for this, containing candidates' names and results from more than 100,000 local elections, has been deposited at the ESRC Data Archive at the University of Essex as the British Local Elections Database where it may be accessed by all bona fide researchers.

Elections buffs were satisfied with the data they had to play with, but many others suggested to us that they needed a guide to enable them to see the wood from the trees. This book is our initial attempt to make some sense of the processes by which local elections have changed and developed in the last two decades. The time and facilities to carry out the analyses were provided through another grant from the ESRC (grant no. R000234540), although they, as we, will be only too aware that we have barely scratched the surface. Our aim on this occasion has been to produce a book which is comprehensive, accessible and does not assume too much prior knowledge or statistical expertise on the part of the reader. We believe that that is our obligation given that most of the data it contains are being put in the public domain for the first time. There are still many questions to be asked about local elections, some of which we address in shorter, academic articles which are referenced at appropriate places in this book. There may even be a 'theory of local elections' to expound. The present volume lays the groundwork for that activity.

Needless to say we have accumulated a large number of debts in the course of writing this book. To explain the detail of everybody's contribution would take up too much space, so we simply thank for their varying efforts (and apologise to whomever we may have inadvertently left out): Mark Besley, John and Hugh Bochel, Bill Bush, David Butler, Brian Cheal, Rob Clements, David Cowling, Phyllis Craig, David Denver, Crispin Derby, Christine Gunter, Paul Jeffery, Peter Kellner, Adrian Lee, Michel Le Lohé, John Mark, Michael Temple, Paul Wilder, Alan Willis, Caroline Wintersgill, John Woollard.

Colin Rallings and Michael Thrasher,
August 1996

1 Local elections – a case of mystery, intrigue and neglect

Local elections in Britain are a mystery to the general public, intriguing to the media and somewhat neglected by academics. There are good reasons for all three of these assessments. Most of the electorate are puzzled about the local government system for the simple reason that it is puzzling. The structure is already complex and recent structural changes will only serve to add to that complexity. In 1991 the government established a Local Government Commission for England. At the same time it asked the respective Secretaries of State for Scotland and Wales to review the local government structure in those countries. There followed wholesale structural changes in both Scotland and Wales with the replacement of a two-tier system by all-purpose or unitary authorities. In England changes have been piecemeal, resulting in a local government structure which comprises a mix of single- and two-tier authorities. The cycle of local elections is an intellectual challenge in itself. Some authorities have elections when others of the same type do not. There are even occasions when, within a single local authority, electors in some wards are able to vote in an election but their neighbours in adjacent wards, literally across the street in some cases, are not. At least with general and European elections every elector realises something is expected of them, even if some still prefer not to exercise their right to vote.

Arguably, the British local government system is as much of a mystery to the electorate in the 1990s as it was when it was reorganised more than twenty years ago. Before 1973, local government in England – excluding London which had been reorganised in 1964 – consisted of 48 county councils, 79 county boroughs, 285 municipal boroughs, 491 urban districts and 415 rural districts, not to mention approximately 10,000 parish councils and meetings. Many of these authorities were extremely small, with fewer than half the county districts having populations above 20,000 (Redcliffe-Maud and Wood 1974). The position in Scotland and Wales was no less complex. Reorganised in 1929, Scottish local government consisted of 33 county councils alongside 4 all-purpose councils of cities which covered the major population centres of Glasgow, Edinburgh, Aberdeen and Dundee. Below the counties were some 21 large burghs, 176 small burghs and 196 district councils. The pattern in Wales resembled more the

English structure with a varied collection of county boroughs for the cities and a two-tier structure of county and district authorities elsewhere. Throughout the 1950s and 1960s various reviews of these structures were undertaken and although there was consensus about the need to reduce the number of authorities opinion remained divided over the specific direction reform should take.

The reform debate was dominated by the general feeling that local government should become more efficient, effective and democratically accountable: that an essentially Victorian structure should be transformed into something able to respond to the needs and demands of the late twentieth century. It was also believed that local government needed to be streamlined, that it should be much easier for ordinary citizens to understand its structure, functions and finances. While reorganisation in the early 1970s certainly reduced the number of directly elected authorities, from more than 1,300 to just over 400 in England alone, an opportunity to simplify the electoral system was missed. As we shall show later, the existence of different electoral systems, coupled with a new and strange structure, served merely to confuse voters and frustrate efforts to persuade them to identify strongly with these new authorities. More than twenty years after the system was reformed the evidence from opinion surveys confirms that the public are often ignorant about the functions carried out by local authorities and puzzled about the allocation of responsibilities between the various tiers of local government (Widdicombe 1986c; Lynn 1992; Parry *et al.* 1992). Despite this confusion, the electorate is then asked to play its part in the local democratic process. When large numbers of electors choose to abstain rather than engage in this process, it is local government which is blamed and local democracy which is perceived to be weak. Strangely, those who created this Byzantine folly in the first place receive little censure.

Large sections of the media share this state of ignorance with the general public but here the imperative of producing copy or preparing a broadcast is such that they feel the need to develop 'an angle' while simultaneously concealing their own confusion. The approach normally pursued is a response to the standard questions – what can these local elections tell us about the next general election/the future of the Prime Minister/the current state of the parties, and so on. We would not wish to deny the value of such questions nor, indeed, the appropriateness of using local voting data to detect changes in national trends. The problem is that the media often seem obsessed with such an interpretation and appear indifferent and oblivious to all else. Local elections have become nationalised to the extent that the media seem unconcerned about their consequences for local council control, the conduct of local authority business or the effects on local services. Naturally, this upsets many people who want to view local elections as precisely local elections and not merely as surrogate indicators of developments in national politics. Commenting on media coverage of the 1981 elections, for example, Jones and Stewart remarked, 'It did not enter into the minds of most commentators that these results were from *local* elections, and that in some cases people were voting about the behaviour of their local councillors' (Jones and Stewart 1983: 16, emphasis in original). This sense of frustration is echoed by many who feel that the media's failure to broaden its election coverage to accommodate local influences and effects does local government and the political system a disservice. That said, the quality of local election coverage by the press and broadcasters alike has improved markedly over the past decade. There are a number of factors, some technological, some attitudinal, which have allowed a broader media agenda. Local broadcasting organisations, particularly the BBC's own network of radio stations, have certainly helped to strengthen the local interpretation of such elections. Nevertheless, the relevance of local elections for national politics is still a dominant theme for the media.

SURVEY DATA

The study of local elections and electoral behaviour by academics has similarly been patchy. Given the healthy state of electoral studies in Britain we might have expected local government elections to be a topic of extensive scrutiny and analysis. Unfortunately, survey data, used as a major source by political scientists because it explores individual attitudes and voting behaviour, has largely been missing as a resource for local electoral studies. Opinion polls generally ask questions about national, not local, voting intentions. Funding for academic surveys of attitudes before, during and after general elections has been secured. Those data have proved invaluable in helping us to understand some of the essential dynamics of electoral behaviour in Britain. Similar surveys, set in the context of local elections, have only rarely been conducted and never in the same depth as their national equivalents. Compared with the amount of survey data on parliamentary elections, that specifically concerned with attitudes to local voting is minuscule. Ironically, far more is known and written about individual-level voting behaviour of Britons at elections for the European Parliament, despite the fact that even fewer people participate in these than in local elections (Atkinson and Braunholtz 1996; Franklin and Curtice 1995; ICM 1994; Reif (ed.) 1985).

The main demand for surveys of specifically local attitudes has come from government appointed committees of inquiry, with a very few commissioned purely for academic research. The Maud committee, which investigated management in local government in the 1960s, published findings from its own survey of the local government elector but little of this report dealt with voting behaviour (Maud 1967). Amongst the findings that did relate to voting attitudes, however, the committee's survey found that men (as opposed to women), middle-aged respondents and those in professional and managerial occupations were more likely to take their responsibilities as local citizens seriously. The research also found a core of electors who appeared either uninterested in or ignorant about local government. For such people the electoral process was of little importance or too complex to understand (Maud 1967: 72–82).

Smaller scale opinion surveys conducted within individual local authorities produced virtually identical findings. The public were generally ignorant about the local government structure, the administration of services and the methods for raising local taxes (Birch 1959; Bealey and Bartholomew 1962; Bealey *et al.* 1965; Budge 1965; Budge *et al.* 1972).

It was not until the mid-1980s that another government sponsored survey of public opinion was carried out, this time for the Widdicombe committee investigating the conduct of local authority business. In addition to a series of questions designed to examine the public's awareness of local government and its services, the survey also sought clues about attitudes towards local voting. One of the more interesting findings from this study was that while most voters' partisanship did not vary between local and national elections it did for a sizeable minority of about 20 per cent of respondents. This led to the conclusion that 'there is some scope for the impact of local influences on local voting' (Widdicombe 1986c). In short, roughly one in five voters viewed local elections as more than just an annual general election.

Further evidence that some voters have evolved different party allegiances according to the electoral context can be gleaned from various opinion polls. A poll conducted for the *Sunday Times* in 1984, for example, noted that Labour's lead over the Conservatives increased by 8 per cent when respondents were asked about local voting intention rather than how they might behave if a general election was being held. In a survey conducted by National Opinion Polls (NOP) in 1987 a similar local electoral advantage for Labour of 7 per cent was found (Gyford *et al.* 1989). A more recent NOP survey conducted before the 1994 local elections confirmed these earlier findings with approximately one in five supporters of the three main parties revealing that they were either undecided about supporting their national party or had already decided to switch their vote to a rival party at the forthcoming local elections.

Survey data can also be a useful way to explore public opinion over time. A survey conducted in 1990 (Bloch and John 1991), for example, replicated some of the questions from the Maud survey. These data give an opportunity to study what had happened to attitudes over a twenty-five-year period. Compared with the 1960s the public appeared more cynical about local politicians. In 1965, 56 per cent of respondents agreed with the statement 'The people you vote for say they'll do things for you, but once they're in they forget what they've said'. By 1990 67 per cent agreed. Interestingly, the proportions agreeing with the statement 'Local council elections are sometimes so complicated that I don't really know who to vote for' were exactly the same at 29 per cent in both surveys (Bloch and John 1991: 34–5). Local government reorganisation in the 1970s, therefore, had clearly not had the effect of simplifying the electoral process in the minds of electors.

As well as monitoring changing attitudes over a long period surveys can also be constructed so as to measure short-term fluctuations in opinion. Such a technique was employed in one of the few book-length studies on the subject of local elections in Britain. Miller's *Irrelevant Elections?* (Miller 1988) ingeniously used evidence from the first survey conducted on behalf of the Widdicombe inquiry and combined it with a follow-up poll carried out after the May elections in 1986. Altogether some 65 per cent of the original sample of 1,145 respondents were interviewed again. The use of two surveys allowed Miller to construct a panel of respondents and to test for any change in their attitudes over a six-month period and, more importantly, to examine the relationship between attitudes to local voting and voting itself.

Using these data Miller addressed such questions as whether local election outcomes reflected attitudes to local or national politics? Did local voters concern themselves with the concept of local autonomy? How did their assessment of local government performance affect their voting behaviour? Amongst the main findings were that while some groups, principally the elderly, better educated, and middle-class respondents, expressed a positive attitude towards local voting, such differences were less noticeable when it came to actual voting. Although a majority of voters often abstain in local elections Miller found that there were few voters who consistently abstained. While a third of respondents said they voted for the candidate rather than the party in local elections a majority indicated little interest in local politics. Such work is immensely valuable in identifying those sections of the electorate more likely to vote or abstain in local elections and in exploring the impact of individual attitudes on behaviour. Ultimately, however, survey data should form but a part of any serious investigation of local voting. Generally speaking they tell us little about local election results, the nature and state of party competition, the characteristics of candidates and councillors, the nature of the electoral cycle, the operation of the electoral system and much else. Such topics can best be analysed using aggregate voting data.

AGGREGATE DATA

One of the first (and almost the last) major studies of local voting to use actual election results was published thirty years ago. *Voting in Cities* (Sharpe (ed.) 1967) presents a series of case studies of the 1964 local elections in boroughs such as Bradford, Exeter and Wolverhampton. It examines the state of party competition, the characteristics of candidates and councillors, the nature of local campaigns as well as the election results themselves in terms of turnout, ward marginality and electoral swing. Although specifically concerned with one set of elections, a number of contributors drew on their local knowledge and available electoral statistics to provide the reader with a fascinating account of the evolution of party politics in some local authorities. Hill's study of Leeds (Hill 1967), for example, gives aggregate vote shares for the three main parties in that borough dating back to 1945, analyses local councillors in terms of years of service, and shows how the electoral system helped distort the relationship between votes and seats. Published in an age with no personal computers to help process the data it represents a remarkable achievement of data collection, organisation and analysis. Technologically speaking we have moved on a great deal since and it is surprising, not to say disappointing, to discover that Sharpe's book still remains the sole example of its type. Austin Ranney's comments on the utility of aggregate data analysis remain pertinent. He wrote:

> the availability and inexpensiveness of aggregate data invite replicative and comparative studies on a wide scale. . . . Aggregate election returns are the 'hardest' data we can get, in the sense that their meaning and comparability vary less from area to area, from time to time, and from study to study than do most survey data. . . . Whatever complex socio-psychological processes may underlie the voter's decisions to make particular allocations, the votes themselves constitute a basic medium of political exchange. Thus their relative 'hardness' as much as their accessibility, makes election returns a significant body of data for political analysis.
>
> (Ranney 1962: 96)

A number of shorter pieces of aggregate data analysis have been published, however, which all serve to show that local election results can prove an invaluable source of data for electoral analysis. Some of these studies have concentrated on specific sets of local election results, concerned with describing winners and losers, reporting vote shares, changes in council control and assessing the dominant electoral issues (Bristow 1981; Bartley and Gordon 1982). More detailed analyses of specific local election cycles have also featured in books whose main purpose has been to provide a record of ward by ward results. Bochel (firstly John and later his son, Hugh) and Denver, for example, have published the results of all Scottish local elections since 1974 and in each of their books there is a chapter of analysis and summary tables covering such topics as candidature, party competition, turnout, changing party vote and seat shares (Bochel and Denver 1974 onwards). While Bochel and Denver systematically covered the Scottish results the treatment of local elections south of the border was piecemeal. Results for elections in London have been published but until the early 1960s these reports contained summary data only and little, if any, commentary (see Minors and Grenham 1994).

For many years, outside London there was no systematic publication of election results and coverage was restricted. There was, for example, a guide to voting in Greater Manchester produced prior to the inaugural elections held in 1973 (Clark 1973) and the same author went on to publish a similar guide to the 1977 county elections (Clark 1977). An investigation into the viability of the six new metropolitan county councils contained an analysis of voting patterns in those authorities from 1973 to 1981. The study observed that voting patterns and electoral swing were fairly uniform across these authorities and concluded that national, rather than local factors were most influential in deciding the outcome (Bristow 1984). It was not until the 1985 local elections, however, that something comparable to the Scottish election series was produced for England.

Starting in that year we published the results of the English county elections (Rallings and Thrasher 1985) and since then have expanded our election coverage to all types of local authority elections in England and Wales. Later (Rallings and Thrasher (eds) 1993), we published a statistical digest of local election results for all authorities in Great Britain which recorded summary aggregate data for each and every cycle of local elections held since 1973.

Interest in local voting statistics has also led some researchers to more specific types of inquiry. The practice of using multimember electoral divisions in British local government has facilitated research into the effects of ballot structure on voting patterns. One study (Upton and Brook 1974) examined the relationship between a candidate's position on the ballot paper and the level of voter support. This was followed by another piece of research (Denver and Hands 1975) which focused on the spread of votes amongst candidates from the same political party. As we shall show in later chapters complex local government ballot structures continue to be a useful source for observing patterns of voting.

Another relatively popular topic has been the possible relationship between levels of local taxation and voting behaviour in local elections. The most favoured approach has been to address the question of whether voters react negatively to a party seen as responsible for raising local taxes. While research on councillors has often found them to claim concern about the electoral impact of their actions (Gregory 1969; Hampton 1970; Newton 1976), analysis of the tax/vote relationship has proved more difficult. A study of four sets of elections in London over a ten-year period, for example, found rate increases related strongly to a party's electoral fate for only one set of elections (Ferry 1979). Typical of this type of analysis are the conclusions reached by two studies conducted in the early 1980s which identified very little relationship between rate increases and local voting behaviour (*Economist* 1980; Bristow 1982). More recently Gibson (1988) has cast doubt on the method employed by earlier researchers. His argument has been that it is wrong to focus on seat changes when investigating the effects of taxation and better to measure vote change. Using this approach suggested that 'rate changes are a statistically significant determinant of local election results' (Gibson 1988: 205). The community charge or 'poll tax', which replaced the rates, was primarily intended by the government to strengthen any relationship between voting and taxation. At the 1990 local elections when this proposition was first tested in England a study for the *Economist* observed 'the poll tax could yet achieve the principal aim for which it was designed' (*Economist* 1990). A more technical analysis of the possible effects of the poll tax on party vote shares was less confident in its conclusion, remarking simply that the relationship was stronger in Conservative controlled London boroughs than in their Labour equivalents (Gibson and Stewart 1992). Our own analysis of the 1990 elections led us to conclude that 'the poll tax was not itself the prime cause of the variation in results either between types of local authority or individual councils' (Rallings and Thrasher 1992a).

Another important application of local voting data has been in the investigation of factors affecting electoral turnout. Addressing the issue of why so few people vote in local elections has, of course, significant implications for the role and status of local government in a modern democracy (Rallings *et al.* 1994; Rallings and Thrasher 1994). Research has targeted a number of variables which might improve our understanding of electoral participation. Some studies have highlighted the importance of local party organisation and its effectiveness in publicising the existence of local elections (Bulpitt 1967; Pimlott 1972; Pimlott 1973). Others have concentrated on the effects of canvassing and campaigning by parties and the extent to which the targeting of voters has an impact upon their willingness to participate in the election (Brown 1958; Bruce and Lee 1982; Bochel and Denver 1971; Bochel and Denver 1972). A different line of inquiry has been to focus on the candidates themselves to see whether differences in race or gender have any impact on turnout (Spiers and Le Lohé 1964; Studlar and Welch 1988). Ward marginality has also been seen as an important variable, with highly marginal wards possibly generating fierce party competition and thus greater public awareness and higher turnouts (Fletcher 1967; Newton 1972). Yet another focus has been to look at individual ward characteristics to see whether these have any relationship with levels of turnout (Taylor 1973; Dyer and Jordan 1985; Rallings and Thrasher 1990; Rallings and Thrasher 1994). Does, for example, the relative affluence of a ward affect levels of electoral participation? Is there a neighbourhood effect such that turnout in some wards is higher because surrounding wards have a history of high turnout? How important is electorate size – are wards with small populations more likely to witness greater public involvement in their elections than wards with large populations? Are electors who live close to a polling station more likely to vote than those who live further away?

Aggregate voting data can also be used to support or counter the findings gathered from survey data. Repeatedly, as we noted above, opinion surveys have asked people to reveal attitudes to local and national voting. Some respondents have said they think differently about parties in terms of electoral context but do they actually vote differently? The evidence, using aggregate data, suggests that they do. An analysis of local voting in two cities in the 1950s and 1960s showed then that while the operation of national influences accounted for almost three-quarters of the electoral swing the remainder appeared to be a function of influences operating only at the authority and ward level (Green 1972). In 1979, when the general election was held on the same day as the local elections, it became possible to compare voting patterns in both sets of election. One study found that voters in rural areas were more likely to cast their vote differently in the local and general elections than were those residing in urban areas (Waller 1980). Another calculated that up to one million more voters supported the Liberals locally than had supported them in the general election (Steed 1979). Such an estimate is borne out by a study of voting in Liverpool which revealed widespread defections from Labour and the Conservatives to the Liberals when voters were electing councillors and not Members of Parliament (Cox and Laver 1979). In short, survey and voting data concur that a proportion of voters do cast their ballot differently in local and national elections. Survey and voting data, however, do not agree on all aspects of local electoral behaviour. As we shall show later, in recent years the outcome of each May's local elections have been forecast better using an extrapolation of real votes cast in local by-elections than by relying on individual voting intentions as reported to opinion pollsters.

This brief review of the research literature demonstrates how studies using aggregate data have shed light on some important aspects of local elections and electoral behaviour. Arguably, the main obstacle to more extensive and detailed academic research has been the absence of comprehensive data. Before the widespread use of computers, collecting literally thousands of local election results and then analysing them was virtually impossible. Even as computing power became more widely available the sheer scale of the task involved in converting several years' worth of results into a machine-readable format has remained an important barrier to analysis. The relative neglect by academics, therefore, has largely been the result of the practical difficulties involved in data collection and processing rather than any intrinsic lack of interest in the study of local elections.

LOCAL ELECTIONS AND THE POLITICAL SYSTEM

Local elections provide us with important indicators about the state of local government. Concerns about the health of local democracy can be addressed by comparing past and present levels of voter participation, the extent of competition and contestation for council seats, the role of non-party, minor and fringe party candidates, and other related issues. Controversy, both national and local, often forms a backdrop to local elections and the way in which the electorate responds can have a crucial impact on policy. The 1990 local elections, for example, were dominated by the poll tax issue and their outcome played a critical part in the subsequent abolition of the tax (Butler *et al.* 1994). Similar, though more local, controversies have dominated election proceedings in different authorities at different times. During the 1980s, for example, when legislative changes to local government finances provoked fierce opposition, some authorities, including Lambeth and Liverpool, held elections which effectively became plebiscites on the issue of central government's right to alter the rules for raising local revenue.

To a significant degree we should talk of the local political system in the plural rather than the singular. Each local authority's elections are affected by local issues and the peculiar local application of national issues. While national trends do operate, and the growing party politicisation of local government indirectly contributes to that picture of uniformity, important differences continue. It is still possible, for example, to observe local elections in what are effectively one-party-dominated authorities taking place alongside other authorities where party competition is fierce and the result always in doubt. Over time the impact of increased party competition combined with a more volatile local electorate, has meant that more local authorities than ever before are 'hung' with no single party enjoying an overall council majority. The nature and outcome of local party competition, therefore, is of more than immediate interest, providing us with valuable information about the wider political system and how politicians might have to adapt to changes in their environment. It is interesting to note how local politicians are able to act in ways which their national counterparts would find difficult, if not impossible, to emulate. Though there has been much talk of Labour and the Liberal Democrats declaring an electoral truce to insure against another Conservative general election victory, there is little prospect of such an event taking place. Similar constraints did not appear relevant in the 1993 county elections when a limited electoral pact did, in fact, occur in Berkshire. Equally, national politicians agonise over their reactions were there to be a hung parliament, while in local government councillors have long ceased to worry about the mechanics and have, relatively smoothly, put in place joint decision taking and policy making arrangements. As in so many other ways, local government sets the example for central government to follow.

Local elections can be particularly sensitive to changes in the nature and substance of party competition. National parties and politicians are acutely aware of the value of such elections in charting the ebb and flow of national popular support. In both 1983 and 1987, for example, Mrs Thatcher called a general election one month after receiving what she rightly took to be a clear vote of confidence at the May local elections. In 1991 the local results were sufficiently ambiguous to persuade her successor, John Major, to delay the widely anticipated general election for a further year. Clearly, local voting behaviour can, and should, be analysed within both a local and a national political context. The annual local elections, though a useful measure of the electoral mood, are limited by the fact that they occur only in May. Local by-elections, however, numbering on average some 25–30 contests each month, provide us with a more regular political barometer which reacts to quite small fluctuations in party support. While such elections cannot, of course, replicate the function of opinion polls in probing individual attitudes about politics they can be interpreted in similar ways.

PLAN OF CHAPTERS

This book is a product of the fact that comprehensive data on local elections now exist. It aims to present for the first time a wide-ranging, though preliminary, analysis of local elections in Britain. The information it contains on patterns of turnout and party competition, the operation of the electoral system, trends in electoral support and much else besides has been gathered by us over more than a decade. The commentary identifies some key themes within the local electoral process and comments on their wider relevance for both local government and the political system as a whole. If this leads others to want to explore the data further for themselves, then so much the better.

The first two chapters are necessary scene setters. Chapter 2 takes a historical view and examines those ideas which fuelled the nineteenth-century campaign to democratise local government and the reforms designed to translate theory into practice. Prominent in these discussions were issues of electoral representation, the frequency of elections and how the local franchise should maintain a strong link between taxation and representation. Just as the process of reform became piecemeal so also did the pattern of political development. Using electoral data from elections before the 1970s reorganisation we show that in some local authorities party machines were quickly developed and elections followed a pattern similar to that of the national parliament. In other areas, however, party politics was largely absent and local elections, even until quite recently, were traditionally fought on non-party lines. Such developments, both in ideas and practical politics, have contributed significantly to attitudes about the nature and purpose of local government elections in the modern age.

Chapter 3 is largely a description of the current local electoral system. To begin, we describe the nature of the electoral cycle, the source of so much confusion in the minds of voters and commentators alike. Next we describe how the essential building blocks of the electoral system, local wards and divisions, are constructed. From there we move on to outline the qualifications for voting in and contesting local elections. The sheer volume of local elections means that Murphy's Law – 'if it can go wrong it will go wrong' – will probably be evident more often than in national elections. It is not uncommon, for example, for local contests to finish in a dead heat or for local elections to be the subject of legal cases involving electoral malpractice. We examine a number of recent cases which have helped expose weaknesses in the electoral system.

The following six chapters consider the related themes of voters, candidates and parties. In Chapter 4 we explore electoral turnout, comparing Britain with other systems in order to test the conventional wisdom that voters here are relatively indifferent to local elections. A number of different lines of inquiry are used to address this issue. One important source of information is survey data which examine voter participation at the individual level. In addition we will use aggregate data, at the ward and authority levels, so that we may uncover any possible structural influences on turnout. Our aim is to identify those circumstances operating at individual, ward and authority level which appear to increase or decrease the level of participation in local elections.

Chapter 5 looks at candidates and councillors in local elections. One important measure of the health of local democracy has traditionally been the overall level of contestation for council seats. Large numbers of uncontested seats are seen as evidence of a lack of public interest in the work of local government. We will examine the different rates of contestation, both over time and across different types of local authority, in order to shed light on this important aspect of local democracy. Elected councillors are largely expected to carry out their duties without proper remuneration or other kinds of support. By measuring the rate of turnover amongst councillors, whether from defeat at the ballot box or other causes, we can begin to observe the electoral advantages, if any, of local political incumbency. At the same time we can also discover whether councillor turnover operates at a level that might threaten continuity of membership in local authorities. Two important considerations in discussions about the state of democracy in Britain are the under-representation of women and that of people drawn from ethnic minorities. We are especially able to examine here the electoral relevance of gender differences amongst candidates and councillors. Local elections and authorities appear generally to offer more favourable conditions for women to become actively involved in politics. Any analysis of their relative success in contesting, and winning, local elections has clear implications for the wider debate on gender equality in British politics.

Chapters 6, 7, 8 and 9 each deal with different aspects of the impact of parties on local elections. The changing nature of party competition is the main theme of Chapter 6. Fought over relatively small constituencies, sometimes a mere thousand electors, local elections offer ideal opportunities for parties and less formal political groupings to enter and become established within the political system. As no financial deposit is required from candidates, unlike the £500 required from those wishing to contest parliamentary elections, conducting a local election campaign can be a relatively inexpensive business. Since reorganisation, the nature of party competition and thus the party system has changed dramatically. In the first few years following legislation local elections were dominated by two-party (Conservative and Labour) politics. The appearance of the Social Democrat party and its subsequent partnership with the Liberals in the early 1980s transformed the shape of electoral competition virtually overnight. Following an acrimonious split between elements in the two parties in 1987 a new party, the Liberal Democrats, emerged from the ashes, and it has been joined in the contest for local council seats by other parties, representing the interests of the Far Right, Far Left and alternative visions of the political future. In both Scotland and Wales the respective nationalist parties continue to challenge for council control. This extension of party competition has led to a decline in the combined vote share for the two major parties, and a complex pattern of council composition for many authorities. In Chapter 7 we trace the way in which votes have been distributed over time in the different parts of British local government and examine the importance of the relationship between vote shares and seat shares in structuring electoral outcomes.

Chapters 8 and 9 focus more specifically on the political parties themselves. Chapter 8 charts the ebb and flow of electoral fortune for each of three main political parties – Conservative, Labour and the Liberal Democrats and their various previous incarnations. For Labour and the Conservatives our interest lies in how the base of their support in local government has changed and the extent to which their performances still tend to mirror each other. One of the most important electoral features of the past twenty-five years has been the growth in support for centre parties. The Social Democrats and the Liberals grew out of quite different political traditions but together formed the Alliance in 1981. Organisationally, the SDP were essentially a national party without local foundation while the Liberals could rely on strong roots in local government. We will explore the extent to which such organisational differences affected their respective development at the local electoral level. Subsequently the Liberal Democrats have made an impact which amounts to one of the biggest and most rapid advances by any political party contesting local elections. In 1995 they became the second largest party in terms of both seats and party control of councils in Britain.

In Chapter 9 we examine the fortunes of candidates standing for minor parties or, as in the case of many Independents, for no party at all. There has been a traditional view that parties have no place in the activities of local government and the decline in the number and success of Independents has been a great source of regret for its adherents (Maud 1967: 110–1). Although local elections still offer much better opportunities for Independents than can be found at the parliamentary level, party politicisation of local government has undermined their role, even in rural areas. Minor parties also experience difficulties in combating the superior organisation and campaigning of the major parties. Nevertheless, as we shall show, there are still areas of the country where minor party candidates as well as Independents have successfully challenged the dominance of national parties.

In Chapters 10 and 11 we return to the main question addressed by Miller and others – should we treat local election outcomes as reflecting voter concern with local or national issues? Chapter 10 considers the degree to which local elections can be treated as the outcome of local issues and controversies. In every electoral cycle there are invariably some authorities which appear to buck the national trend and where election results are influenced by dominant local factors. In the 1994 London borough elections, for example, the Liberal Democrats captured control of Kingston upon Thames but lost Tower Hamlets; Labour in its turn lost Waltham Forest but won boroughs such as Ealing and Croydon; the Conservatives, although in aggregate losing heavily in both seats and council control across the capital, improved their position in Richmond on Thames and successfully defended Westminster and Wandsworth. Such results seriously undermine the case for treating local elections as little more than a large-scale national opinion poll. Focusing exclusively on the consequences for the broader national picture is to ignore the vitality and variety clearly present within the local electoral process.

Chapter 11, however, addresses the same question from the opposite perspective and examines whether, and how, local election results reflect national politics and electoral trends. For some time we have investigated the extent to which contests for local council seats can be used as pointers for future parliamentary elections. The raw materials used in this exercise have been local by-elections together with the annual diet of local election results. The use of by-elections to monitor the fluctuations in national party support can be set alongside opinion polls which regularly ask the public a question along the lines of, 'If there were a general election tomorrow, which party would you support?' The accuracy of such polls has been questioned recently but there can be little dispute that they are effective in capturing broad trends in public opinion (Rallings and Thrasher 1993b; Curtice 1996). In Chapter 11 we show the extent to which results from local elections can similarly be used to measure national voting patterns.

In the final analysis, of course, local elections have both local and national outcomes. How well or badly a party performs has implications for both its political stake in local authorities and its status nationally. In Chapter 12 we consider the consequences of voting in terms of such outcomes. The idiosyncrasies of our 'first past the post' electoral system are well known at the national level. What is little understood is its effect in individual local authorities where wards with relatively small electorates determine council composition. Differences between a party's share of votes and seats have sometimes been large and these have had implications for the size of majorities on those local councils. In some cases the distortion is such that virtual 'one party states' are created with the inevitable decline in morale and competition for the other parties denied fair representation. The degree of disproportionality in local council composition will be examined as parties are variously over- or under-represented in seats by the operation of the electoral system.

Over the past decade, however, the electoral grip of the two main parties in many local authorities has been effectively broken. The number of councils with no single party in overall control has increased considerably. Coalition government is now very much a fact of life for many councils and councillors but inevitably, in the first instance, political tensions were prominent. Originally, both Labour and Conservative politicians were hostile to the idea of sharing power with another party. Labour councillors were even forbidden by the national party to join local coalition administrations. In most cases such prejudices proved short lived, however, and when the traditional two-party grip on local government did not return as expected a more tolerant attitude began to prevail. Now coalition government, of varying degrees of formality, operates in councils throughout Britain. Moreover, the implications of such changes for national politics cannot be ignored. Parties which find themselves sharing power in local government will have their attitudes to coalition in national government influenced by such experiences. In this way local election outcomes which might, in the first instance, have been significantly influenced by national issues could, in their turn, influence future national events.

In our final, concluding chapter we raise a number of questions and issues by way of setting a future research agenda. Local elections have been a relatively neglected area of academic study but with more voting data becoming available it is an appropriate time to identify some key themes and normative issues which might form the basis of further inquiries into the nature of local electoral behaviour in Britain. What, if any, is the relationship between the electoral and policy processes? Can local politicians claim a mandate when elections are determined partly by national, partly by local issues? Do councillors with apparently impregnable majorities behave differently from those for whom the slightest shift in electoral opinion will see them voted out of office? If we acknowledge that low turnout is a problem for local government what remedies are there for improving that situation? Does the local electoral system require overhaul? Is the current system ill-suited to the kinds of responsibilities increasingly expected of local government? If it is, what should replace it?

2   The evolution of local democracy

INTRODUCTION

The concept of local democracy is highly valued in the public imagination. Although constitutionally subordinate to a sovereign parliament it would be unthinkable for central government to challenge the principle of a democratically elected system of local government. Surveys of public opinion regularly report that a majority of respondents claim to vote in local elections when the reality is that less than half the electorate actually do. It is indeed a powerful political symbol when citizens conceal the truth for fear of appearing to fall down on their civic responsibilities. Despite the steady erosion of local government's powers, particularly since 1979, even radical reformers have steered away from a direct confrontation with the elective principle. Support for democratically accountable local government, therefore, lies deep within our political culture. It occupies this position largely because of its historical development. Like other British political institutions local government has evolved its traditions, rituals and legitimacy over a considerable period of time.

   The aim of this chapter is to examine the evolution of local democracy with particular reference to the place of elections and voting. It will begin by focusing on the ideas put forward by Victorian reformers who were the architects of a 'system' of local government. We will examine the arguments in favour of directly elected local authorities, noting the dissenting voices which demanded that the power of elected representatives should be balanced by some proportion of non-elected councillors. Another favoured method for controlling the pressure released by a democratic electoral system was to pay close attention to the length of the electoral cycle. Throughout the nineteenth century those wanting annual elections to maximise accountability debated with those wanting a longer cycle in the belief that too frequent elections would deter the 'right sort' from standing. The complexity of current local arrangements is, in large part, a reflection of the conflict and compromise which characterised this debate more than a century ago. Democratic local government required an electorate, of course, and various extensions of the franchise were introduced to strengthen the association between local taxation and the right to vote. The Victorians were as concerned to stop people from voting when they had no financial stake in the public policies resulting as were those advocating the principle of a community charge more than a century later. What was the correspondence between theory and practice as local government developed under the Victorians and beyond? In the final section we look at the way in which the local electoral process evolved and became increasingly influenced by the growth of party politics. As it developed local government sometimes reflected, sometimes led changes in the national political system.

LOCAL DEMOCRACY AND DIRECT ELECTION

The origins of modern local government can be traced to the 1830s. These were prompted by the Great Reform Act of 1832 which broadened the franchise for the House of Commons. Extending the parliamentary franchise merely created the anomaly of a democratic parliament with, arrayed underneath, an outmoded and motley collection of parishes, corporations and other antiquated forms of local administration. Critics of this corrupt, inefficient and largely non-elected system had been given a reform momentum on which to build. After 1832 the problems of municipal government became politically important for two reasons. First, wealthy patrons withdrew financial support from the boroughs once their power to affect directly the composition of the House of Commons had been reduced. Second, although legislation had extended the parliamentary franchise to the large industrial towns, many of these had poorly developed systems of local administration, and in some cases had no local authority at all. Press attacks on the unreformed system began in earnest with *The Times* protesting:

> The most active spring of election-bribery and villainy everywhere is known to be the Corporation System. The members of Corporations throughout England, are, for the most part, self-elected and wholly irresponsible but to themselves alone. They have contrived by a dextrous series of manoeuvres to oust the inhabitants, for whose benefit the Charters were originally granted, of all right of succession to their own benefit the funds of which they were lawfully but trustees. There is scarcely an instance of any town sending representatives to Parliament where the Mayor, Aldermen etc., have not regularly seized upon, or clutched at, the nomination of the Members, and, if induced to it by opposition, where they have not, without scruple, mortgaged the town estates or wasted the capital, to find means for the most iniquitous and barefaced corruption of voter.
> (*The Times*, 25 June 1833, quoted in S. and B. Webb 1963, vol. 3: 755)

There was certainly the will to introduce reform; only the means remained to be resolved. In the vanguard of a new reform movement came followers of the political philosopher, Jeremy Bentham. The leader of a group which became known as the 'Philosophical Radicals', Bentham's views were to influence a generation of philosophers, notably J. S. Mill and, more importantly in terms of local government reform, political activists anxious to translate theory into practice. The most celebrated of these activists was Edwin Chadwick, the inspiration behind the 1834 Poor Law Amendment Act and later the 1848 Public Health Act. The ideas underpinning this legislation can be readily identified in Bentham's writings, principally his Constitutional Code (Bentham 1843). The Code was a blueprint for a future state and contains Bentham's detailed thoughts about the optimum structure and organisation for a system of democratic local government. Before it was completed, however, Bentham died and evidence suggests Chadwick himself completed parts of the scheme (Everett 1966). Although Bentham advocated the concept of a unitary state he believed the needs of particular areas should be met by some form of sub-national government. Below the national legislature, therefore, he recommended a system of sublegislatures. 'By sublegislature, understand a political body exercising under the authority of the legislature, either as to the whole or as to a part of its logical field of service, functions of the same nature as those of the legislature' (Bentham 1843: 640). Local government, therefore, was to be a minor version of central government, faithfully reflecting its organisation and methods of management and administration. Bentham was firm in his advocacy of democratically elected government. Stung by an earlier government rejection of his scheme for a model prison system, Bentham concluded that those in authority must be made to conform with the public interest. A process of direct election was thought to be the most suitable mechanism for ensuring such compliance. Legislatures, at all levels, therefore, should be elected annually by secret ballot by voters who would qualify for the franchise by virtue of age and literacy. A strict regime of attendance on the part of elected members would be required and unexcused absences would result in the member concerned having to vacate their seat (Peardon 1951).

Support for annual elections conducted by secret ballot featured prominently in the campaign to expand the parliamentary franchise and was reiterated by some of those supporting local government reform. In 1834 the Royal Commission on Municipal Corporations found widespread dissatisfaction with the system of non-elected municipal authorities 'where powers are subject to no popular control and where acts and proceedings being secret, are unchecked by the influence of public opinion' (Municipal Corporations Commission 1835). As with the Poor Law Commission report, largely authored by Edwin Chadwick, the strategy of the Philosophical Radicals was to pack the Royal Commission with political sympathisers, thereby guaranteeing that the official report would concur with Bentham's theories. In the case of the Municipal Corporations Commission, Chadwick's equivalent as political driving-force was Joseph Parkes, a Birmingham solicitor and ardent Benthamite. The Commission would, in time, investigate a total of 285 corporations and produce over three and a half thousand pages of evidence. Before the work had begun, however, Parkes revealed his desire to get to grips with the 'rascally corporators' (Buckley 1926) and the inquiry duly responded.

These rascally corporators were eventually undermined by the 1835 Municipal Corporations Act, but before that legislation was passed, a dispute arose over the timing of elections. J. A. Roebuck, for example, believed in an extensive system of local elections and, in the case of administrative and legislative functionaries, annual election. His primary motive was to reduce the opportunities for political corruption (Roebuck 1835). Parkes himself favoured a system of triennial elections, believing this would still permit electoral accountability whilst establishing some degree of legislative continuity (Parkes 1835). In the event there was a compromise. Local councillors would be elected for three years but one third of the council would have to seek re-election every year. Not for the last time the local electoral structure would reflect more the reality of political bargaining and less a carefully crafted and logical idea.

Before the Bill bringing in the municipal corporations could proceed, however, it had to pass through the House of Lords, where another ambush on its democratic credentials awaited. There, a former Conservative Lord Chancellor, Lord Lyndhurst, proposed an amendment that a portion of the council should be appointed as aldermen for life. After considerable debate the government adopted another compromise – one third of the council would be aldermen. These would be selected by the elected councillors and would sit on the council for a six-year term. Parliamentary opinion was clear – too much local democracy too soon might produce a tyranny of the majority. Some form of stabilising influence was considered necessary and it was thought that aldermen would provide this.

Although reform covered many of the towns and cities the principle of elected local government was not extended to rural areas, where the appointed Justices of the Peace reigned supreme. In fact, vested interests succeeded in preventing a reform of rural England until the late 1880s. While a modicum of local democracy had been established, controversy persisted. An extensive debate was conducted about the need for checks and balances within the new local democracy. From 1850 to 1888 no less than nine Parliamentary Bills were introduced, all differing in their recommendations (Leach 1888). What fears were expressed about the growth of local democracy? Chief amongst the complaints was that the 'wrong sort' were being attracted to public office. George Brodrick, for example, commented, 'elections supply ample proof of the fact that local busybodies, with no qualification but the capacity of active canvassing, constantly prevail against candidates of the highest ability and mature experience' (Brodrick 1883: 702). Brodrick was not alone in expressing such sentiments. His close friend, George Goschen, introduced a Bill which would have reserved seats on the council for local magistrates (Goschen 1872) while William Rathbone and others believed the important powers of any future county councils were sufficient reason for wanting a third of the council to be selected by the magistrates (Rathbone *et al.* (eds) 1885).

Yet another scheme for diluting the principle of direct election was devised by Lord Edmund Fitzmaurice, later to win the backing of Charles Dilke as President of the Local Government Board. Fitzmaurice's scheme argued for a directly elected council but one which would also contain the Lord Lieutenant and local Members of Parliament (Fitzmaurice 1882). When legislation setting up the new county councils and boroughs was finally presented to Parliament in 1888 the government avoided a nominated element on the council, favouring instead an extension of the aldermanic principle. According to Walter Long, who as Parliamentary Secretary at the Local Government Board guided the Bill's passage through the House of Commons, having a mixed elected and nominated element together on the councils would prompt 'odious comparisons'. The hidden subtext, however, appears to have been the belief that the sheer size of the proposed county authorities would be such as to discourage from standing all but those individuals with considerable free time to devote to council duties (Petrie 1936). In this way legislators could be seen to extend the principle of local democracy at the same time as keeping potential troublemakers out of the governmental system.

Others were fiercely opposed to any relaxation of the elective principle. While Mill admired the practice of magistrates sitting as ex-officio Guardians on the Poor Law Boards, he was not prepared to depart from the concept of a fully elected local council (Mill 1968). Another observer claimed aldermen had become a 'malign influence' and that to extend the system was to create a 'selected gentry' (Leach 1888). The debate attracted the attention of liberal academics. As Edward Freeman, Professor of History at Oxford remarked, 'in bringing in an elective system, it is better to do it thoroughly, and to trust to the good sense of the present magistrates to come forward for election like other people, and to the good sense of the electors to choose them when they deserve it' (Freeman 1888: 603). Despite such views the Liberal Unionist, Joseph Chamberlain, supported the aldermanic principle claiming: 'in the vast majority of cases, the election of aldermen does secure the presence of experienced men in the Council, and of many men who, having done a great deal of public work are unwilling to undergo the continual fatigue and annoyance of public election' (Hansard 1888, v.324, c.1363). Significantly, the Liberal MP Henry Fowler supported the principle of selected members as a convenient way of rewarding individuals for services to the community. In 1894 Fowler, then President of the Local Government Board and himself a former mayor and alderman of Wolverhampton, would ignore his earlier advocacy and refuse to extend the aldermanic principle to the urban and rural district councils. Such debates revealed Victorian uncertainty about the advantages of local democracy and these would be echoed in further arguments about the frequency of local elections.

THE ELECTORAL CYCLE

Frequent elections were seen as providing the electors with more influence. The choice appeared to be one of annual versus triennial elections. For some, however, the 1835 compromise of annual election for a third of the council had been a success. The liberal-minded *Westminster Review* claimed, 'At all events frequent elections are the best specific yet discovered for the prevention of apathy, stagnation, and jobbing in the governing body, and the promotion of life and intelligence in the governed' (Leach 1888: 283; Acland 1882). But the political tide was running against such sentiments and the idea of less frequent elections grew more popular. Rathbone, protesting about electoral exhaustion, claimed, 'Even a man with comparative leisure found it extremely difficult to take an interest in the numerous elections which now take place' (Hansard 1888, v.326, c.1843). Continuity of council membership proved a central plank of the case against annual elections. Chamberlain, while supportive of a close relationship between electors and councillors, thought this should not be at the expense of consistent local government. Briefly, the government appeared to relent in favour of more frequent elections, supporting biennial elections for a third of the council but the scheme was dropped after it was claimed it would increase 'the power of canvassers and wire-pullers' (Boyle 1888: 258–9). This fear of electoral engineering appears to have persuaded the government in favour of triennial elections for the entire county council although even this system still evoked fears that such elections would become 'emotional events' decided by a single issue or that council policy could be disrupted by these occasional visits to the electorate. Selected aldermen were also to be permitted on the new county councils.

The need to appease diverse opinion thus delivered a local electoral system which contained contradictory elements. While the towns and cities were elected by thirds on an annual basis, the new county councils were to be elected *en masse* every three years. An element would not be elected, but rather selected, by the remaining councillors. Such inconsistencies were to remain in place until the 1972 local government reorganisation, and, in the case of different electoral cycles, would survive to the present day. The earlier faith in annual elections had taken a pounding in the middle part of the nineteenth century. Violence and corruption were common at local elections and it was argued that their increased frequency would simply exacerbate the problem. The middle classes' fear of Chartism and growing working-class radicalism quelled the urge for more frequent testing of public opinion. While these factors were undoubtedly present they were seldom expressed publicly. Instead, the debate fixed on three main issues. First, there was the need to maintain continuity of council membership. Second, reformers were concerned that too much turnover amongst council members would be bad for consistent policy making. Third, and not least, was the fear that suitably qualified councillors, able to take on the expanded administrative responsibilities of county government, would be dissuaded from seeking office if they had to place themselves regularly before the electorate. With hindsight, it seems that debates about the breadth and frequency of local elections were driven more by views about the electorate, actual and potential, than the advantages and disadvantages of differing electoral systems.

THE LOCAL FRANCHISE

It was not until the 1945 Representation of the People Act that the franchise in local and national elections became identical. Before then the local franchise had, in some ways, been more restrictive than the parliamentary voting qualification. The essential difference between the two franchises related to payment of local rates. For nineteenth-century reformers there was a critical relationship between taxation and representation. Various Acts defining the franchise were quite specific about the need to maintain this link between payment for local services and the power to elect the stewards of such budgets. The local franchise, therefore, developed into a curious mix of enlightened attitudes set alongside support for such principles as weighting voting according to an individual's local tax burden. In the case of the poor law, for example, there was such intensity of feeling about the need to equalise voting with taxation that in 1818 the Vestries Act adopted the principle of plural voting. Under this legislation those rated at less than £50 would have one vote, while those above this figure were to have an additional vote for every incremental rate rise of £25. There was to be a maximum of six votes. The same Act, however, also said that women could vote in these vestries, although this right was denied married women on the grounds that their husbands would vote on their behalf (Keith-Lucas 1952). Equally enlightened for the time were the terms of Hobhouse's Act (1831) which first introduced election by secret ballot into the constitution. Although not compulsory, it required nothing more than five ratepayers to demand that the open ballot be replaced by a secret one for the scheme to be adopted. In such ways the local franchise developed as both more and less enlightened than its parliamentary equivalent. The reasons for these differences are worth exploring in a little detail because they provide an important historical context for contemporary discussions about the nature and purpose of local elections.

The Reform Act of 1832 extended the vote to various types of leaseholders, copyholders and householders. The people brought onto the voting register were likely to be small landowners, tenant farmers and shopkeepers. Three years later the franchise for the Municipal Corporations Act was introduced and critical differences between the two franchises appeared. First, the period for qualification under the parliamentary franchise was one year while in the case of the local franchise it was over two years. Second, freemen who could vote in parliamentary elections were not eligible for local elections. Third, the local vote was given to all resident ratepayers, regardless of amount, but the parliamentary franchise specified a minimum of £10 per annum. Fourth, the parliamentary franchise allowed some people to qualify under certain types of age-old precedents related to tithes and taxation, for example, 'scot and lot' voters and 'pot wallopers' (Keith-Lucas 1952). These differences clearly affected the size of the respective voting registers.

By analysing 39 boroughs where parliamentary and local boundaries coincided Keith-Lucas was able to study the electoral differences produced by these franchises. Overall, the number of parliamentary voters on the 1837 registers was 53,134 while municipal voters numbered 45,958. The picture, however, was far from uniform with some boroughs having more local than parliamentary voters. Stockport, for example had 1,278 electors on the parliamentary register but 3,320 on the municipal register. The variability between the registers appears to have been related to two main factors. Where the parliamentary register was larger, there was a greater number of freemen on the electoral roll. Where the local electoral register was larger, the preponderance of ratepayers paying less than the £10 qualification for the parliamentary vote accounted for the difference. Excluding people from the local voting register appeared to be a matter of no representation without taxation. That said, there was no attempt to limit the application of that principle, unlike the parliamentary franchise which by having the £10 ratepaying limit effectively made an association between voting and the supposed quality of the electorate. In general, the Victorians were clearly unconcerned about the discrepancy between the qualifications needed to vote in local and general elections.

Another important area where differences were permitted was that of female emancipation. Women were not given the right to vote in national elections until the 1918 Representation of the People Act and even then the franchise was restricted to those aged 30 and over. Universal adult suffrage was not achieved until 10 years later when the 1928 Representation of the People (Equal Franchise) Act was introduced. In respect of votes for women the local franchise was more enlightened than its parliamentary equivalent. As we noted earlier, independent women ratepayers were given the vote under the Sturges-Bourne Acts of 1818 and 1819 but this had applied only to parish vestries. In 1869, however, women were given the vote following an amendment to the Municipal Franchise Bill instigated by Dr Pankhurst (Keith-Lucas 1952). A subsequent court case, however, established that the vote should be restricted to single women and could not include the wives and daughters of ratepayers. Two years before this legislation John Stuart Mill had argued in the House of Commons that denying women the vote breached the principle of no taxation without representation and periodically thereafter various attempts were made to give women the parliamentary vote (Seymour 1970).

This period, therefore, helps us to understand the respective thinking which lay behind the composition of the local as opposed to the parliamentary franchise. In the case of local voting the relationship between taxation and representation was much more to the fore than was the case with the parliamentary franchise. It is not entirely clear why this view was so dominant. It might have been a case of national politicians tolerating codes of conduct in local government which they would have found intolerable when applied to the country as a whole. There is, however, a clue to Victorian thinking in the work of J. S. Mill. Although an advocate of votes for women it was Mill's views on plural voting which encapsulated the implied relationship between local democracy and local taxation. Defending the existence of plural voting (i.e. the greater the tax burden, the more votes for the individual) Mill wrote,

> the honest and frugal dispensation of money forms so much larger a part of the business of the local than of the national body, that there is more justice as well as policy in allowing a greater proportional influence to those who have a large money interest at stake.

(quoted in Keith-Lucas 1952: 27)

It should be noted that local government expenditure was at this time greater than that spent by Whitehall and that it was not until the first decade of the twentieth century that the balance changed. Nevertheless, Mill was expressing a commonly held view that local democracy was buttressed by a strong association between taxation and representation, even though that might permit such practices as plural voting and give women a political voice. With the merging of the two franchises following the Second World War, although the business vote survived as part of the local franchise until 1969 (Byrne 1985: 281), this distinction was subsumed beneath the wider claims of universal adult suffrage. It could be argued that this Victorian view of the local government franchise never fully disappeared. Mrs Thatcher's support for the community charge was a resurrection of this fundamental idea of binding spending to voting.

In many ways Victorian reformers were taking an enormous risk. Local authorities accounted for the bulk of total government expenditure and elections were unpredictable in their outcomes. It was unclear what sorts of people would put themselves forward for election. Would the 'right sort' be deterred from standing for fear of being rejected by local ratepayers? The growth of parties, while overcoming some of the organisational problems, opened up new difficulties. The fear was that candidates who had party and not community at heart might serve the wrong interests. Voters too were an unknown quantity. Associating local voting with ratepaying was supposed automatically to impose spending restraints on elected authorities but there was no accounting for bribery and corruption by unscrupulous candidates. Government, therefore, learnt to keep a watchful eye on the fledgling local democracies before extending their scope and powers still further.

DEMOCRACY IN PRACTICE?

The evolution of local democracy and the development of political parties have been inextricably linked. To a considerable extent the latter helped determine the pace and direction of that evolution. Gyford, Leach and Game (1989) divided one hundred and fifty years of local government into five stages of party political development – diversity, crystallisation, realignment, nationalisation, and reappraisal. The first of these stages, 'diversity' lasted from 1835 to the late 1860s and was characterised by a multitude of local parties and deep schisms within them. Such parties were as immature as local government itself. The hopes for a democratised system of local government were slow to materialise. In MacDonagh's view, what was accomplished by the reforms of the 1830s was simply, 'a great deal in terms of "civil and religious liberty" and egalitarian principle, but almost nothing in terms of day-to-day living' (MacDonagh 1977). It was his view that the municipal corporations became little more than vehicles for a newly vitalised party struggle which came at the expense of administrative improvement. The belief that corruption would be driven out by the elective process proved short-lived. By the middle of the nineteenth century the borough councils were accused of jobbery, nepotism and other corrupt practices just as their non-elected predecessors had been (Cole and Postgate 1961).

In truth, local democracy existed in name only. Extensions of the local franchise and elected councillors were fine in theory but the practice was less than impressive. By 1851, for example, only 3 per cent of Birmingham's population were eligible to vote in municipal elections (Hennock 1973). Sceptics, such as the libertarian lawyer and polemicist Joshua Toulmin-Smith, expressed serious doubts about the role elections played in providing popular control over elected officials. He advocated regular and open public meetings to combat the secrecy of many municipal authorities (Toulmin-Smith 1851). There were, however, some local authorities which prospered under the new democratic regime. Progressive local authorities such as those in Liverpool and Glasgow expanded their powers through Private Acts of Parliament (Cole and Postgate 1961). In Birmingham the great experiment in what became known as 'municipal socialism' gathered momentum under the leadership of Joseph Chamberlain and many of the more enlightened authorities began to follow these innovations.

There followed a period of party 'crystallisation' which lasted until the turn of the century. As the structure of local government was consolidated and expanded local parties became better organised. One of the most dramatic improvements came in the management of elections. For politicians the reform of local government provided new opportunities and challenges. The expansion of the electorate, albeit on a small scale, gave the impetus for the development of local party machines, capable of canvassing and mounting viable election campaigns. By the end of the nineteenth century some of these parties had adopted practices seen in parliamentary elections and were able, at least in the more urban authorities, to conduct competitive elections (Fraser 1976). On occasions, however, local parties demonstrated their electioneering inexperience. Keith-Lucas recounts how, in the elections to school boards, a system of cumulative voting was employed. This gave each voter multiple votes up to the number of available vacancies. The voter could distribute these votes amongst the candidates as they thought fit, either spreading them evenly or awarding them all to a single candidate. In Birmingham, the Progressive party led by George Dixon and Joseph Chamberlain fielded fifteen candidates, one for each vacancy. The opposition, instead, fielded a smaller slate of candidates, thereby concentrating its support. Although the Progressives had greater numerical strength they actually won fewer seats (Keith-Lucas 1952).

The reformers' tactic in opting for an electoral system which would not deter the right kind of people from standing succeeded. In the urban municipal boroughs, for example, most seats were contested by the main parties and by the turn of the century most of these authorities were controlled by one political party or another (Redlich and Hirst 1970). In contrast, the shire counties and smaller urban and rural districts appeared void of candidates sporting party labels. Here 'Independents' dominated, quite often in the person of the local squire or large landowner. In the first round of county elections no fewer than 131 peers of the realm were returned. Rural local government continued prominently to feature non-party candidates, and in a handful of areas this persisted almost to the present day. One estimate of Independent strength on the county councils suggests that during the period 1949–70 their numbers never fell below 26 per cent of all councillors, reaching a peak of 33 per cent in 1964 (Gyford and James 1983). Nevertheless, as early as the 1870s the Conservative party at least had begun to interpret local election results in terms of likely parliamentary contests and 'with the creation of the first county councils in 1889 party managers from both camps began to see such contests not merely as indicators but as useful dress rehearsals for subsequent general elections' (Gyford *et al.* 1989).

This century there have been three stages of party political development. By the end of the nineteenth century local politics had become dominated by the Conservative and Liberal parties. This dominance was to be contested in a period of 'realignment' which saw the Conservative–Liberal contest joined by the fledgling Labour party. Over a period of forty years from the beginning of the century the Labour party gradually replaced the Liberals in many parts of the country, but principally in the urban authorities. With the growth of Labour the scope of party competition grew and brought further complications. Suddenly, local parties became engaged in formal and informal alliances as means were sought to block the path of their new opponents. In Wolverhampton, for example, local Liberals formed electoral pacts with Conservatives to frustrate Labour's advance (Jones 1969). Elsewhere, the Conservative party was content to allow candidates to use ratepayer associations as a front, believing that subsequent administrative cooperation with Liberals in the battle against Labour was facilitated by using a non-partisan title (Young 1975). Despite such tactics the Labour party began to flourish in some local authorities. Labour councillors doubled in number between 1914 and 1919 (Gyford *et al.* 1989). In London the party won half the borough councils in the 1919 elections and in 1934 gained control of that highly prized target, the London County Council (Thompson 1967). Labour's success mirrored the Liberal decline. Losing heavily in the 1919 elections the Liberal party continued to lose seats steadily throughout the next decade. By 1929 Liberals were almost a spent force and accounted for just one in eight of all candidates in that year's local elections (Cook 1975).

To an extent, however, the pattern of party development reflected important urban/rural differences in local government. An analysis of voting in four counties during the 1930s shows that in elections to the county councils the majority of councillors were returned unopposed. Within the boundaries of these counties were autonomous county boroughs where the level of contestation was much higher. In terms of turnout the county councils once again compared unfavourably with the county boroughs. In none of the contested county divisions did the turnout rise above 30 per cent but in the county boroughs more than two-thirds of contested seats had turnouts in excess of that figure (Self and 'Administrator' 1947; see also Denver and Hands 1977). A study of municipal elections throughout the 1920s revealed a similar picture with turnout averaging some 52 per cent in these more urban authorities (Rhodes 1938). Immediately after the Second World War electoral turnout in the county boroughs still averaged around 50 per cent but fell back again the following decade (Newton 1976). Such examples help illustrate the vital connection between the growth of party and the development of local democracy. In rural areas, where party politics was less visible, more seats went uncontested and turnout was invariably lower than in the more party-politicised urban authorities.

At the end of the Second World War there began a period of 'nationalisation' of party politics which would last until local government reorganisation in the 1970s. During this phase attempts were made to bind national and local parties together in a series of organisational changes. The party politicisation of local government continued, but only to the point where in 1971 just over half of all councils could be counted as partisan in the sense that more than half their councillors sported party labels (Gyford *et al.* 1989). The conduct of local elections dominated by national political parties raised doubts about the nature and direction of modern local democracy. Local elections, fought on local issues, played out before a local electorate, lay at the core of Victorian reform thinking. More and more, however, local elections fought by national parties appeared to have had an homogenising effect (Bristow 1978) to a point which threatened their 'localness'. Newton, in a study of Birmingham, went so far as to comment,

> The conclusion must be that local factors have a relatively insignificant impact on local election results. In fact, the term 'local election' is something of a misnomer, for there is very little that is local about them, and they tell us practically nothing about the preferences and attitudes of citizens to purely local issues and events. They are determined overwhelmingly by national political considerations. Local elections are a sort of annual general election.
>
> (Newton 1976: 16)

In their analysis of party organisation, however, Gyford and James challenged this view, concluding, 'the distribution of resources is such that neither national nor local politicians can command the loyalty and obedience of their party colleagues at the other level of government' (Gyford and James 1983: 200). Summarising the findings of various case studies of individual local authorities Bulpitt remarked that the 'conventions of party government vary according to local physical, economic and social factors, even local personalities and the history of party politics will play their part in determining the style of local politics' (Bulpitt 1967: 97).

While the local political parties may not have been homogeneous in their outlook and behaviour, the electorate often appeared blissfully unaware of the differences, voting in local elections according to national loyalties. After analysing the 1964 local election results one writer reluctantly conceded, 'There is little support in all this for a theory of local government that is based on the notion of the self-governing community, limited to an area that can encompass the local loyalty of its population' (Fletcher 1967: 321). A panel survey of voters conducted at the same time supported such a view, noting that 90 per cent of respondents stayed with their national party allegiance when voting in local elections (Butler and Stokes 1971). Even so some areas appeared to buck the national trend. A survey of politics in Glossop, for example, suggested a combination of an ill-defined party political conflict together with a dogged resistance by local Liberals contributed to a pattern of local voting which did not conform entirely with the nationalisation thesis (Birch 1959).

The period following reorganisation in the 1970s Gyford, Leach and Game (1989) termed 'reappraisal'. Although this period has seen a decline in the number of non-partisan councils, its most distinguishing characteristic has been, perhaps, a new sense of ideological urgency in local party politics. Local parties have issued lengthy and detailed manifestos and the parties themselves have come to define the way in which individual local authorities conduct their business. A more detailed analysis of this period will follow in subsequent chapters but in electoral terms it might properly be termed a period of dealignment. From 1973 onwards the domination of local government by the two main parties was systematically challenged in the same way that their grip on parliamentary voting was loosened in the two elections held in 1974. In the 1970 general election, for example, the combined support for Conservative and Labour amounted to 90 per cent of votes cast. Four years later it had fallen to just three-quarters of all votes. Over the period between 1964 and 1970 an average of 40 per cent of electors 'very strongly' identified with either the Conservative or Labour parties. By the second general election of 1974, in October, this figure had fallen to just 26 per cent (Denver 1994: 47). An electorate which no longer strongly identified with one or other of the two major parties nationally also appeared more willing to transfer its loyalties when voting in local elections. We might even argue that the party politicisation of local government has come full circle with increasing local diversity replacing a uniform national swing of the electoral pendulum.

CONCLUSIONS

The local democratic tradition has developed over a period of more than a century and a half dating from the 1830s. In that time legislation has tackled the organisation and administration of local government in a piecemeal fashion.

First the rapidly growing towns and cities of industrialising Britain were democratised, followed much later by the more rural areas of the country. The early radical reforms were succeeded by more conservative approaches. The desire to maximise electoral influence was superseded by a greater concern with local government's administrative efficiency and competence. The growth of a national party system came to shape the way in which local democracy manifested itself on the ground. Before party machines became more organised, however, local authorities developed their own particular characteristics and cultures. The peak of this localness probably occurred in the last decades of the nineteenth century before the nationalisation of local politics took a firmer grip in the second half of this century.

But elections are as much about electorates as they are about parties. The detail of the local franchise revealed key assumptions about the nature of local democracy and the role of voting. The link between taxation and representation was clearly perceived. Reformers were acutely aware of the need to use the electoral system to introduce suitable mechanisms for financial accountability. This overarching concern led to some innovations which were enlightened for their time. Ratepayers were enfranchised regardless of their taxable investment. Women were not treated as second-class citizens. But the path of reform also developed in less enlightened fashion. Plural voting, the business rate and the cycle of local elections were all used as measures to buttress the voting power of economic wealth. Such concerns would still not be far away when the time came to shape an electoral system for the new local authorities created by the major reorganisation which took place in the early 1970s.

3 The local electoral system

INTRODUCTION

Describing the local electoral system in Britain is not unlike trying to describe cricket. Most people when viewing a group (usually males) dressed in white and running, standing, or sometimes sitting, in a field will realise that if bats are to be seen and a red ball is in evidence then cricket might be the activity. The deeper elements of the game will, however, remain a mystery to most observers. They will not know about the many ways in which the batsman can be given out. They will seldom have need to discover the intricacies of the law regarding leg before wicket. The concept of a no ball being called when three fielders are situated backward of square leg would be as alien to most humans as it would be to a Martian. It will also be completely irrelevant to them to know that only one of the authors of this book has ever scored a half century but that the other one has accomplished the hat trick. The local electoral system is similarly confusing but there is a crucial difference between it and cricket. Unless one is actually playing or a serious watcher of cricket, a knowledge of its arcane laws is very much an optional extra for the vast majority of people. Local elections, however, are a key aspect of the democratic process and their outcome affects us all. Even if we choose not to participate in them, an understanding of their character and rules ought to be readily accessible. Currently it is doubtful whether this is the case.

Britain has an irregular, rather than uniform, local electoral system. While many people might be aware that local elections are held each May, the majority would be ignorant about which authorities are holding elections in a particular year. More confusing still is the fact that in some cases elections covering only part of the council area are held at any one time – an election in one ward does not necessarily mean an election in every other ward. Moreover, the cycle and timing of elections, though crucial to public participation, is but one part of the overall system. There is, in addition, the question of how the electoral units are devised for each election. Which body is responsible for the creation of local wards, what criteria are used to construct ward boundaries and what sorts of consequence flow from these activities? Then there is the matter of the election itself. Who is qualified to vote in local elections and, just as important, what qualifications do people require in order to stand as a candidate in local elections?

While the answers to some of these questions are, admittedly, of only passing interest to the average voter, those intimately involved in the local democratic process should demonstrate greater awareness. Yet, over the years, we have fielded enquiries even from the local authority associations themselves seeking guidance on the operation of *their* electoral system. Moreover, as we shall see later, there have been frequent occasions when local parties have been unable to contest wards because of a failure to deliver their nomination papers in time. Similarly, seats have been won by a party only for the election to be declared void because the winning candidate was below the statutory age for qualification as a candidate. The purpose of this chapter, therefore, is to outline some of the essential features of the current local electoral system. We begin by describing the electoral cycle, noting how different local authorities use different methods for electing their councils. Second, we consider how local electoral boundaries are constructed. Given that parliamentary constituency boundaries are built from the aggregation of smaller local wards, the procedure for creating those wards takes on added significance. In a third section we examine the qualifications required to become either a voter or a candidate in a local election, highlighting those factors which might disqualify an individual from each. Finally, we describe the organisation of local elections, the electoral timetable and what happens when the process does not run according to plan.

THE LOCAL ELECTORAL CYCLE

Major reorganisation of local government in Britain took place in the early 1970s, except for London where the process had occurred a decade earlier. The new system contained two administrative levels. In England and Wales the upper tier consisted of 47 shire counties and 6 metropolitan counties while in Scotland there were 9 regional councils (and 3 unitary Islands councils). The lower tier in all three countries was the district council – 333 shire districts in England and Wales, 36 metropolitan boroughs and 53 Scottish districts. This structural pattern replicated the earlier London reforms which had created the Greater London Council (GLC) as an upper tier with 32 London boroughs as well as the City of London as lower tier authorities. This structure remained in place until 1986 when the six metropolitan counties and the GLC were abolished. More recently local government has been restructured in Scotland and Wales and parts of England. In both Scotland and Wales a system of single tier, or unitary, authorities has been introduced with the first elections to these authorities conducted during 1995. In England, four administrative counties have so far been abolished – Avon, Cleveland, Humberside and the Isle of Wight. In each case the remaining authorities have become unitary councils, sometimes following the amalgamation of former district councils. Further structural changes will be phased in during 1996 and beyond as the government completes its programme of change instigated by the Local Government Commission.

Reorganisation in the 1970s also determined that each councillor would serve for a fixed period of four years and not three, as had been the case since the 1830s. This change meant that London had to be brought into line with the new electoral cycle. Given that all councillors were now to be elected for the same period of time (the office of alderman was abolished) one method of giving these elections a higher profile might have been to hold them all simultaneously. The reality, however, was a rather complex timetable of elections and different methods for electing councils.

One basic difference among local authorities' electoral arrangements in the United Kingdom has to do with the special case of Northern Ireland. Although local government in the province was also reorganised in the early 1970s it was decided that the simple plurality system, or 'first past the post', would not be applied there. An electoral system which awarded local council seats on a winner takes all basis was seen as divisive in a country where voting followed sectarian lines. In the event the 26 district councils were to elect their members using the single transferable vote (STV). Although STV was first introduced as a temporary measure it was made a permanent fixture of the electoral process in 1977 (Connolly and Knox 1986; Lucy 1994).

Although the simple plurality electoral system is used throughout England, Wales and Scotland, there are a surprising number of variations on this method. One basic difference stems from whether an authority uses single or multimember wards. While each local authority ward has at least one councillor as its elected representative, a significant proportion of wards in Britain have more than one. Unfortunately, from the viewpoint of clear understanding, wards within the same tier of local government, even within the same authority, sometimes have differing numbers of councillors to elect. Currently, for example, there are 759 wards in the 32 London boroughs. Of these wards, just 15 elect one councillor, 330 elect two and 414 three – making a grand total of 1,917 councillors. By contrast, the metropolitan boroughs have a total of 827 wards all represented by three councillors each. In Scotland the electoral system has been a rare example of simplicity. All regional and district wards elected a single-member and this model has been copied in the new unitary authorities. The shire counties in England and Wales at first operated with a baffling array of single and multimember wards (known as divisions), but by 1989 all had been converted to single-member. Wards in shire districts in England and Wales currently range in size from single-member wards to one ward in East Cambridgeshire (Soham), one in South Oxfordshire (Henley) and two in the Forest of Dean (Cinderford and Lydney) which each elect a total of five councillors. The new unitary authorities in both England and Wales have a mix of single and multimember wards.

If the ratio of councillors per ward is one main difference between local authorities, a second is the scope of their elections. Some authorities hold 'whole-council' elections when every council seat becomes due for re-election every four years. Other authorities, including all of the metropolitan boroughs, operate a system of 'partial' elections where a fraction of the council (normally, but not always, one third) are required to stand for re-election. In Scotland there were whole-council elections for both regional and district authorities, with the English and Welsh county councils and London boroughs also adopting a similar method. These procedures were largely a legacy of the nineteenth century when, as we noted in Chapter 2, the county boroughs held annual elections for a third of the council while the shire counties were elected *en bloc* every three years.

Thus far the electoral system would not appear too confusing, but let us introduce a number of qualifications. First, there is the case of the shire districts in England. Under the terms of the 1972 Local Government Act shire districts were allowed to choose between 'whole-council' or 'partial' elections. Currently, approximately one-third operate a system of 'partial' elections with the remaining two-thirds using the 'whole-council' arrangement. Those authorities that employ the partial method will hold elections in each of three years for only some of their councillors. At the end of this cycle there will be a fallow year used to elect county councillors for the area. For those districts using whole-council elections there would only be an election every fourth year, with the county contests falling midway through the cycle. The system was made even more complicated, however, when district councils were allowed to move from one system of election to the other. Since the late 1970s a number of districts, for example Torbay and Tonbridge and Malling, have abandoned the practice of partial elections and now employ the whole-council method: none have opted to move in the opposite direction. This opportunity for district authorities to choose their method of election means that in some areas neighbouring councils of the same type operate with different electoral cycles. The only factor in common is that all councillors sit for a four-year period.

A further cause of misunderstanding relates to those districts which use partial election. In only a minority of cases is the practice of the metropolitan boroughs followed whereby each ward elects three councillors, one at each set of annual elections. More commonly, wards have varying numbers of councillors and thus varying cycles of election. In any one year of the electoral cycle there will be some proportion of the local electorate which does have the opportunity to vote and some which does not. In Exeter and in Bristol we find a further variation on the theme. All wards are two-member, with two-thirds of them – but not the same two-thirds – having elections each year. Moreover, although the new unitary authorities in Wales will all have 'all out' elections, England is to retain its mixed pattern. One unitary council, Hartlepool, has even uniquely been allowed to hold its first partial election – for one councillor in each of 15 of its 17 wards – just one year after its inaugural elections in 1995. It is little wonder that the voters are confused or feel less impetus to participate in contests which are not true tests of opinion across the whole authority.

Another source of confusion relating to the electoral system stems from the fact that the metropolitan and London boroughs, although broadly similar in size, function and status, use different methods of election. As noted above the metropolitan boroughs are organised into wards, all of which are represented by three councillors. These authorities hold partial elections with a third of the council re-elected each year, together with a fallow year, once reserved for elections to the now abolished metropolitan counties. The London boroughs, however, follow the 'whole-council' method. We are left, therefore, with a situation where large cities such as Birmingham, Manchester, Liverpool, Leeds and Newcastle upon Tyne hold elections in years when there are no corresponding elections for London. A case can be made for annual elections and a case can be made for quadrennial elections. Keith-Lucas, however, is adamant, 'There can be no justification whatever for the system used in London boroughs of multimember wards combined with triennial [sic] general elections, for they both deny an annual opportunity to test opinion and help obliterate minority views' (Keith-Lucas 1978: 117). The description above simply confirms that the only consistency about the local electoral system in Britain is its inconsistency.

To try to summarise: during the period 1991 to 1999 the local electoral cycle in Britain is as outlined in Table 3.1. The county councils have elections once every four years, in 1993 and 1997. The metropolitan boroughs hold elections every year except when county contests are due. The London borough elections occur only in 1994 and 1998 because these authorities hold elections for the entire council. Shire districts in England using the 'whole-council' method had elections in 1991 and 1995 and are due them again in 1999. Those using 'partial' elections have, like the metropolitan boroughs, contests in three years out of four. The Scottish regions and districts used to have quadrennial elections in even numbered years. Their successor unitary authorities, and their Welsh counterparts, will have a similar cycle, but in odd numbered years beginning with 1995. The English unitary authorities will continue as a mix between annual and quadrennial elections, with the annual contests not always featuring elections in every ward. Nor is this the end of the matter. Periodically the boundaries of wards are revised and electoral arrangements consequently altered. In these cases it is necessary to re-elect the council on the basis of the new wards and if, as in Colchester in 1990 or in Basingstoke and Deane in 1992, the authority has opted for annual elections it can hold elections for its entire membership in what would normally be a partial or 'off' year.

The question must be asked: is this a sensible arrangement for the conduct of local elections in Britain? To some extent the pattern, if pattern there is, reflects tradition. Many of the metropolitan boroughs and some of the shire districts were, prior to local government reorganisation, county boroughs. Following the legislation of 1835 and 1888 these authorities developed a tradition of partial and annual elections. County councils, however, were established in 1889 with a three-yearly electoral cycle for the whole council. The 1972 Local Government Act clearly wished to honour those different traditions by allowing the new

Table 3.1 The local electoral timetable in Britain 1991–1999

Authority	Year of election								
	1991	1992	1993	1994	1995	1996	1997	1998	1999
County			x				x		
District (whole-council)	x				x				x
District (partial)	x	x		x	x	x		x	x
London borough				x				x	
Metropolitan borough	x	x		x	x	x		x	x
Scottish region				x					
Scottish district		x							
English unitary				x	x	x	x	x	x
Scottish unitary					x				x
Welsh unitary					x				x

authorities to continue with their pattern of election. There was, therefore, a problem of honouring tradition while at the same time making the system understandable. However, since one of the stated aims of the 1972 reorganisation was to facilitate electoral participation, there might have been a greater premium placed on simplicity. It is significant that the recent reorganisations of local government in Scotland and Wales, carried out under the aegis of the respective Secretaries of State, have been far more *dirigiste* in their treatment of electoral arrangements than has the similar reorganisation in England conducted by the independent Local Government Commission. It is a fair bet that this is one area where the English local elector might have welcomed a rational and clear solution being imposed 'top down' rather than a continuing tolerance of sometimes contradictory and always confusing arrangements emerging from the 'bottom up'.

THE DRAWING OF BOUNDARIES

Wards, the units into which local authorities are divided, are the basic building blocks in our local and parliamentary electoral system. Who determines their size and number, and do they then remain unaltered over time? Until quite recently the answers to such questions could be determined by reference to the work of the independent Local Government Boundary Commissions separately established for England, Scotland and Wales. In principle these Commissions had the power to review the areas covered by local authorities and to make changes consistent with 'the interests of effective and convenient local government'. Accordingly, they could recommend the abolition of an authority and its redistribution amongst other authorities. In practice those changes to local authority boundaries which were made were invariably piecemeal and involved small areas of land and relatively few voters.

The principal task of the Commissions was to undertake a periodic review of local ward boundaries. In the late 1970s, for example, the English Local

Government Boundary Commission made wholesale changes to district council wards before moving on to examine ward boundaries in the metropolitan boroughs in the early 1980s. Such a review of the borough and district wards and county divisions, which had been used for the initial elections in 1973 and which had been put in place at that time by the Home Office, had a knock-on effect on electoral arrangements. The work of the Commission was governed by specific rules.

The commissioners, for example, were asked to create electoral divisions within a county which contained approximately equal numbers of electors. Their ability to do this was limited by other demands. County divisions should not cross the boundaries either of the lower tier district councils or of civil parishes. Within these parameters the commissioners were also instructed to construct boundaries which would be easily identifiable, that recognised local ties and that paid at least some acknowledgement to the boundaries of district council wards in the county. Similar conditions were also laid down for the drawing of ward boundaries in Greater London and the London boroughs as well as the district authorities. Conforming with all of these requirements simultaneously often proved impossible for the Commission, with the result that various anomalies arose. In the majority of cases county divisions did cut across district ward boundaries. This has been much regretted by election analysts, among others, who have found it difficult to make comparisons of voting at county and district council elections except at a higher level of aggregation. In some places, principally in the larger towns and cities, county divisions are either congruent with district wards or are aggregations of two or more whole such wards, but these are the exception rather than the rule.

Similarly, the different Boundary Commissions found it difficult to comply with the requirement that wards within counties should approximate to one another in electoral size. Although obliged to take projected population growth into account when proposing boundaries, Table 3.2 shows the extent of variation by 1993 amongst electoral divisions in eleven counties which had been re-warded in 1981 or 1985. Hampshire, for example, contained a division with less than 8,000 voters while another had more than 21,000 electors. In Northamptonshire the largest division contained almost four times as many electors as the smallest. In other words in some counties the voting power of electors in the smallest divisions can be more than three times that of those in the largest. This is not to say the boundary commissions failed to observe their guidelines but rather, to reiterate, that the terms under which they were asked to operate were bound to prove mutually exclusive. This experience closely parallels that of the various Parliamentary Boundary Commissions which face similar difficulties in satisfying apparently contradictory criteria (McLean and Mortimore 1992; Butler 1992; Rossiter *et al.* 1996).

The current organisation of ward boundaries is certainly better than that which the commissioners inherited from the 1972 reorganisation. The practice of dividing local authorities into wards stemmed from the 1835 municipal corporations reform. Conservative politicians, concerned that they might not

Table 3.2 Variations in size of electoral divisions, English counties 1993

	Minimum	Maximum	Standard deviation
Cheshire	7,003	15,202	1,697
Cleveland	3,873	8,541	841
Derbyshire	5,913	14,721	1,403
Essex	8,943	19,647	1,875
Hampshire	7,977	21,265	1,939
Humberside	4,796	12,776	1,233
Lancashire	6,474	17,331	1,744
Northamptonshire	4,517	15,539	2,049
Northumberland	1,878	7,128	1,394
Oxfordshire	3,951	11,656	1,292
Somerset	3,388	9,839	1,673

win any seats if the council was elected by the town as a whole, succeeded in dividing the area into smaller units which became known as wards. In this way concentrations of middle-class voters who might be expected to vote Conservative would ensure the party some representation on the council (Keith-Lucas 1978: 20–1). The additional requirement that these authorities should have annual elections gave rise to multimember wards, often of three or six members. The existence of wards with multiple councillors simplified the task of drawing ward boundaries within authorities, and in some cases enabled authorities to avoid it altogether. Following reorganisation in the 1970s, and before the Local Government Boundary Commissions could properly review arrangements, elections had to be organised for the new authorities. To save time, ward boundaries from the old authorities were used and councillor quotas were assessed according to electorate. This gave rise to some ludicrous extensions of the multimember arrangement. In Table 3.3 we reproduce the 1973 result for the Clitheroe ward of Ribble Valley district council. The ward elected no fewer than ten councillors (there were some examples of twelve-member wards in Beverley) and a total of 31 candidates contested the inaugural election. Unfortunately we do not posses a copy of the ballot paper itself, but it must have been of considerable length. Is it coincidence that the only two non-Conservative candidates to be elected would both have been at the head of the ballot paper? Proponents of a fairer electoral system could doubtless identify any number of other inequities produced by such electoral arrangements.

Such wards were subsequently reorganised, although some examples of four- and five-member wards remain. Although little understood and often ignored, local government boundary reviews are of immense importance for the future conduct of parliamentary elections. While responsibility for the revision of parliamentary boundaries lies with a completely separate set of authorities (the Parliamentary Boundary Commissions for England, Wales and Scotland), the

Table 3.3 Result for Clitheroe ward, Ribble Valley, 1973 elections (ten councillors to be elected)

Candidate	Party	Vote
Turner R.	Con	2,139
Blackburn J.	Con	1,956
Robinson T.	Con	1,909
Ainsworth R.	Ind	1,840
Chatburn C.	Con	1,763
Akker D.	Lab	1,759
Rushton T.	Con	1,755
Todd J.	Con	1,754
Wells L.	Con	1,713
Taylor W.	Con	1,617
Jackson G.	Lab	1,522
Jones B.	Lab	1,502
Foulkes E. Ms.	Lab	1,499
Moore S.	Con	1,489
Steele R.	Con	1,472
Sharples W.	Lab	1,401
Penny E. Ms.	Lab	1,384
Cooper A.	Lib	1,363
Chadwick R.	Lab	1,339
Joynson B.	Lab	1,215
Earnshaw V.	Lab	1,104
Spencer F.	Lab	1,039
Gordin J.	Lib	944
Bradshaw B. Ms.	Lib	921
Aspden J.	Lib	796
Crook B.	Lib	673
Fulton R.	Lib	652
Kay J.	Lib	648
Mellor F.	Lib	636
Kane J.	Lib	603
McCrerie M.	Lib	490

work of one directly impinges upon the work of the other. Parliamentary constituencies are built as amalgams of whole local authority wards. It follows, therefore, that the consequences of any local government ward boundary revisions feed into the next review of parliamentary boundaries. A party which finds itself systematically disadvantaged in an area by the direction a ward boundary line takes will see that disadvantage carried over into any constituency which encompasses that ward. In short, while the results of redrawing wards can be felt immediately in local elections their effects may take a decade to have an impact at a general election.

In 1992 the Local Government Boundary Commission for England was abolished and its functions transferred to the new Local Government Commission. That body's initial task was to conduct a review of the structure of local government in shire England. It has now begun work on a *Periodic Electoral Review* and has published a helpful guide to its approach and procedures (Local Government Commission for England 1996).

WHO CAN VOTE?

The 1945 Representation of the People Act stated that those eligible for the parliamentary vote should also have a vote in local elections. The principle established in the nineteenth century of tying the local voting qualification to occupation and ratepaying was thus finally overturned. Since then there have been a number of alterations to the local franchise and anyone aged eighteen or over can now vote except individuals subject to certain conditions which may disqualify them. These include individuals detained in mental institutions, certain types of prisoner and those who have been convicted of electoral malpractice. The electoral register of persons qualified to vote is compiled by each district authority's Electoral Registration Office. County councils do not compile their own registers, relying instead on those compiled by the constituent districts. An individual may live at more than one address and thereby be listed more than once on the electoral register, although it is, of course, an offence to vote more than once. Electoral registers are compiled each October and come into operation in the middle of the following February.

Normally, the compiling of the electoral register does not generate great interest but in recent years this has changed. In the mid-1980s it was noted that the register was becoming both less and less accurate and increasingly out of step with the separately compiled estimates of population. The register's inaccuracy stemmed from a combination of factors. First, being compiled in October, it was already some months old when it came into effect – time enough for a sizeable number of people to move residence and, of course, to die. Second, some electoral registration officers, in order to save time and money, took to using old registers to make up for the absence of information from their annual registration returns. This resulted in some names being included on the register which should not have been and others who should have been but were excluded (Pinto-Duschinsky and Pinto-Duschinsky 1987; Todd and Dodd 1982). Estimates suggested the electoral register was already 10 per cent inaccurate on the day it became official. Another trend, of a more worrying nature, became apparent in the late 1980s. The introduction of the community charge, or 'poll tax', was linked to a further significant decline in the electoral register's accuracy. The Office of Population, Censuses and Surveys (OPCS) makes its own calculations of the adult population eligible to vote. When these estimates were compared with local authority registers it became clear there was a shortfall in the number of people actually registered to vote. Moreover, this shortfall grew as it appeared that more potential electors anticipated the introduction of the poll tax and made no effort to register. Their motive for removing themselves from the electoral register was clear – the less visible they became as citizens the easier it would be for them to avoid paying the poll tax. The government expected the electoral register to be used to help compile the community charge register and many local authorities soon discovered its utility (Department of the Environment 1986; Wadsworth and Morley 1989). The decline in the size of the electoral register was quite dramatic in some local authorities, particularly in the inner cities, although the fall of 20,000 in the electoral roll in the London borough of Hackney between 1989 and 1990 seems to have had as much to do with the drawing up of a more accurate register (Curtice and Steed 1992). Overall, McLean and Smith have calculated that the total shortfall from the electoral registers in Great Britain as a whole is in the region of six hundred thousand people (McLean and Smith 1995). Arguably the electoral effects of the poll tax legislation will remain for some years to come despite abolition of the tax in 1991.

Following a local election the electoral register is marked in the sense that those electors who voted are identified as such. The marked register is retained for public inspection for a period of six months. Rennard suggests that local parties may wish to study these registers for two main purposes. First, if the outcome was close and a handful of votes separated victor from vanquished, a close scrutiny of the register might reveal illegal voting. Should discrepancies such as someone voting twice or, as happened in one election, dead people apparently managing to put a cross on the ballot paper, then the marked register would be a vital piece of evidence in a legal case. A second reason for studying the marked register is to enable a party to know which electors actually voted and which did not. Cross comparisons with party canvass returns may then reveal potential members or supporters who might require forms for postal or proxy votes at the next election (Rennard 1988: 141–2). From a psephological point of view study of the marked register could also reveal turnout details reduced to the level of streets and the use of census data would facilitate an analysis of any possible relationship between socio-economic status and turnout in local elections (Dyer and Jordan 1985; Swaddle and Heath 1989).

ELIGIBILITY FOR ELECTION

Although individuals are eligible to vote as soon as they reach eighteen years of age, the right to stand for election does not come until twenty-one. At least one further condition from a list has to be fulfilled before an individual becomes eligible to contest an election. The list, as set out in section 79 of the 1972 Local Government Act, can be summarised as follows:

a If the individual is a local government elector for the authority.
b If the individual has, during the previous twelve months, occupied land or other premises in the area as either tenant or owner.

c If the individual's principal place of work during the previous twelve months has been in the authority.

d If the individual has resided in the area for the previous twelve months.

At least one of the above conditions has to be satisfied in terms of both the date of nomination for candidates and election day itself. In Scotland the same conditions operate but the twelve-month period is timed from nomination day only. Each candidate is also required to have a formal proposer and seconder and, in addition, the assenting signature of eight other registered electors of the authority. There have been instances when these rules have been breached and new elections have had to be called. Rennard reports that in the 1986 London Borough elections two councillors were forced to resign because they were twenty-one on polling day but had not reached this age on nomination day (Rennard 1988: 120). A successful candidate in Exeter was taken to court by one of his opponents in 1992 following a claim that he fulfilled none of the criteria (a)–(d) in the list above. The councillor won his case on appeal by arguing that, as he devoted the whole of his time to council work, he could justify calling the Civic Centre his principal place of work even though he resided outside the authority area and was not one of its electors.

INELIGIBILITY FOR ELECTION

Assuming that an individual meets the various conditions set out above it could still be the case that he or she is not allowed to stand as a candidate in a local election. There are a number of reasons why a person may be ineligible as a candidate:

a If the individual holds paid office with the authority.

b If the individual is a declared bankrupt or has made a composition or arrangement with creditors.

c If the individual has been surcharged as a councillor by the auditor for an amount in excess of £2,000 within the previous five years.

d If the individual has within five years before the day of election or since election been convicted in the United Kingdom (and including the Channel Islands and Isle of Man) of any offence carrying a sentence of three months or more (whether suspended or not) without the option of a fine.

e If the individual has been disqualified from office following corrupt or illegal electoral practices.

These conditions are themselves subject to further elaboration and modification within the 1972 Local Government Act. Further restrictions on the political activity of local authority employees were established by the 1989 Local Government and Housing Act. The Act laid down that certain sections of staff working in local government might have access to politically sensitive information and that it was reasonable to make them ineligible for election.

Estimates vary as to the number of people affected by this legislation, but certainly more than 10,000 local authority workers are now disqualified from standing for election even in an authority for which they do not work. Instances of people prevented from standing because of conviction on charges of electoral malpractice are rare, but do exist. In December 1993, for example, the *Sunday Times* reported that a former Conservative mayor had been jailed for six months for fielding a bogus candidate at the 1991 local elections. His intention had been to draw opposition votes to the Independent candidate, thereby easing the path to a Conservative victory. The police were alerted when a local journalist failed to contact the candidate for an interview and a subsequent raid on the defendant's flat revealed campaign literature for the bogus contestant (*Sunday Times*, 20 December 1993).

THE ORGANISATION OF ELECTIONS

Local elections are held on the first Thursday in May unless the Secretary of State makes an order 'not later than February 1st in the year preceding the first year in which the order is to take effect' (Local Government Act 1972, sect. 43). In 1995, for example, the elections to the new Scottish unitary authorities were held on 6 April. Local returning officers and their electoral administration officers are responsible for the organisation of local elections and have to abide strictly by laid-down rules and regulations (Lasham and Smith (eds) 1992). These vary slightly according to whether the election is being conducted in England and Wales or in Scotland. The election proper in England and Wales begins when the returning officer publishes the notice of election, the latest occasion on which this can happen being twenty-five days before the contest. When calculating the number of days leading to an election it is important to remember that certain days are excluded. The term 'days' refers to 'working days' and therefore excludes Saturdays and Sundays, as well as Christmas Day, Good Friday and other public holidays. The next critical date in the process is when candidates lodge their nomination papers with the returning officer. This deadline has often caused problems for local parties. In the 1993 county council elections, for example, two Labour candidates in Cumbria failed to make the deadline, thus missing the election in two critical divisions which the party had won four years previously. As well as jeopardising party chances, such instances of inefficiency may not impress the electorate in other wards. Following the submission of nominations there is a period for 'second thoughts', with a candidate being allowed formally to withdraw before noon on the sixteenth day before the election. The parties must also during this time keep a close watch on the various deadlines for the registration of postal or proxy voters. There are signs that, with a growing elderly electorate, this aspect of electioneering is becoming more developed and parties have until thirteen days before the election to encourage their supporters who do not or cannot vote in person to register for an absent vote. In the event of unforeseen absence there is a further opportunity to apply for an absent vote no later than the sixth day prior to the election.

The polling stations are open from 8a.m. to 9p.m. at local elections, an hour less on either side than for parliamentary elections. The first count is often that of the postal votes and this may take place on polling day or the day before. Postal votes have to be returned in the official envelope which must carry a voter's declaration of identity, signed and witnessed, together with a valid ballot paper inside. Candidates' agents observe the legal niceties and can lodge appeals against the officials allowing or preventing certain votes from being counted. At the count of ballot papers following the election candidates may be present together with a number of agents already nominated to the returning officer. The role of counting agents can be vital to a candidate's chances. Their role is to scrutinise the activities of the officials, making sure a vote for their candidate is properly accounted. Long before the final vote is announced an astute counting agent will have recorded the number of votes from each polling station and by extension the turnout. The electoral fortunes of some parties are closely allied to the overall level of turnout and this act of counting can give an early indication of the final outcome. Where multimember wards exist the actual counting of votes at local elections may be much more complicated than that experienced at parliamentary contests. Imagine the count for the election in the Clitheroe ward described above where 31 candidates contested the ten seats available.

Strictly speaking the election is not over until some time after the votes have been counted. A victorious candidate does not become a councillor until he or she has completed a declaration of acceptance of office. This process must be completed within two months of the election. Complaints concerning the conduct of the election have to be lodged no later than twenty-one days following the election. Complaints relating to the return of candidates' expenses can be made later than this since the business of declaring expenses runs to a different timetable. Candidates are allowed to incur expenses not exceeding £250 plus 3 pence per elector and, unlike parliamentary and European Parliament elections, no financial deposit is required in order to stand. Where a party fields more than one candidate, as in wards with multiple seats, the amount allowed to be spent is reduced. Two candidates are limited to three-quarters of an individual candidate's spending while three candidates can only spend up to two-thirds each of an individual's spending.

WHAT HAPPENS WHEN THINGS GO WRONG?

Local elections appear to attract a fair share of incidents which cause results to be delayed and, in some cases, legally overturned. Part of the explanation for this has to do with the sheer volume of local elections. At the 1992 general election 651 MPs were returned to the Commons. At the 1991 local elections over 12,000 councillors were elected to more than 300 local authorities. Inevitably, with these kinds of numbers, we should expect the occasional hiccup in electoral procedure.

Some of the incidents surrounding local elections require the ingenuity of electoral administrators and returning officers to resolve but others are covered by electoral law and a legal outcome results.

Close results in parliamentary elections are much less common than in local elections. The closest outcome in a parliamentary election was in Ilkeston North in 1931 when just two votes separated the winner from second (Craig 1989: 180). In local elections close results of this order are not unusual (statistically speaking, a smaller electorate will produce closer results and the frequency of close results will be greater because of the sheer number of elections involved) and ties have been recorded. In such an event the process for settling on the winner is legally stated. The returning officer must decide the issue by drawing lots, the winner of which is deemed to have received an additional vote. In the past returning officers have used a variety of methods to settle the issue, including tossing a coin and drawing cards from a pack, but best practice would appear to involve ballot papers marked with the names of the tying candidates enclosed in sealed envelopes and then drawn out by the returning officer. Interestingly, in some local elections in France ties are resolved by reference to the age of the candidates with the elder or eldest being declared the winner (Cole *et al.* forthcoming).

Elections are sometimes postponed because of the death of a candidate and the law is clear about such circumstances. The poll is countermanded and if polling has already commenced it must be abandoned and all papers collected and sent to the returning officer. The last occasion on which a parliamentary election was postponed was in Barnsley in 1951 (Craig 1989: 196). Such examples are, in fact, quite common in local elections. In the 1993 county elections, for example, no less than four elections were postponed (out of a total of 3,500) because one of the candidates had died subsequent to nomination. In every case the rearranged election was held within the thirty-five days as laid down by statute.

Election results can be challenged if there is a suspicion that the law has been broken. Following the 1994 European elections the Liberal Democrats tried to get the result in the Devon and East Plymouth constituency overturned. The basis of their argument was that the nomination of a candidate calling himself a 'Literal Democrat' should not have been allowed because it was too similar to their own party label and caused confusion among the electorate. In the event they lost the case. It is worth noting that in local elections it is common to find candidates with identical party descriptions contesting the same seat and, as far we are aware, no successful legal challenge to this has ever been made. Nevertheless, electoral laws are broken in the conduct of local elections. In September 1994, for example, a former chairman of the Greater London Conservative Agents Association was convicted of forging votes in a local by-election. The offence took place when RPF9 forms were illegally altered changing a request for a postal vote into one for a proxy vote. The matter would have gone undetected but for the fact that the couple who had apparently requested a postal vote changed their holiday plans and decided to vote in the by-election. On reaching the polling station, however, they were informed that they had already voted, or rather that their proxy had voted on their behalf (*Guardian*, 2 November 1994). Further examples of this practice, known colloquially as 'granny farming' because of the tendency of those applying for postal votes to be elderly women living in retirement homes, have been identified but successful prosecutions have been few. In local elections, especially where wards are marginal, electors few and turnout low, some party campaigners clearly find transgressing the rules a considerable temptation.

CONCLUSIONS

Local elections in Britain depend on a complex set of rules and conventions. Some aspects, such as eligibility to vote or stand for election, are tightly prescribed; others, such as drawing up the boundaries of local government wards, are based on mutually contradictory guidelines and thus allow scope for the exercise of influence and discretion. Voters themselves probably ask no more of the electoral system than that it is easy to understand and clearly lays down their role within it. On that dimension it seems sadly lacking. The existence side by side of annual and quadrennial electoral cycles, of single and multimember wards, and of whole-council and partial contests are a recipe for confusion. As in other facets of life, one way to cope with such uncertainty and confusion is to ignore its cause. For local government one manifestation of this may be a level of electoral turnout which is frequently less than half that achieved at general elections in the same area. As the Widdicombe Committee itself commented, 'a system which is as complex and inconsistent as the present one is hardly calculated to encourage electoral participation' (Widdicombe 1986a: para. 7.5). In the next chapter we turn our attention to the much discussed matter of participation in British local elections. How bad is it? What is there that distinguishes those authorities with a record of unusually high or low turnouts? Can anything be done to improve electoral participation?

4   Turnout in local elections

INTRODUCTION

It is popularly assumed that in Britain only about a third of electors bother to vote in local elections. Low turnout is believed to weaken the democratic base of local government – local councillors find it difficult to argue that they have a strong electoral mandate when they have been elected by only a small minority of the adult population. Supporters of the poll tax cited low turnout as a central part of their claim that local government was not properly accountable, and that steps should be taken to strengthen the link between voting rights and the local tax burden. Indeed, compared with other countries within the European Union, Britain does lag some distance behind in a league table of local turnouts. Table 4.1 provides recent illustrative data for sub-national elections in various EU countries and shows a clear gap between this country and our European partners. Although some of these countries have either a legal or quasi-legal regulation to make voting compulsory, this does not wholly explain the disparity. Britain, for example, is the only one of these countries to use 'first past the post' (FPTP) in local elections, while all the others use different forms of more proportional systems. Various advocates of proportional representation (PR) have claimed that its introduction would enhance electoral participation (Lakeman 1974), and academic research has shown turnout in PR systems to be on average some 7 per cent higher than for FPTP (Blais and Carty 1990). We assess the impact of the electoral system in detail in Chapter 12 but here our focus will to be to identify and understand some of those factors, which may or may not be directly related to the particular operation of electoral rules, which contribute to low turnout in British local elections.

At this point, however, it is worth sounding a note of caution. Interpreting local turnout figures is not as straightforward as it might seem. First, turnout may have been higher in the 1970s than our figures indicate. Twenty years ago electoral registration officers did not have the access to computers they enjoy today. This meant that updating the register from one year to the next was time consuming and expensive and in many areas the register was only changed infrequently (Todd and Dodd 1982; Todd and Eldridge 1987; Pinto-Duschinsky

Table 4.1 Average turnout in sub-national elections in European Union

	% turnout
Luxembourg	93
Italy	85
Belgium	80
Denmark	80
Germany	72
France	68
Spain	64
Ireland	62
Portugal	60
Netherlands	54
Great Britain	40

Source: These data were obtained from official sources in all cases. For most countries the most recent sub-national elections have been used to compile the mean percentage. For further discussion see Cole *et al.* forthcoming.

and Pinto-Duschinsky 1987). Thus, people who should have been taken off the register, for example the deceased and those moving and registering elsewhere, were often left on and registers would be larger than they should have been. In such circumstances recorded turnout would have been smaller than it might have been with a more accurate register. More recently the turnout statistics might have been affected in the opposite direction and represent an overestimation of effective participation. In the years leading to the introduction of the poll tax registration officers found more and more eligible voters failing to register and the numbers on the roll thereby falling. On the assumption that those leaving the register would always have been less likely to vote in any local election than those remaining on it, turnout may artificially appear to rise.

Notwithstanding such difficulties turnout in local elections can and ought to be examined in some detail, not least in a bid to shed light on why and when turnout is sometimes high and sometimes low. In this chapter, therefore, the issue of turnout is approached from a number of directions using different types of data. First, we examine findings from surveys which have sought to identify the characteristics of voters and non-voters alike. Second, exogenous factors such as the imminence of a general election are analysed in terms of their relationship with fluctuations in local turnout. Third, differences in turnout amongst various types of local authority will be considered, to identify any possible relationship between electoral participation and local government structure. Fourth, we look more closely at differences between authorities of the same type in order to identify the impact of local political culture on electoral participation. Our fifth section again uses aggregate data but at the ward, not authority level. Variously, we consider the effects of party competition, ward size, and ward marginality on turnout.

TURNOUT AND SURVEY EVIDENCE

Examination of the relevance of individual social and psychological characteristics to electoral participation requires survey data. Given that the majority of electors do not vote in local elections it is, perhaps, appropriate to begin by asking not who votes but rather what sorts of people abstain. Using British Election Study data for the period 1966–1974 Crewe, Alt and Fox (1977) examined the background and attitudes of those who abstained from voting in parliamentary elections. They observed patterns of voting/non-voting across a sequence of four elections, thereby allowing for the possibility that abstention was random, not systematic. Their most significant finding, perhaps, was the absence of what we might call the 'serial abstainer'. A mere 1 per cent of respondents had abstained in all four elections. As the authors note, 'Non-voters in a particular election are not part of a substantial body within the electorate who persistently opt out of elections' (Crewe *et al.* 1977: 47).

An examination of respondents' socio-economic backgrounds revealed only small differences between voters and non-voters at national level. There were, however, three characteristics of some statistical significance. These were associated with a respondent's residential mobility, housing tenure and age. Abstention was greatest among newcomers to an area. The costs of voting, for example, in having to apply for a postal vote or return to a former ward to vote, were greater for such electors and may have outweighed the perceived benefits of voting. Another explanation which would appeal to those who see a strong link between community of interest and local voting would be that newcomers would have had little time to develop local ties and would be less likely to vote than those who had.

The significant association between frequency of voting and housing tenure was not about owner-occupiers versus council tenants but rather between private sector and council tenants. The latter tended to vote because of peer pressure within a well-defined community whereas the former were scattered and not exposed to such influences. In terms of age the association with electoral participation appeared simple, 'the younger an elector, the less likely he or she will vote regularly' (Crewe *et al.* 1977: 56). On closer inspection, however, this relationship had much to do with residential mobility rather than age alone. In short, the younger the respondent, the more likely that person was to be residentially mobile and live in private rented accommodation, with each of those factors contributing to perceived higher social costs of voting. Surprisingly, the analysis did not find any significant relationship between turnout rate and educational attainment which one US study believed to be of 'transcendent importance' in that country (Wolfinger and Rosenstone 1980).

In addition to sociological factors affecting turnout the research also examined psychological effects. Respondents expressing a strong sense of partisan commitment were more likely to vote than were those without. Those who had voted in all four general elections covered by the study were much more likely to be found amongst the 'strong party identifiers' and those who perceived real differences between the parties than amongst those who expressed no interest in the party political struggle and were indifferent to the electoral outcome.

More recent research, by Swaddle and Heath (1989), matching survey data about individuals with the official record of whether or not they voted at the 1987 general election, tends to confirm Crewe, Alt and Fox's findings about the importance of age and length of residence, but, further, claims that class and income are important. They conclude 'the common belief that those in the highest income and status brackets participate most in politics is thus shown to be true after all' (Swaddle and Heath 1989: 549).

Both these pieces of research, although identifying a number of factors related to individuals' likelihood to vote, were concerned with national elections. Would the same conditions and attitudes operate at the local level? Surveys conducted first for the Widdicombe Committee and a second follow-up study commissioned by the Economic and Social Research Council can help us answer that question. The first survey interviewed 1,000 respondents during November 1985 and 745 of the original sample were then re-interviewed in May 1986 in a project led by William Miller. Miller's findings show that 'local turn-out behaviour *does* vary over time, and the electorate is *not* divided into regular local election voters and regular local election abstainers' (Miller 1988: 91, emphasis in original). This is precisely the evidence unearthed in the analysis of general election voting but it is surely of greater significance given the differences in abstention rates between local and general elections. In short, the majority who abstain in one set of elections are not necessarily the same majority who abstain in another.

What of the characteristics of local voters and local non-voters? To a significant extent the findings are compatible with the national data. The propensity to vote correlated with age and length of residence. Older voters were more likely to vote than other age groups while longer-term residents also had better voting records than other groups. The other variable which analysis of parliamentary elections had identified as significant was housing tenure, noting that council house tenants were more likely to vote than those in the privately rented sector. The size of Miller's sample precluded this distinction within the rented sector but it is worth noting his observation that council tenants were more likely to vote than owner-occupiers (Miller 1988: 96). Other things being equal, council tenants have more direct stake in their local authority in the sense of it being their landlord and it should not be too surprising that this greater level of investment should manifest itself in their willingness to vote.

A sense of psychological involvement in politics was also positively correlated with the likelihood of local voting, although it was difficult to distinguish between the local and national dimensions of this variable. Miller found that turnout was closely related to an elector's knowledge of, and interest in, politics. Of those who discussed local politics regularly 74 per cent reported actually voting in the elections compared with a 46 per cent turnout amongst those who never discussed local politics. There was also a strong correlation between turnout and those who could correctly identify their local councillors (Miller 1988: 98). Yet, interestingly, there was little evidence to suggest the pattern of participation would have the effect of skewing the results of any election in favour of a particular party or class. Miller is keen to emphasise that the minority who do vote is 'almost perfectly representative of the full electorate in terms of partisanship and issue attitudes' (Miller 1986: 143).

At the level of the individual, Miller's analysis of local turnout patterns is clearly the most extensive and sophisticated yet undertaken. A person's age, length of residence and sense of psychological involvement in local politics and the strength of their party identification all appear critical factors in determining the propensity to vote. Miller suggests, however, that while these variables correlated well with turnout they are not necessarily good for predicting turnout itself. The reason for their weak predictive ability appears to stem from the instability of the party identification variable. The process of partisan dealignment, a weakening in the intensity of support for the political parties, has effectively injected a degree of instability into the whole question of a person's sense of party identification. We can no longer be certain that people who identify strongly with a party at one interview will necessarily respond in the same way at a subsequent interview. In short, predicting local turnout on the basis of survey data has become more of a problem than it once might have been. In subsequent sections we shall see whether an analysis of aggregate, as opposed to individual, level data can provide an insight into levels of local electoral participation.

EXOGENOUS INFLUENCES ON LOCAL TURNOUT

The 40 per cent level of local turnout which places Britain firmly at the bottom of the EU league is, of course, an average figure. There is evidence that the actual level of turnout in any year can be heavily influenced, both positively and negatively, by external factors. In 1979, for example, Prime Minister James Callaghan called a general election for the same day as the local elections. Turnout in the local contests naturally rose as electors took advantage of a rare opportunity, though the percentage voting in the national election remained higher than the local in most of the areas where they were concurrent. The proximity of a general election, perceived or otherwise, also has an effect on local turnout. Turnout is above average in years when local elections immediately precede an anticipated general election – see Table 4.2, p. 53 – falling back quite sharply the following year. In both 1983 and 1987 Mrs Thatcher used the local elections as a test of her government's popularity before calling a general election. In 1991 John Major made it clear he too was contemplating a summer general election and turnout rose once again, although on this occasion the results were such that the Conservatives put back the election for another year.

General elections, however, can also have the opposite effect and serve to depress local turnout. Examination of turnout in district and metropolitan council elections reveals slumps in the years subsequent to a general election. On some occasions there even appears to be a widespread epidemic of voter fatigue. One of the lowest turnouts in the metropolitan boroughs came in 1975 after the electorate had been asked to vote in two general elections the previous year. In 1992 the general election came just one month before the local elections and that fact was reflected in turnout. The English shire districts recorded their lowest ever turnout with little over a third of voters being prepared to make a return visit to the polling stations. The metropolitan authorities had an even lower turnout, with voter fatigue possibly compounded here by frustration among Labour voters convinced that general election defeat had been snatched from the jaws of victory.

This is not to say that overall local turnout can only be increased or decreased because of the proximity of a general election. The introduction of the poll tax in 1990 proved to be a considerable stimulus as normally placid citizens took to the streets to protest at what they viewed as an unfair method of raising local taxation. Such was the strength of their disquiet that, discounting the 1979 figures, turnout rose to record levels. This was a clear example of the way in which turnout can be raised if the salience of local elections is heightened. In 1995 the opposite effect came into play, with low turnout reflecting the fact that the elections were widely perceived as a foregone conclusion. For the third year running the Conservatives were heading for a local electoral disaster. Neither of the two opposition parties appeared to be threatened in their own wards. Conservative ministers subsequently argued that the party had suffered badly because of the low turnout. In actual fact turnout declined by more in Labour and Liberal Democrat seats than it did in Conservative controlled wards. The Conservatives suffered so many losses not because of differential turnout but simply because the national party was deeply unpopular. What accounted for the relatively low turnout in 1995, therefore, was a combination of complacency among non-Conservative voters and disaffection amongst previous Conservative supporters.

TURNOUT AND LOCAL GOVERNMENT STRUCTURE

Such factors as the proximity of a general election or the national standings of the main parties produce generalised effects upon the level of local turnout. Beneath that general tide, however, there are other currents which account for differences in turnout between different types of local authority. Such differences are revealed in Table 4.2, which breaks down turnout between local authority types. Before discussing turnout in any detail, however, we should note that deriving accurate data for local turnout is fraught with difficulties. A proper figure requires the number of votes cast expressed as a percentage of the total electorate in all wards with contested elections within the tier of local government under consideration. Local authorities, however, have not always been able to provide figures for the number of valid ballot papers issued in multimember wards. Furthermore, electorate figures are often inconsistent in the sense that they may either include, exclude or calculate exactly the number of attainers eligible to vote. In such circumstances we have to rely upon the electorate figures provided by the local authorities, knowing that some will have been adjusted and others unadjusted. In respect of the number of votes cast in multimember wards we have used an algorithm based on averaging votes cast for party slates (Rallings and Thrasher 1993c; but see also Rallings and Thrasher 1996b). When we show turnout for a particular level of local government the actual figure used is the overall turnout.

Comparing the London and metropolitan boroughs in Table 4.2, for example, we find that London consistently has turnouts between 1 and 5 per cent higher. Even when the electoral cycles coincide and any national effects are therefore constant, London's lead is still evident. Surprisingly, when turnout in general elections is studied, the reverse relationship appears to be true. At the 1987 election turnout in constituencies located within the metropolitan boroughs was 74.1 per cent while in London it was 70.7 per cent. In 1992 the turnout in London was 73.7 per cent but in the metropolitan areas it was again higher at 74.9 per cent. There is no simple explanation for these discrepancies, especially given that these are the two-tiers of local government most similar in terms of their socio-economic characteristics. Nonetheless, it is likely to be of some significance that the London boroughs operate a system of all-out quadrennial elections and the metropolitan boroughs hold annual elections for a third of council seats. In the former, voters know that this is a relatively infrequent opportunity to change the political control of their council but, in the latter, such an option depends upon the ruling party's numerical majority and which party controls the seats which happen to come up for re-election each year.

Having said that, the difference in levels of turnout between those shire district authorities with quadrennial whole-council elections and those with annual ones is much smaller than that between the London and metropolitan boroughs. Moreover, there is no consistency in terms of which set of councils can boast the higher overall figure. Of course, it is possible that the electoral system will still prove to be an important independent determinant of turnout in these cases once other factors have been taken into account, but such an analysis in beyond our scope here. What does seem clear is that turnouts in each type of district rise and fall together, adding support for our contention about the importance of exogenous national factors in encouraging local electoral participation.

Another important point of inter-authority comparison worth noting in Table 4.2 is that between the shire counties and districts. Turnout for the English county councils peaked in 1981 since when it has been falling steadily. Turnout in the shire district authorities has, however, been on a generally rising curve, notwithstanding the dramatic slump in 1992. Although the differences between

Table 4.2 Variations in overall turnout at local elections in Britain

Year	London boroughs	Metropolitan boroughs	English counties	English districts (w)	English districts (p)	Welsh counties	Welsh districts	Scottish regions	Scottish districts
1973		33.4	42.6	39.6	39.2				
1974	36.4							50.6	51.4
1975		32.7							
1976		38.1		44.7	44.4			44.7	
1977			42.3						
1978	43.1	37.2			42.4				47.8
1979		74.7		72.1	73.5				
1980		36.3			38.9				45.7
1981			43.7						
1982	43.9	38.8			41.8			42.9	
1983		42.0		45.0	45.6				
1984		39.8			40.2				44.4
1985			41.6						
1986	45.4	39.9		48.8	41.9			45.6	
1987		44.7			50.6				
1988		40.1			41.5				45.5
1989			39.2			44.2			
1990	48.1	46.2		48.2	48.6			45.9	
1991		40.8			46.2		53.4		
1992		32.5			37.8				41.4
1993			37.2			38.8			
1994	46.0	38.9			42.6			45.1	
1995		33.8		41.9	39.2		48.8		44.9

Note: Figures for 1995 in both Scotland and Wales refer to turnout at the unitary council elections. Turnout data for English districts have been separately calculated for authorities that use 'whole council' (w) and 'partial' (p) elections. Reliable data for Welsh local authorities are unavailable for the earlier years.

the counties and districts are not great it should be borne in mind that the distribution of functions, and therefore responsibility for spending, heavily favours the county councils. If there was a clear relationship between spending and accountability in local government we should expect to find turnout considerably higher for the county authorities responsible for such services as education and social services. That relationship is plainly not evident. How, then, might we explain this apparent anomaly? One possible important factor could lie with the Victorians' ideal that local authorities should reflect, as far as possible, an existing sense of community. The smaller scale district authorities, although boundaries have been criticised in some, are arguably a closer approximation of that spirit than the shire counties whose areas are much larger and where, in some cases, the administrative centre is quite distant from a large proportion of the population. In that case the difference in turnout between district and county authorities is in the right direction and almost to be welcomed since it shows greater voter identity with the true local community.

The planned growth in unitary authorities, designed to be closer to the community whilst at the same time providing all major local government services, should by this token lead to higher turnouts. Limited evidence from London and the metropolitan boroughs suggests that turnout has increased quite sharply since they became single tier authorities following the abolition of the GLC and the metropolitan counties in 1986. In London, comparing the pre- and post-abolition periods, average borough turnout is up from 38.9 to 46.5 per cent, and up from 37.3 to 39.6 per cent in the metropolitan areas. This will be one indicator of performance which it will be useful to monitor as the electoral cycle unfolds in the new English, Scottish and Welsh unitary councils.

LOCAL AUTHORITIES AND TURNOUT

Having discussed local voter participation in terms of the influence of external factors as well as variations across the local authority structure, we now turn our attention to differences between authorities of the same type. In 1993 we were commissioned by the Department of Environment to undertake the most comprehensive statistical examination of local turnout in Britain to date (Rallings and Thrasher 1994). In this section we report on some of the main findings of that research.

When looking at patterns of turnout over time we noticed that the standard deviation in turnout levels between authorities within each tier of local government has remained fairly constant or slightly decreased. This suggests that most authorities within each tier have conformed to a general trend. Ignoring the artificial figures for 1979, the highest mean turnout figure in each tier is accompanied by relatively high minimum and maximum scores among individual councils. Similarly, the lowest mean turnout for a tier of local government produces low minimum and maximum individual turnouts. In short, when turnout rises in a tier of local government it does so across the board and, when it falls, it does so across all the constituent authorities. Thus the importance of exogenous influences is reinforced.

It is also the case that individual councils tend to occupy a largely unchanging position in any league table of turnout. Two pieces of evidence can be used to support this claim. In the first place, there is a high correlation in turnout across local authorities between pairs of elections. What this means is that a local authority which enjoys high turnout in one election is likely to have a high turnout at subsequent elections. Although the relationship is strongest between adjacent elections, it is impressive that it is still present for elections more than ten years apart. The correlations between contests in 1990 (poll tax elections) and 1992 (aftermath of general election), which produced first the highest and then the lowest local turnouts for more than a decade, are especially interesting. In both the metropolitan boroughs and shire districts the inter-election correlations of turnout were in excess of 0.8, suggesting that the absolute change in turnout levels had little impact on individual local authorities' records as relatively good or relatively poor performers. Voters in some authorities appear good at participating while in other authorities they show a marked reluctance to use their vote.

This pattern of enthusiasm or indifference can be confirmed by looking at where local authorities appear in the rank order of turnout in their tier. The same authorities appear time and again at the top or the bottom of the respective lists. Thus, for example, the London borough of Richmond upon Thames consistently finishes in the top three of a league table of London authority turnouts while Hackney repeatedly picks up the metaphorical wooden spoon. Among the metropolitan authorities it is Sunderland which finishes at or near the bottom of the 36 boroughs while Stockport is rarely far from first place. Of course, local authorities may find that their position in the league table of turnout rises or falls. Where changes do take place there is usually a prima facie explanation readily available. For example, the movement of Liverpool and Westminster from near the bottom to near the top of their respective 'leagues' and the unusually high turnout in Bradford in 1990 would appear to be related to specifically local political events in those authorities which we discuss in more detail in Chapter 10.

We noted earlier in this chapter how an individual's social circumstances can influence his or her willingness to participate in local elections. The conclusions of a series of multiple regression analyses designed to determine how much of the variation in turnout between local authorities can be explained by their socio-economic and electoral characteristics were unequivocal (Rallings and Thrasher 1994: ch. 4). In four sets of elections between 1978 and 1990 in the London boroughs, for example, there was a clear relationship between levels of turnout and the affluence of the local authority. Boroughs with high unemployment, high levels of council housing and an overcrowded housing stock were particularly prone to record low turnouts. Moreover, on every occasion such variables proved to be statistically more important than political ones, such as the size of the leading party's majority on the council, in accounting for turnout differences.

Some boroughs, however, consistently appear to either out- or under-perform their predicted turnout. Richmond upon Thames is more than one standard deviation above its 'natural' turnout at every election; Barking and Dagenham and Newham are always at least that far below theirs.

The only general explanation for differences in turnout between metropolitan authorities lies in their socio-economic characteristics. Political variables do not exert an independent influence in any of the 12 sets of elections between 1978 and 1992 that we studied. Census variables, particularly those relating to housing tenure and employment status, consistently loaded heavily into the regression equation and they explained between 29.8 per cent and 55.8 per cent of the variance in turnout between boroughs. As in London, several metropolitan boroughs habitually appear in the list of those authorities with turnouts more than one standard deviation above or below the level predicted by the model. What this means is that a regression model of turnout is unable in itself to explain why turnout in Stockport and Wolverhampton should be consistently and unexpectedly high or that in Wigan and Sefton similarly low. As in London it may well be that presently unmeasureable aspects of local political culture offer an explanation.

Social and economic variables do not appear to be as powerful an influence on turnout variation in the shires as they are in London and the big conurbations. Although socio-economic variables prove to be the more consistent and powerful predictors of turnout, such that the proportion of pensioners is positively related to turnout and the level of male unemployment negatively so, their more limited role is perhaps explained by two connected factors relating to the composition of district councils. First, in those shire districts which are socially quite homogeneous, factors influencing levels of turnout may work against each other. For example, areas of high social status may be predisposed to recording higher than average turnouts except for the countervailing influence that these areas might also be politically 'non-competitive'. Second, during the period of study dominant Labour councils were rare in the shires and thus the occasions on which socio-economic and political variables acted to reinforce each other in explaining turnout were of limited influence in a model of turnout. Taking all this into account, it was still the case that turnouts in Rossendale and Exeter, for example, were consistently higher than predicted and those in Hull and Stoke-on-Trent consistently low. Once again our data do not permit us to provide an explanation as to why this should be the case.

TURNOUT AND WARD CHARACTERISTICS

Using aggregate data one final level of analysis of the factors affecting local turnout is available to us – the ward. As might be expected the variation in turnout levels between wards is huge. In the 1995 district council elections, for example, turnout in the Chenies ward of Chiltern district was 77 per cent and that in the St Endellion ward in North Cornwall 73.4 per cent. By contrast, only

17.2 per cent of the electorate voted in the Noddle ward in Hull and only 17.5 per cent in Queens, Rushmoor. In this section we analyse the impact of party competition, ward size, ward marginality and socio-economic character on turnout and their utility in explaining such variations.

A number of studies have highlighted the development of a competitive party system in local elections. By the end of the last century party politics was a fact of life in the vast majority of the largest towns and cities (Redlich and Hirst 1970). In rural authorities the spread of party was not as great and elections in these authorities contrasted with their urban counterparts in two important respects. First, the absence of competition meant that many councillors were returned unopposed. An analysis conducted in the 1930s showed that the majority of councillors did not have to fight a contested election and turnout in the case of the county councils only averaged between 11 per cent and 20 per cent (Self and 'Administrator' 1947). Second, many councillors held no overt party allegiance and fought elections as 'Independents'. In the absence of a party machine such candidates were often left to their own devices in terms of campaigning and canvassing. Many studies have examined the link between local party activity and the level of turnout in elections (Gregory 1969; Pimlott 1972; Pimlott 1973; Bruce and Lee 1982). Public interest seems to be stimulated through election campaigning and competitive parties present policies for debate, attract media attention and generally instil some vitality into the election atmosphere. In the 1964 local elections, for example, Fletcher noted that 'average turnout in non-marginal wards contested by Liberals was more than one third higher than in non-marginal contests where no Liberal stood' (Fletcher 1967: 301). Other things being equal, the more parties contest and campaign for the seat the higher the turnout (Capron and Kruseman 1988).

The figures in Table 4.3 do point to a relationship between the level of party competition and levels of turnout at the most recent elections in the different types of local authority. In the 1993 English county elections, for example, the mean percentage turnout in divisions where just two of the main parties competed was 36.2 per cent whereas in those divisions with candidates from all three parties, turnout was more than 1 per cent higher. A similar boost from three-party competition can also be found in the metropolitan and London boroughs, although in the English districts, turnouts are almost identical in cases of two- and three-party contestation. In Scotland, there has been an increase in four-party competition and it is interesting to note that higher turnout does appear to be associated with greater party competition. In the 1992 district elections, for example, turnout averaged 44.4 per cent in wards with four-party competition but only 39.5 per cent in those wards with just two-party contests. In the 1994 regional elections the pattern was less pronounced, however, while in the unitary council elections held in 1995 turnout was on average identical in wards with four-party or two-party contests.

Overall, however, these figures appear to suggest that the electorate are marginally more interested in an election when the range of parties to choose

Table 4.3 Turnout and party competition

	Year	2-party % mean turnout	2-party N =	3-party % mean turnout	3-party N =
English counties	1993	36.2	717	37.6	2,150
English districts	1995	41.7	2,170	41.5	3,003
London	1994	43.0	101	46.5	657
Metropolitan boroughs	1995	32.3	183	34.5	591

from is greater and when a potential voter is not faced with choosing between either voting for an alternative party because their 'own' has not fielded a candidate or staying at home. At the local authority level the intervention of third party candidates can have a dramatic effect upon turnout. In the London borough of Sutton, for example, the Liberals contested most wards in the 1964 elections and turnout was 44.0 per cent. At the following two sets of elections in 1968 and 1971 the party contested many fewer wards and turnout in the borough fell by 6 per cent, despite the fact that turnout levels in London as a whole rose. In 1974 the Liberal party fought all wards in the borough for the first time and turnout immediately rose to 46.6 per cent, this time in contrast to a mean fall across London.

What evidence exists that electors actually respond to local parties? Jordan and Dyer's (1985) analysis of a marked electoral register allowed them to identify which electors had actually voted, thereby avoiding the problem of respondents' faulty recall which often bedevils opinion surveys. The authors concluded that two factors appeared particularly influential in persuading people to vote. First, there was the strength of party identification, a sense of psychological involvement which earlier studies had uncovered. The second factor, however, was the level of party activity in the ward. This suggests that, other things being equal, political parties have a critical role to play in promoting the competitiveness of local elections and in stimulating turnout (see also Hill 1967: 140). Similar effects were noted by Bochel and Denver when they conducted Labour ward campaigns in Lancaster and Dundee. Frequent canvassing of party supporters in targeted areas resulted in increased turnouts in those wards relative to other wards in the authorities (Bochel and Denver 1972). In another study the same team selected two blocks of flats in a ward, each a similar distance from the polling station. One block was heavily canvassed with each voter receiving three visits while the other was ignored. Interviews with residents from the respective flats then revealed that 54 per cent had voted from the ignored block but in the canvassed block turnout was 64 per cent (Bochel and Denver 1971). The evidence suggests, therefore, that a link exists between levels of party organisation, party activity and party competition, and ward turnout.

Given that the concept of local democracy emphasises a sense of community identity, and given numerous studies which have shown that sense of identity is usually felt in geographically relatively small areas, it would be reasonable to expect that turnout might be related to the ward size. Cutright and Rossi (1958) found that in the United States candidates did better in their home precincts than elsewhere in the district, indicating that voters were more inclined to support someone they knew when they recognised names on ballot papers. Further studies have pointed to the importance of what can be termed the 'friends and neighbours effect' on voting patterns (O'Loughlin 1981; Eagles and Erfle 1989). Taylor's study of voting in Swansea demonstrated that the distance an elector had to travel to the polling station appeared to have an effect on the likelihood of voting. Of those electors estimated to be within a minute's walk of the polling station no less than 65 per cent voted but of those who lived more than five minutes away only 35 per cent voted (Taylor 1973). It is also claimed that as local authorities grow in size and lose the traditional trappings of a close-knit community, interest in local elections appears to subside (Verba and Nie 1972). However, it can be the case that small communities discourage competition. Turnout may be higher in smaller wards, but so too may be the rate of unopposed returns. In Scottish local elections it was found that individuals did not wish to stand against an incumbent who was well known in the district for fear of giving offence (Masterson and Masterson 1980). In terms of ward size and electoral participation there appears to be a happy medium. If wards are too small there is a risk that the friends and neighbours effect will be taken too far – to the point, indeed, where electoral competition is avoided because of its threat to community bonds. If wards are too big then there is a risk that they will cease to reflect a sense of community of identity and electors fail to see the salience of local elections.

The evidence from recent British local elections does suggest that small communities appear to have a better voting record than larger ones. In the shire districts, where the wards are smaller than other types of local authority, turnout in single-member wards of less than 2,000 electors averaged 52 per cent in 1991 while in larger wards it was some 3–4 per cent lower. Indeed both the wards noted above (pp. 56–7) with turnout in excess of 70 per cent in 1995 had very small electorates – 943 electors in St Endellion and a tiny 190 in Chenies, the smallest electorate in the country. In the shire counties a similar relationship between the number of electors in a division and turnout exists. In the 1993 English county elections, for example, mean percentage turnout in divisions of less than 3,000 electors was 43.5 per cent but for the largest divisions, with electorates exceeding 12,000, turnout was on average only 35.7 per cent. A similar pattern exists in Scotland. In district wards of less than 2,000 electors the mean turnout at the 1992 elections was 45.1 per cent but in those wards with electorates in excess of 5,000 the average turnout fell to just 40.3 per cent.

The relationship between turnout and the ward electorate is much less pronounced, however, in the urban areas of London and the metropolitan boroughs. There are only 21 wards in London with electorates of under 3,000 and the mean turnout in these wards in the 1990 elections was 50.6 per cent. At the other end of the scale there are just 5 wards with electorates larger than 12,000 and here turnout averaged 51.9 per cent. Naturally, such a small number of cases might lead to distortions. Moving up and down the electorate scale, however, merely confirms the absence of a relationship between ward size and turnout in London. In wards with electorates in the range 3–5,000 turnout averaged 48.5 per cent in 1990 and it was 48.8 per cent in those wards with a range of 9–12,000 electors. In the metropolitan boroughs the relationship between size and turnout is in fact the reverse of that expected. Turnout in the wards with fewer than 7,000 electors averaged 36.2 per cent in 1991, but 40.8 per cent in the 168 wards with more than 12,000 voters on the register. A possible explanation is that ward boundaries are less likely to reflect defined communities in London and the metropolitan areas than in the shires, and thus party activity will be more important than mere size in influencing levels of participation.

The evidence regarding ward size and local turnout does not, therefore, appear to be uni-directional. Is the same true for the impact of ward marginality on turnout? If party campaigns and party activists are able to exert an influence on overall rates of turnout, and assuming that parties will be most active in the most marginal wards, the closeness of the result on the last occasion the ward was contested should be positively correlated with turnout. Previous studies offer conflicting evidence. Fletcher (1967), for example, concluded that the major effect on turnout was the closeness of the result – the more marginal the seat the more parties campaigned and canvassed, the more interest it evoked and the more electors were inclined to vote. In her study of voting in Leeds Hill remarked, 'The general level of political activity (as measured by the turn-out in local elections) upholds the generalisation that it is the marginal wards which have the highest turn-out' (Hill 1967: 139). Similar findings were reported by Denver and Hands (1985) and from a study of London borough elections (Rowley 1971). However, a rather different conclusion was drawn by Newton who argued that local voting and turnout were more likely to be affected by national politics and the prevailing mood of the day rather than by the marginality of particular wards (Newton 1972).

Our evidence suggests that ward marginality – defined as the percentage lead of the first over the second placed party at the previous election – does appear to be a major influence on turnout in most types of authority. As shown in Table 4.4, there is a consistent relationship between turnout and marginality at recent elections, suggesting that when electors believe the outcome in their ward is in doubt they are more willing to incur the costs associated with voting. Newton is right in the sense that the sudden rise in turnout at the 'poll tax' elections in 1990, for example, points to the impact of a national controversy on overall levels of electoral participation, but wrong in that turnout was still demonstrably higher in marginal wards than safe wards even at those particular elections. In

Table 4.4 Turnout and marginality

	Year	Wards with <5% majority		Wards with >35% majority	
		% mean turnout	*N =*	*% mean turnout*	*N =*
English counties	1993	39.7	350	33.4	713
English districts	1995	42.8	751	40.9	1,030
London	1994	49.7	79	42.1	193
Metropolitan boroughs	1995	34.4	88	28.2	258

London, for example, the mean turnout in that year in marginal wards was 51.4 per cent and in safe ones 44.5 per cent – both figures higher than in 1994, but with a similar gap between them.

We also conducted a limited multiple regression analysis of our ward level data enabling us to consider the interrelation of these political variables together with socio-economic characteristics on turnout (Rallings and Thrasher 1990). It appeared that socio-economic and political factors made an almost equal and independent contribution to that proportion of variance in ward turnout which we could explain. Citizens living in low status areas are less likely to participate both because of that fact, and because they are located more frequently in non-competitive wards. On the other hand, those in wards with a large Conservative share of the vote and majority may be discouraged from voting because they feel they already 'know' the result *despite* generally living in an area of high status and thus assumed high predisposition to participate. It is also interesting to note a positive correlation between Alliance/Liberal Democrat share of the vote and turnout, where the party's success in winning wards seems related to persuading an absolutely larger number of people to vote.

For individual wards, as for local authorities, there is a considerable variance in the degree of 'fit' between actual and predicted levels of turnout. Wards whose turnout is especially above or below that suggested by the regression model can be divided into four types:

1 Wards which appear to have unusually high or low turnouts just once.
2 Wards which habitually appear as 'outliers', but which are not clustered with others from the same authority.
3 Wards which appear to have unusually high or low turnouts just once, but which are clustered with others from the same authority.
4 Wards which habitually appear as 'outliers' and which are clustered with others from the same authority.

We have, in other words, 'habitual' and 'one-off' over- or under-achievers. Wards in categories 1 and 3 are likely to be exhibiting a response to currently salient local issues or to a particular set of political circumstances. Where an authority-wide cluster is identified, as in Liverpool in 1984, Thanet (Kent) in 1985 or Bradford in 1990, a qualitative examination of the local campaign will usually provide supportive evidence for the statistical phenomenon. Wards in categories 2 and 4 appear time and again. Why some individual wards feature is not readily apparent and appears to have little to do with patterns of party contestation. The Queens ward in Rushmoor, for example, had candidates from all three parties plus the Greens in 1995. The key factor here is that the ward covers an army housing estate in Aldershot, with a large number of absent 'service voters' reluctant to take steps to enable them to vote in an election for an area with which they are likely to have little identity. By contrast, the Chenies ward has a tiny high status electorate and a clear pattern of voting for the candidate rather than the party. In between the extremes, however, one is again forced back almost to cultural explanations focusing on history and tradition as to why some wards habitually under- or over-perform.

CONCLUSION

We have analysed local electoral participation from a number of different perspectives. First, we reviewed the findings from survey data which gave an insight into what sorts of individual voted or did not vote in elections. Next, we used actual turnout data to assess the impact of a wider set of variables, ranging from national influences down to ward level characteristics. Combining these approaches what can we conclude?

The evidence from survey data suggested that age, residential mobility and housing tenure were significant factors in determining the propensity to vote. In addition an individual's psychological investment in the political process also appeared critical. Miller's later two-wave panel survey confirmed many of these earlier findings with the additional observation that council tenants were more likely to vote than owner-occupiers. Arguably, the most important finding of the survey data is that there do not appear to be electors who habitually abstain from voting in either national or local elections. There does not appear to be any significant element of the electorate which is alienated from the voting experience. That suggests that if the circumstances are propitious then people who abstained in one cycle of local elections could be persuaded to vote in another.

Next, we analysed the data from local elections over a period of more than twenty years. Over time turnout in local elections appears to have increased slightly, although issues concerning the accuracy and comprehensiveness of the electoral register mean that the data should be treated with caution. The examination of the link between party competition, marginality and turnout showed that a healthy local democracy (judged in terms of local turnout) is most likely to exist where party competition is high and where no seat can be adjudged safe. By contrast the existence of local authorities and wards where one party has a secure majority has a negative effect on turnout. Depending on local context such political factors tend either to reinforce or cancel out the impact of the socio-economic character of an authority or ward on turnout levels.

There were also a number of external political factors which seemed to have a significant effect upon turnout. Unsurprisingly, the holding of a general election in 1979 on the same day as the local elections had an obvious and positive effect on turnout. In Sweden, for example, it is commonplace to hold elections for the national and local tiers of government simultaneously. Even the proximity of general elections appears to galvanise the local electorate – perhaps by way of enhanced party activity and media coverage – and persuade more to vote than otherwise might be the case. Equally, there is a sense of election weariness with turnout falling in the set of local elections which follow a general election. Political controversy also appears to have a beneficial effect on turnout. As a general case the 1990 elections proved beyond doubt that the electorate will vote if stimulated, or perhaps provoked would be a better description. Localised examples of the same kind of stimulus can also be found in authorities such as Liverpool, Westminster, Bradford and Basildon. In the last mentioned case the turnout rose dramatically in 1992 as the electors appeared to celebrate their newly discovered status as the touchstone of Conservative fortunes within the country as a whole.

This still leaves those authorities and wards which either defy the trends or whose turnout differs markedly from that in similar areas. Regardless of socio-economic status, regardless of the scale of party competition, regardless of the state of council and ward marginality voters in authorities such as Rossendale, Richmond upon Thames and Stockport appear to turn out in greater numbers than we might expect. At the other extreme the particular reluctance of voters in Newham, Barking and Dagenham, Wigan, Sandwell, Stoke on Trent and Hull to go to the polls cannot satisfactorily be explained with reference to those variables. Analysis of quantitative data, we suspect, can only take us so far in answering questions about which factors serve to encourage or discourage local electoral turnout. The next stage is the detailed examination of electoral and political processes in those authorities to try to determine if they provide the clue (see Rallings *et al.* 1996).

5 Contestation, candidates and incumbency

INTRODUCTION

The popular impression that very few people bother to vote in local elections is closely linked with another which contends that many seats are uncontested and that those which are are attract few candidates. Our purpose in the first section of this chapter, therefore, will be to compare this conventional wisdom with reality. As with the data on electoral turnout, the truth is more complex than is commonly realised, but certainly on this issue the health of local democracy should not give undue cause for concern. Indeed, we may go further and argue there are positive signs of increasing competition. Such improvement in levels of contestation has done little, however, to reduce concerns about the 'calibre' of those individuals putting themselves forward for election. This has been a traditional complaint, encountered throughout the nineteenth century. Arguably, it is based on snobbishness rather than on empirical evidence (Dearlove, 1979: ch. 4). We have no new data available to us here on the occupation, age, educational background or attitudes of individual candidates and councillors, but in one sense we can examine the extent to which councillors remain, in Stanyer's memorable phrase, a 'male, bourgeois gerontocracy' (Stanyer 1976: 109).

In the second section we examine the changing representation of women in local government. The decision by the Labour party in 1993 to introduce all-women short lists for the selection of prospective parliamentary candidates in certain marginal seats was intended to address the problem whereby fewer than 10 per cent of MPs elected in 1992 were women. Though few disagreed with that objective, controversy surrounded the means and Labour had to abandon the policy following a judgment in 1996 that it was illegal. As we shall show, women have been more successful in winning a presence in local government and currently about a quarter of councillors are female.

A third section briefly presents some new data on the ethnic background of councillors. In the final part of the chapter the value to a candidate of political incumbency will be explored in some detail. Can some councillors count on a 'personal vote', can it be measured, and is it sufficient to provide a buttress against a more general swing away from their party?

CONTESTATION AND COMPETITION

At the initial elections to the post-reorganisation county councils held in 1973, no fewer than 500 of the new councillors were elected unopposed. This meant that more than one in eight of all shire councillors entrusted with spending ratepayers' money in such vital areas as education, social services, libraries and roads could lay no claim to an electoral mandate or even popular support. The same year also saw elections for the smaller shire districts. In 166 of the 333 districts in England and Wales at least one ward was uncontested. That no other candidate had chosen to contest the election in their ward or division was no fault of these particular councillors, of course, but for many the high level of non-contestation did not bode well for the newly-reformed structure. Prior to reorganisation many seats had been uncontested but one of the stated aims of the legislation had been to make local government more democratic and accountable as well as more efficient and effective. There was not even support for the idea that while potential candidates might dislike the large and possibly remote counties they would feel differently about the smaller, and possibly more accessible, district councils and present themselves for election. In the first elections to these authorities the percentage of councillors returned unopposed was even higher than for the county councils. Virtually one in five district council seats did not have an election. In the public imagination at least the sense that local government elections were unimportant and poorly contested had been reinforced by these events.

Lack of contestation has, however, largely been a rural/suburban phenomenon. In those, mainly more urban, shire districts which opted for annual elections, contestation rates reached 93 per cent as early as 1978 and have risen since. In the metropolitan and London boroughs, moreover, it has been relatively rare for seats to be uncontested, even in the early years following reorganisation. In the 1973 elections a mere 3.7 per cent of seats for the metropolitan counties were unopposed while the metropolitan boroughs enjoyed an even higher level of contestation with just 2.6 per cent of seats unopposed. Some individual boroughs, though, did not have a good record of contestation. In St Helens in 1973 as many as 13 per cent of seats went uncontested, making it one of six boroughs where all the seats were not fought. In 1975 30 per cent of the wards in North Tyneside saw their councillor(s) elected unopposed but the number of boroughs with unopposed returns dropped to just four. By the end of the decade, both the overall level of uncontested seats and the number of affected metropolitan boroughs had fallen still further. Within this generally improving picture some wards with notoriously bad records of non-contestation resisted the trend. The boroughs of Barnsley and Knowsley remain the worst affected in this respect. Barnsley has two wards, Dearne South and Athersley, where elections have been held at only two out of every three opportunities. In the same borough the electors of Dearne Thurnscoe ward have not been offered a contest in half of the eighteen elections between 1973 and 1996. This low rate of contestation is matched by the Princess ward in Knowsley, with Cantril Farm ward only marginally better. All are extremely safe Labour wards.

By contrast the Greater London Council, created in 1964 and abolished in 1986, never once in its six electoral cycles had an uncontested seat. The record of the London boroughs was also not far from perfect with the highest level of non-contestation occurring in the 1968 elections when 1.7 per cent of seats were uncontested. This figure was largely a product of the absence of candidates in Tower Hamlets where less than two-thirds of all seats were contested. Indeed in nine electoral cycles since 1964 the borough has had contests in all its wards on only five occasions. This situation is not without irony. One of the wards with the worst record in terms of contestation in the whole of London is Tower Hamlets' Millwall. In a third of elections held since 1964 this ward failed to attract sufficient candidates to force a contest. Yet it was this same ward which was the scene of the British National party's by-election victory in September 1993 and which, in the May 1994 quadrennial elections, attracted 14 candidates, massive media attention and a turnout of 66.5 per cent. Overall, however, uncontested seats are statistically insignificant in the capital. Since 1974 they have accounted for less than 0.2 per cent of all seats in London borough elections.

During the 1970s, therefore, the impression that a large proportion of local government seats went uncontested was only ever partially true. It did not apply to the metropolitan authorities nor, in large part, to the larger district councils in the shires. Throughout the 1980s, moreover, rates of uncontested seats fell gradually, even in the English shires. By the 1985 county elections uncontested divisions amounted to little more than 2 per cent of all seats and affected only 32 of the 296 districts in England. Among the shire districts with whole-council elections the improvement was not as marked, although by 1991 the proportion of uncontested seats had fallen to 12.4 per cent and was reduced again to just 8.3 per cent at the 1995 elections. There can be little doubt that the major contributing factor in this steady decline of uncontested seats in the shires has been the growing party politicisation of these areas. The expansion of party competition has meant that fewer Independents than before have gone unchallenged. Even so, of the more than 500 wards uncontested in the 1995 district elections almost half were retained by Independents. While some still decry the role of political parties it cannot be denied that their presence has helped rescue local government from accusations that its decisions lack legitimacy because so many councillors have no real electoral mandate.

What of Scotland and Wales? As Denver (1993) notes the number of uncontested seats were relatively few for the first local elections in Scotland following reorganisation. In the districts one in five councillors were elected unopposed while in the regions the figure fell to just one in ten. After this initial surge of enthusiasm there was a short period in the late 1970s and early 1980s during which the number of unopposed seats rose but thereafter the overall pattern of contestation in Scotland certainly reflects the English trend towards fewer uncontested seats. In the 1980 Scottish district elections, for example, 26 per cent of seats had unopposed returns whereas by 1992 this figure had halved. Contestation for the Scottish regional seats has generally been better. In 1978 one in five regional divisions were uncontested but by 1990 the proportion had fallen to just one in twelve. In April 1995 the first elections to the new 29 Scottish unitary authorities saw yet another reduction in the number of uncontested wards. Only 52 councillors, just 4.5 per cent of the total, were returned unopposed. There is not such good news for defenders of local democracy in Wales, however. At the last county elections in 1993 no less than 22 per cent of the country's 500 county divisions went uncontested. In Powys alone 26 of the county's 46 divisions had councillors returned unopposed, with Independents therefore being guaranteed continued 'control' of the council as soon as nominations closed. In elections held in 1991 for the Welsh district councils the ratio of contested/uncontested wards was even worse with more than one in four wards uncontested. Given a history of so many uncontested seats there was scepticism whether the creation of a single-tier system of 22 new unitary authorities in Wales with clearer lines of accountability would help stimulate more interest in the elections. However in the initial May 1995 elections only 16.3 per cent of wards went uncontested, still large by comparison with other local authorities, but a distinct improvement on the previous pattern in Wales.

Overall, there now appears to be little substance to the general claim that local government elections in Britain are plagued by a large proportion of uncontested seats. There are, admittedly, isolated pockets of poor contestation, notably in some areas of Scotland and Wales, but in England the number of unopposed councillors is rapidly diminishing. Levels of contestation, however, only represent one indicator of the health of local democracy. A further check is to measure the degree of competitiveness in contested seats by calculating the ratio of candidates to seats for any given set of elections. In single-member wards this figure is derived simply by dividing the number of candidates in a ward by one. In multimember wards the total number of candidates has to be divided by the total number of seats to be filled in that ward. The mean ratio of candidates/seats can then be calculated for any tier of local government or for a particular set of local authorities. Table 5.1 illustrates the ratios for selected elections over the last twenty years. It can be seen that for all tiers of local government the mean ratio of candidates has been fairly uniform since the late 1970s, levelling off at about 3 candidates per vacancy and reflecting the growth in three-party competition in most wards (see Chapter 6).

An analysis of mean candidate/seat ratios for individual local authorities does, however, show some interesting variations. In London, for example, Barking and Dagenham has consistently had the poorest ratio. In the 1978 elections its candidate/seat ratio was just 2.4 and its 1990 figure of 2.3 was by some considerable margin the lowest. At the other end of the scale no local authority has consistently finished with the highest ratio – rather it appears specifically local events appear to influence the number of candidates contesting

Table 5.1 Ratio of candidates to seats 1973–1994

English counties	1973	1977	1981	1985	1989	1993
	2.4	2.7	2.9	3.0	3.1	3.1
Metropolitan boroughs	1973	1976	1982	1986	1990	1994
	2.5	3.1	3.0	3.1	3.4	3.0
London boroughs	1974	1978	1982	1986	1990	1994
	3.0	3.2	3.2	3.2	3.2	3.0
Scottish regions	1974	1978	1982	1986	1990	1994
	2.7	2.4	2.9	3.1	3.4	3.4

the available seats. A case in point is Greenwich which, in 1990, saw its candidate/seat ratio rise to 4.4, considerably higher than the borough had witnessed before. The explanation for this lay with the emergence of candidates standing for the so-called Valley party, a single issue group protesting at the proposal to move Charlton Athletic Football Club away from its traditional home – 'The Valley'. Similarly, at the 1982 elections the large number of candidates standing for the 'Save London Action Group' in the borough of Kensington and Chelsea boosted the candidate/seat ratio to 5.2. Four years later, however, that particular protest had dissipated and considerably fewer candidates contested the elections in the borough.

The tendency of candidate/seat ratios to fluctuate within authorities is also noticeable within the metropolitan areas. Wolverhampton, for example, had relatively high ratios in the mid-1970s when its elections attracted candidates from a vigorous ratepayers' movement as well as the National Front. In recent years neither of these groups has fielded candidates and consequently Wolverhampton's seats are less fiercely contested. When one authority subsides, however, there are usually others to take its place. Birmingham's elections in the 1990s have attracted a large number of Green party candidates, placing it consistently amongst the highest candidate/seat ratios for the metropolitan authorities.

The authorities examined thus far have all been principal spending bodies in English local government. We noted in the previous chapter, however, that the electorate appears either ignorant of or uninterested in the distribution of power between the county and district authorities. Despite the fact that most services, and therefore expenditure, are administered by the counties, voters seem more willing to participate in district elections. Such indifference to functional power might not be so pronounced amongst the parties, however, whose primary purpose would be to win political power. We would expect, therefore, that the ratios of candidates to seats would be higher for the counties than for the districts. This, indeed, appears to be the case with a ratio of 2.4 candidates per seat at both the 1991 and 1995 district elections compared with one of 3.1 for the county elections in recent years. In short, while the electorate appear more motivated to participate in district elections, candidates face stiffer competition, in terms both of the proportion of seats contested and the number of challengers per seat, in the counties.

Scotland and Wales, of course, have another dimension to their elections because there are candidates representing the respective nationalist parties. We have already noted that both countries have higher rates of uncontested seats, but is the number of candidates for each seat higher than for the English local authorities? As we saw in Table 5.1 competition for seats in elections to the Scottish regional councils compares favourably with that found amongst English local authorities. The Scottish Nationalist party's commitment to fight more and more local council seats is largely responsible for the improved ratio, particularly since 1990. In the elections held for the new Scottish unitary authorities in 1995, however, the candidate to seat ratio fell to 3.0 although this was largely a result of the failure of Conservative candidates to contest seats. In Wales competition for seats has generally been the lowest in Britain. In the 1995 unitary elections, for example, the candidate to seat ratio was just 2.1. Even removing the impact of the many uncontested wards from the Welsh calculation only increases the competition ratio slightly to 2.4. It would appear, therefore, that the political parties habitually contest a smaller proportion of the total seats in Wales than in England and Scotland and that four-party competition at local elections is relatively unusual. We shall address these issues further in the next chapter.

Taken together, however, the data for uncontested elections and candidates per seat provide us with a relatively straightforward means of gauging the state of local democracy measured in terms of electoral competition. What these figures show is that the rate of contestation is now considerably higher than when the local government system was reorganised in the 1970s. Across all sectors of local government and within each country, the proportion of uncontested seats has been steadily declining. In terms of competition, in most cases voters will find that they have about three candidates to choose from for each seat. In some years, particularly 1990, and in some authorities, this competition for votes has risen in line with the salience of the election. Even in relatively quiet electoral years, however, electors have a reasonable amount of choice between candidates. In the next section we consider the controversial issue of whether those voters are offered, and make equal choices between, male and female candidates.

WOMEN AND LOCAL ELECTIONS

Although women comprise about half of the population their representation on elected bodies is much less. The House of Commons elected in 1992 contained just 60 women or 9.2 per cent of the total membership. At the last UK elections to the European Parliament in 1994 women MEPs accounted for 17.2 per cent of the total. Organised pressure groups, such as the '300 Group', have a commitment to redress this gender imbalance on publicly elected bodies. Nationally, the parties are acutely aware of the issue though responses have varied from all-women short lists to gentle arm-twisting of constituency parties (Norris and Lovenduski 1994). To some extent local government has been more enlightened in its attitude to female participation. As early as the 1830s, for example, women were able to vote for various local boards if they were single and ratepayers and by 1875 women could be and were elected to such authorities as Boards of Guardians.

In this section we will provide the answer to some important questions concerning the current status of women in the local electoral system. Has the overall number of women fighting and winning local elections increased since the 1970s and if so to what extent? Do women appear to be more successful in some spheres of local government than in others? Does there appear to be discrimination against them by voters used more to being ruled by men? Do some political parties appear to discriminate against women, saving their safest seats for men?

Women councillors currently account for slightly more than a quarter of all elected members in England and the trend is for more women to be elected with each electoral cycle. There is a small variation across the different types of local authority. In the English shire districts, for example, 27.8 per cent of councillors elected in 1995 were women but in the shire counties the figure is some four and half points lower. In the more urban metropolitan and London boroughs there are, again, dissimilarities in the number of women councillors. In 1994, for example, while 28 per cent of successful candidates in the London elections were women the proportion fell to 22 per cent in the metropolitan boroughs. Both Scotland and Wales are at the lower end of the scale of female representation. In 1995 22.7 per cent of candidates elected to the Scottish unitary councils were women while the figure in Wales was lower still at 19.3 per cent. In Northern Ireland, just 11.5 per cent of elected district councillors are women (Lucy 1994: 171).

Previous studies have suggested that the schedule of council work discourages women from becoming councillors (Barron *et al.* 1991). Certainly the workload, and the associated problems of travelling to and from council and committee meetings, might well explain the lower proportion of female councillors in the English shires. Another possibility is that women candidates feel happier contesting (and by implication winning) multimember wards on district councils rather than single-member divisions on county councils. Research from the United States suggests that women feel more comfortable campaigning in multimember seats where there are more opportunities to emphasise their own positive attributes rather than single-member seats where the contest more often develops into one of running down one's opponents (Kirkpatrick 1974). Welch and Studlar, however, found little firm evidence to support this view although there was some suggestion that in the more traditional districts women were put off from contesting single-member seats (Welch and Studlar 1990: 400–1). Both explanations, in fact, appear to fit the English experience quite well. In London and the metropolitan boroughs wards are multimember but crucially, perhaps, whereas in London all seats are contested every fourth year, in the metropolitan areas usually only a single seat is at stake in each annual election.

Currently, therefore, women account for one in four councillors but in the early years of local government reorganisation their position was much less favourable. Figure 5.1 shows the percentage of women candidates and councillors in the English shire districts from 1973 to 1995. The graph clarifies a number of points. First, there has been a continual increase in the proportion of women councillors, from about 15 per cent in the 1970s, followed by a fairly steep rise in the late 1980s, with a levelling off in the 1990s. Second, throughout this twenty-year period there has been a consistent gap of always less than 4 per cent between the percentages of women candidates and councillors at each set of elections. Although this suggests little prima facie evidence of discrimination against women candidates by either selectors or voters, we will return to the subject a little later. Finally, there is the question of why there was such a dramatic rise in female candidatures and councillors during the late 1980s? One possible explanation is that the change was brought about by one political party which took it upon itself, rather as the Labour party is currently doing as far as parliamentary representation is concerned, to increase the level of female representation in local government.

Would a woman wishing to enter local politics, therefore, be better advised to ally herself with one party rather than another simply because it seemed more receptive to the proactive recruitment of female candidates? The party with the best record in recruiting women candidates in recent times has been the Greens. At the 1989 county elections no fewer than 35 per cent of the party's candidates

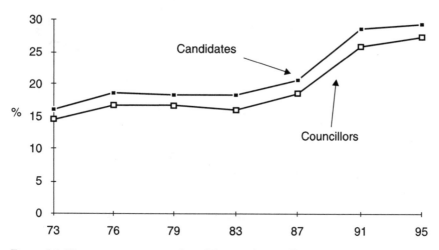

Figure 5.1 Women as percentage of candidates and councillors: English shire districts 1973–1995

were women and in the following year's elections to the shire and metropolitan districts almost 4 in 10 Green candidates were female. The more established parties cannot boast such an approach towards equality. Figure 5.2 compares the ratios of women candidates in the English shire districts over a twenty-year period according to their political party. As can be seen, although there are overall differences between the parties, with women faring less well in the two main parties than in the Liberal/Liberal Democrat 'third' party, there is a remarkable uniformity in the rate of change. Such findings suggest that the reasons for the increase in the numbers of women candidates and councillors lie beyond the political parties themselves and are almost certainly part of a much wider phenomenon affecting the role of women in society. Indeed, an examination of female members of national legislatures in western democracies shows a similarly large increase in numbers in the latter part of the 1980s (Inter-Parliamentary Union 1992).

None of the three parties achieved anything like sexual equality amongst their candidates at the 1991 local elections. A third of Liberal Democrat candidates were women, a little higher than either their Conservative or Labour rivals where in both cases 27 per cent of candidates were female. As with the case of male and female councillors there are systematic differences amongst candidates when we compare district and county elections. In the 1993 county elections all parties had fewer women candidates than in the district elections covering the

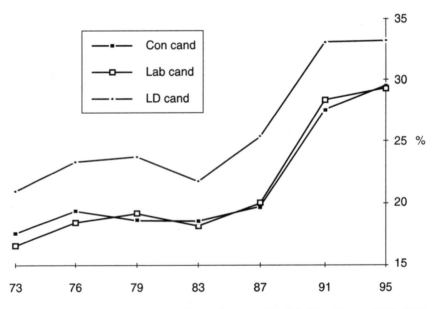

Figure 5.2 Proportion of women candidates by party: English shire districts 1973–1995

same areas. The Liberal Democrats registered slightly under 30 per cent, the Conservatives 25.7 per cent, while fewer than one in four Labour candidates were women. Again it would appear that the size and perceived remoteness of the counties could deter women from putting their names forward as candidates. Moreover, the relatively small number of single-member county seats may lead some local parties to, as they see it, 'play safe' when selecting candidates, thus favouring men over women.

When the figures for women candidates are analysed in more detail at the local authority level, wide variations become apparent. The worst councils in terms of the level of female representation are those dominated by Independents, especially in Wales. In such authorities, of course, most candidates are self-selected rather than chosen from a short list by a group of party peers and thus the absence of women stems from them not presenting themselves for election in the first place. Without survey evidence we can only begin to speculate as to why this might be the case. In councils where party politics dominate, however, there can be a mix of reasons for low numbers of women candidates, incorporating the problems of women not seeing themselves as suitable for a political career in local government as well as discrimination by party selection meetings. Table 5.2 lists those shire districts with the highest and lowest proportion of female candidates at the 1991 elections, together with the change in this proportion between the 1991 and 1995 elections. As can be seen, a large number of women candidates at one election does not guarantee a similar presence at the next – or vice versa. Indeed, between the two cycles, 8 of the initial 'top 10' experienced a decline in women standing for election and 8 of the 'bottom 10' an increase. The performance of the latter group may reflect a desire to do better; it is unlikely that party groups in the former took a conscious decision to cut female representation. Rather the figures are likely to indicate fluctuations, within a generally rising trend, in the number of women making themselves available for election at different times.

Analysis of the role of voters as opposed to selectors in the under-representation of women at national elections has been extensive. Rasmussen, for example, found no real bias against women candidates by voters although there was a greater tendency for them to be selected by parties for their less favourable seats. This is evidence, perhaps, of a prejudice against women built on the unsubstantiated view that the electorate will discriminate against them (Rasmussen 1983). Another study, however, suggested that the electoral disadvantage suffered by women could, in part, be explained by the electorate's reluctance to vote for a woman (Kelley and McAllister 1984). To add further confusion to the picture another analysis, this time of the 1979 British general election, could detect little bias against women with most respondents believing gender had little part to play in determining a candidate's potential to be an MP (Welch and Studlar 1986). Whatever the explanation, minor parties in Britain do have a better record of picking women as candidates in parliamentary seats than either Labour or the Conservatives.

Table 5.2 Proportion of female candidates, district council elections 1991 and 1995

District councils with highest proportion of female candidates in 1991

	% 1991	% 1995	% change
Horsham	47	39	−8
Daventry	42	36	−6
Shrewsbury & Atcham	42	29	−13
Hartlepool	42	30	−12
Stevenage	41	39	−2
Mole Valley	40	43	+3
Bassetlaw	40	38	−2
Carlisle	40	26	−14
Craven	40	38	−2
Wyre Forest	40	40	−

District councils with lowest proportion of female candidates in 1991

	% 1991	% 1995	% change
Nuneaton & Bedworth	5	15	+10
Halton	14	24	+10
Woodspring	16	25	+9
Wansbeck	17	12	−5
Stoke on Trent	17	25	+8
Easington	17	24	+7
East Northamptonshire	18	24	+6
Waveney	18	29	+11
Bolsover	19	17	−2
Gosport	19	39	+20

The question to be addressed here, however, is whether voters discriminate in favour of or against women at British *local* elections? In their study of the 1985 county council elections Welch and Studlar concluded, 'overall, controlling for incumbency and number of opponents faced, women and men candidates win almost identical votes' (Welch and Studlar 1988: 279). It is now possible to broaden the base for our inquiry by looking at the mean percentage share of the vote achieved by women as opposed to men across a range of elections in different types of local government authority.

The best elections from the point of view of examining any differences are those where single-member elections are the norm, principally the English shire counties and metropolitan boroughs. Comparing men and women at the 1993 county elections we find that male candidates won a mean vote share of 33.5 per cent, while women scored a mean of only 30.2 per cent. Over six sets of county elections, however, the gap between male and female candidates varies – ranging from a high of 3.3 per cent in the 1993 example above to a low of just 0.7 per cent in 1973. In the metropolitan areas a similar gap is present – at a maximum of 6.5 per cent in both 1988 and 1990 compared with a 0.8 advantage in average vote share for women candidates in 1976. The latter figure should be treated with some caution as there were relatively few female candidates at the 1976 metropolitan elections.

However, when we control for any possible incumbency effect – that is, the likelihood of predominantly male sitting councillors receiving additional votes in recognition of their past service in the ward – the difference between men and women is less noticeable. The gap of over 3 per cent between all male and female candidates at the 1993 county elections narrowed to just 1 per cent when the mean vote share for male and female incumbent councillors alone was examined. Amongst non-incumbent candidates the gap was wider, with women averaging 2.5 per cent less of the share of the vote than men. When these figures are analysed according to the party allegiance of candidates (see Table 5.3), something of a pattern emerges. Labour non-incumbent women do much less well than their male counterparts, while both incumbent and non-incumbent Liberal/Liberal Democrat women candidates tend to perform better than their male colleagues. The gender gap among incumbent and non-incumbent Conservatives alike is comparatively small throughout. There are, of course, a number of possible explanations for these differences. First, it might be that the Labour process for selecting candidates discriminates against women and that when they are selected women are often given the more difficult seats to contest. A second possibility is that Labour voters discriminate against women candidates. There is less support for this view as recent figures show the gap between Labour's incumbent candidates narrowing sharply to favour women in 1989 and to put male incumbents just 0.9 per cent ahead at the last county elections in 1993. Third, although women may be reluctant actually to be elected to the county councils, many do not object to being 'paper' candidates in hopeless seats, thereby allowing the party to maintain both its quota of female candidates – if not of councillors – and its level of contestation (Barron *et al.* 1991).

Table 5.3 Average percentage vote difference between male and female candidates in English shire county elections 1973–1993

	Incumbents				Non-incumbents			
	All	*Conservative*	*Labour*	*Liberal*	*All*	*Conservative*	*Labour*	*Liberal*
1973	–	–	–	–	0.7	1.4	2.9	−0.3
1977	−1.1	−0.4	−0.3	−1.9	0.8	2.2	3.0	0.2
1981	0.1	0.4	2.5	−5.4	1.4	1.4	4.2	−0.5
1985	1.8	0.5	3.7	−0.1	0.1	0.7	1.9	−1.3
1989	0.3	0.0	−0.2	−1.4	1.6	0.7	3.6	−1.1
1993	1.1	−0.1	0.9	0.5	2.5	0.8	4.6	0.6

Note: Minus sign indicates female lead over male.

In socio-economic terms the metropolitan boroughs are quite different from the shire counties. Politically, they have been dominated by Labour for most of their twenty-year existence. Once again, the gender gap in support for Labour incumbents consistently favours the men, but among non-incumbents Labour women outperformed Labour men in both 1991 and 1992 – see Table 5.4. Does this mean that in the metropolitan authorities Labour's women candidates have not encountered the same difficulties as in the shire counties and that there is discrimination neither by party selection procedures nor by the voters? Unfortunately the data do not allow us to answer such questions unequivocally. Labour's domination in the metropolitan areas is such that the numbers of non-incumbent Labour candidates have reduced considerably over the last decade. In 1986 for example, the number of incumbent Labour councillors comprised some 53.9 per cent of the party's total wards. By 1992 that figure had risen to 66 per cent, leaving relatively few seats where non-incumbents were contesting.

Another way of exploring whether voters discriminate for or against women candidates is to examine voting patterns in multimember wards in the shire districts. Faced with a long list of party candidates, some of whom are male and others female, do electors voting for a party slate discriminate against women? Table 5.5 shows the finishing order for male and female candidates in the 1991 and 1995 English shire district elections. Although a quarter of female candidates finished in first place in 1991 this was lower than the 28.9 per cent of male candidates who finished in the same position. Below first place, however, the percentages become virtually identical. Four years later and the proportion of women candidates finishing in first place was just 2 per cent less than the equivalent figure for male candidates. What this appears to demonstrate is that women candidates, once the decision has been made to stand, appear as likely to be elected as their male counterparts. Further investigation reveals, moreover, that male candidates were much more likely to be incumbents seeking re-election and that some level of personal voting was present. In 1995, for example, amongst non-incumbent candidates finishing in first place, 29.6 per

Table 5.4 Average percentage vote difference between male and female candidates in metropolitan borough elections 1986–1992

	Incumbents				Non-incumbents			
	All	*Conservative*	*Labour*	*Liberal*	*All*	*Conservative*	*Labour*	*Liberal*
1986	6.1	1.3	2.1	4.0	1.6	1.6	2.0	−1.1
1987	2.8	0.4	3.3	2.4	1.9	4.6	1.8	0.9
1988	2.7	4.4	1.2	−1.9	2.5	1.3	1.5	1.2
1990	6.7	4.2	2.7	4.3	2.8	1.2	0.2	1.1
1991	5.9	1.8	5.6	1.4	1.5	2.5	−3.1	−0.9
1992	0.2	−1.8	1.4	−5.8	−0.4	0.9	−2.6	−0.3

Note: Minus sign indicates female lead over male.

Table 5.5 Finishing order of female and male candidates in 1991 and 1995 English shire district elections

Finishing order	1991				1995			
	Female candidate	%	Male candidate	%	Female candidate	%	Male candidate	%
1	1,870	25.3	5,441	28.9	1,777	24.3	4,519	26.3
2	1,740	23.5	4,673	24.8	1,691	23.1	4,193	24.4
3	1,400	18.9	3,353	17.8	1,410	19.2	3,161	18.4
4	865	11.7	2,063	10.9	843	11.5	1,846	10.8
5	568	7.7	1,293	6.9	605	8.3	1,246	7.3
6	415	5.6	901	4.8	400	5.5	988	5.8
7	258	3.5	505	2.7	270	3.7	531	3.1
8	138	1.9	300	1.6	169	2.3	321	1.9
9	91	1.2	208	1.1	98	1.3	237	1.4
10	42	0.6	70	0.4	41	0.6	70	0.4
11	8	0.1	31	0.2	4	0.1	33	0.2
12+	8	0.1	17	0.1	18	0.1	12	0.1

cent were female and 70.4 per cent male. Amongst incumbents, however, women comprised a lower proportion, accounting for 27.2 per cent of incumbents returned in first place. This implies that men have, historically, enjoyed a more privileged position in most parties and have probably occupied the safer seats. That bias would account for the fact that men are more successful pro rata in occupying first place in multiple-member wards. The uniformity amongst men and women below first place suggests there is little prejudice among voters about a candidate's gender. One final piece of evidence which can be put forward to counter any argument that electors discriminate against women is to compare the mean share of the total electorate won by male and female incumbents. It is necessary to examine this particular indicator because the normally used vote share is a summary statistic for parties and not candidates in multiple-member wards. Analysis of the 1995 results in the shire districts shows the mean share of the electorate for 833 female incumbents finishing in first place to be 24.2 per cent while for 2,229 men it was 24.8 per cent. The closeness of these two statistics would suggest that, in the eyes of voters at least, gender is not an issue in selecting councillors.

Equally revealing is an analysis of voting in single-member wards at the 1990 and 1992 district elections. The share of the vote won by male candidates is in both cases 2 per cent higher than that achieved by women. It would be wrong to conclude, however, that this difference results from voter prejudice. When the mean vote shares of male and female incumbents at the 1992 district elections were examined they were identical. This finding suggests once again that voters do not discriminate against women at all but rather that other factors account for the discrepancy in vote shares. One of the most crucial influences on the lower vote share won by women candidates is the fact that parties do not appear to select them for their better seats.

With no real evidence to suggest that the electorate discriminate against women candidates many local parties could work to improve the ratio of women candidates and councillors in local government. The evidence suggests, however, that two factors may operate to depress the number of women in local government. First, it is the case that party selection meetings are often dominated by men who may not be well-disposed towards picking women for the more winnable seats in a district. Whatever the merits of organising candidate selection so as to increase the number of women the various political parties have it within their power to show that local government can once again lead the way in terms of advancing democracy. Second, it does appear that the burden of contesting an election, possibly winning and becoming a councillor, is too great for many women. Surveys show the enormous time councillors have to spend on council-related work and faced with a choice between that and running a home, supporting a family as well as often having a part- or full-time occupation, many women make the decision not to put themselves forward for election. They may, of course, agree to stand in seats where the party has little prospect of victory, fighting little more than a paper campaign. Whatever the process the outcome is the same: women candidates are less likely to be found in a local party's most winnable seats. There is little individual parties can do to rectify this particular problem. If this is the real reason why women are not as involved in local government as much as they might be then a fundamental review of the way our still essentially voluntary system works might be appropriate. At the very least being a councillor needs to be seen as like any other occupation with elected members paid and given the necessary administrative and technical support to fulfil their functions properly.

ETHNIC MINORITIES AND LOCAL ELECTIONS

One other aspect of the demographic composition of candidates and councillors on which all too little information is available is their ethnic background. Michel Le Lohé has kindly provided us with unpublished data on the character of councillors in all those local authorities in England where, according to the 1991 census, the self-ascribed 'white' population was less than 90 per cent of the total. Councillors appear to reflect the population from which they are drawn better in the case of the Asian than the Black community. Indeed in some authorities they are 'over-represented'. In Tower Hamlets, for example, 30 per cent of councillors and 25.7 per cent of the population are of Asian origin. In the same borough, 7.7 per cent of the population, but none of the councillors are Black. More than 20 per cent of councillors are Asian also in Ealing, Leicester, Hounslow, Newham and Slough. The authority with the highest proportion of Black councillors is Lewisham (13.4 per cent), and in Brent, Hackney and Haringey too the proportion exceeds one in ten. With the fuller compilation of such data, and its extension to the level of candidates, it will be possible to conduct the same kind of analysis of the impact of candidature as we were able to do in the case of women.

CANDIDATES AND INCUMBENCY EFFECTS

Compared with the 1960s, when just under half of all councillors had held their seats for ten years or more, only one third of current councillors can boast such longevity (Widdicombe 1986b). Before leaping to the conclusion that increased councillor turnover is a function of greater electoral volatility we should note the comments of one study which remarked, 'In a democratic system there is a natural instinct to imagine that the principal agents of change in the membership of an elected assembly might be the electorate. Not so' (Game *et al.* 1993: 18). This research showed that voluntary resignation and not electoral defeat was the biggest factor in councillor turnover. At the 1990 London borough elections, for example, no less than 53.6 per cent of councillors did not return to the council but only 4.6 per cent were actually defeated at the polls. Although the London authorities have the highest rate of voluntary turnover amongst councillors, even in the shires one in three councillors voluntarily resigned their seats as opposed to one in ten who were defeated during the 1980s. While research has been conducted on the reasons why former councillors have turned their backs on local government – for a lack of continuity in council membership can have important implications for the quality of decision-making – little or no work has been done on why comparatively few councillors face electoral defeat. However, instead of asking why are so few councillors defeated, perhaps we should be asking why are so many, in an age of increasing electoral volatility, successfully re-elected?

There is well-documented evidence from national election studies that in any election incumbents seeking re-election have a head start over their rivals. In the United States, for example, the success rate of incumbents seeking re-election is frequently above 90 per cent for the House of Representatives and only slightly lower for the Senate (Mann 1977; Cover 1977; Parker 1980; Jacobson 1992). Such has been the level of success for incumbents that there have been calls for limitations to be placed on the number of terms which can be served by a legislator. In other countries too, incumbents seem to enjoy similar advantages, although it has not become a political issue in quite the same way as in the United States (Jackson 1994). In the same way that governments are said to have advantages which mean that they can only lose elections by their own hand rather than as the result of the positive appeal of opposition parties, so it is suggested that sitting legislators have a cushion of support denied to their rivals (Mann 1977; Cain *et al.* 1987). Such factors as higher media profiles, opportunities to initiate and identify with successful policy initiatives ('pork barrel politics') as well as an ability to attract support simply because some people like to 'back a winner', all tend to favour incumbents and not their opponents. Occasionally, of course, and especially when a government is embroiled in scandal, political incumbency can prove a handicap (Reed 1994), but on balance once in office certain advantages accrue to legislators when the time comes for them to seek a fresh electoral mandate. Is the same true for local government in Britain? Do incumbent councillors build up a 'personal vote'? In this section we will examine the effects, if any, of incumbency upon the relative performance of candidates in local elections.

First, let us deal with the extent of re-election. How do the different types of local authority compare in terms of sitting councillors successfully returned? In the 1992 elections 59 per cent of retiring councillors in the metropolitan boroughs and 54 per cent in the shire districts were returned. Even in the 1993 county elections, which saw the Conservatives lose control of all but one of their councils, 61 per cent of retiring councillors were re-elected for a further term of office. In the 1995 shire district contests, another election in which the Conservatives experienced devastating losses, no fewer than 78 per cent of incumbent councillors seeking re-election were successful. In other words, even in times of electoral landslides, continuity of council membership is preserved to a much greater extent than one might expect.

So, how much does it help a candidate in local elections in Britain to be standing for re-election? One method for measuring the possible effects of incumbency, or the existence of a 'personal vote', is to examine how retiring councillors perform compared with new candidates in multimember wards controlling for party allegiance.

At the 1991 district council elections incumbents were more than twice as likely to finish in first place in a three-member ward as were non-incumbent candidates. When we controlled for party, however, differences emerged. The largest gap between incumbent and non-incumbents was amongst Conservative candidates where the value of incumbency was almost four times greater than non-incumbency in terms of finishing top of that party's slate of candidates. Incumbency was of less value to Labour candidates, although sitting councillors were still more than twice as likely to finish at the top of the party's list. Liberal Democrat candidates enjoyed the least advantage of incumbency, although even here councillors seeking re-election did perform better than the party's candidates without that experience. Another point perhaps worth noting about Liberal Democrats is that until very recently the party has controlled many fewer councils than the two main parties, and indeed in some authorities there have been but a handful of Liberal Democrat councillors. In such a situation it might be more difficult to acquire the publicity and power which incumbents find necessary to develop their personal following.

In order to circumvent the possibility that an electoral snapshot might be misleading, we repeated our analysis of incumbency for the equivalent cycle of elections in 1995. This time 41 per cent of re-elected incumbents finished in first place in three-member wards compared with 25 per cent who finished in third place. The mean share of the electorate for re-elected incumbents was 21.7 per cent; for newly elected candidates it was 2 per cent lower. Closer inspection of the data controlling for party shows incumbents consistently doing better than non-incumbents, albeit with some variation in the margin between parties – see Table 5.6. Among Conservatives, whose losses were considerable in this particular set of elections, incumbents averaged just under 2 per cent more than non-incumbents. The gap was smaller still for Liberal Democrat candidates, though Labour incumbents did enjoy a slightly larger lead of some 3.2 per cent over non-incumbents, Perhaps surprisingly among Independent candidates, where a priori we might expect evidence of a greater personal vote than amongst those sporting a party label, the difference in mean share of the electorate between incumbents and non-incumbents was also less than 2 per cent.

To what extent were incumbents in the smaller shire districts enjoying a level of 'personal vote' denied to councillors seeking re-election to the larger authorities in areas characterised by greater population mobility? Part of the answer to this question might be discovered by examining three-member wards in the London boroughs. In these wards, with exactly the same structure as those found in the shire districts, the advantages of incumbency did appear to be smaller, although some relationship between finishing position and incumbency was still observable. Overall, incumbents standing for re-election to the London boroughs were one and half times more likely to finish ahead of non-incumbents in those wards won by the same party. The relationship was stronger for Conservatives, whose incumbents were almost twice as successful in coming at the top of the party's slate, than for Labour where incumbency hardly appeared to matter. Although not as plentiful in London as councillors from the two main parties, Liberal Democrat incumbents also reaped an electoral benefit when standing for re-election.

The data for multimember wards and the likelihood of incumbents finishing ahead of non-incumbents on a party slate of candidates suggest that there is such a thing as a personal vote, albeit a rather uncertain and small one. What is notable is that voters in shire districts appear either more able or more willing to recognise a former councillor than those voting in London authorities. This suggests that individuals from smaller and more rural areas have a better chance of becoming known as councillors and thereby establishing a 'personal vote' than do their counterparts on the more urban and larger councils.

Table 5.6 Mean percentage share of the electorate for incumbents and non-incumbents elected in three-member wards at the 1995 English shire district elections

Party	% Incumbents	% Non-incumbents	% Difference
Conservative	19.4	17.5	1.9
Labour	24.0	20.8	3.2
Liberal Democrat	18.2	17.0	1.2
Independent	20.3	18.4	1.9

Another method for measuring the electoral significance of incumbency is to compare the change in vote share for candidates in single-member wards. If voters appear to recognise former councillors on the ballot paper how much of an impact does this have and is it always to a person's advantage to receive such recognition? An analysis of local elections demonstrates that there is an 'incumbency vote' but its direction is not always positive. Table 5.7 shows how incumbent candidates for the three main parties compared with non-incumbents in metropolitan, county and district council elections. In the metropolitan boroughs Conservative incumbents saw their vote rise 8.4 per cent between 1988 and 1992 while support for non-incumbents increased by 3 per cent less. The gap in the districts, however, was much less noticeable – slightly more than 1 per cent. The 1992 elections were particularly bad for the Labour party coming one month after a general election defeat. Labour lost vote share and seats throughout the country. Labour councillors seeking re-election to both metropolitan borough and district councils found their vote share decline by some 3 per cent more than non-incumbents. Liberal Democrat councillors seeking re-election in the metropolitan areas saw their vote rise twice as much as for non-incumbents, but in the shire districts the pattern was reversed with non-incumbents securing an average increase in vote share of 2.1 per cent compared to just 1.4 per cent for incumbents. In the county elections Conservative incumbents fared worse, and there was little difference between the categories for the other two parties. Without further analysis it is difficult to conclude whether the fate of incumbents was due to voters wishing to punish recognised faces or a case of the bigger the initial vote share, the greater the decline. The important point, however, is that incumbency does not always bring advantages in local elections.

This brief examination of incumbency effects in local elections suggests that councillors do not appear to enjoy the same sorts of benefits of holding office as enjoyed by members of national legislatures. In the context of a single election for a multimember ward, incumbents do appear more successful than their non-incumbent party colleagues. The data from single-member wards, however, suggest that incumbency is no safeguard to a candidate when the tide of electoral opinion is running against their party. Indeed, incumbents, because they are

Table 5.7 Mean vote change for incumbent and non-incumbent candidates

	Conservative		Labour		Liberal Democrat	
	Incumbent	*Non-incumbent*	*Incumbent*	*Non-incumbent*	*Incumbent*	*Non-incumbent*
Counties 1989–93	−8.4	−5.6	+1.1	+1.1	+7.0	+6.7
Metropolitan boroughs 1988–92	+8.4	+5.7	−11.9	−9.1	+5.9	+2.6
Districts 1988–92	+3.3	+2.1	−7.0	−4.1	+1.4	+2.1

often defending a vote share higher than non-incumbents, appear to suffer even bigger swings against them. Certainly, political incumbency appears no match for the much more influential factor of a generally higher level of electoral volatility. These observations must still be regarded as preliminary. As yet we have not examined the full circumstances surrounding the re-election of councillors. Does the fate of incumbents vary according to the party in power locally and/or nationally? Are incumbents more prone to defeat when ward turnout declines? Are incumbents cushioned from defeat when electors are given more parties to choose from or is their exit from local politics hastened when voters are given a wider range of choices? Doubtless some councillors would even maintain that while many of their colleagues do not enjoy a personal vote they, of course, do! This is certainly one area of the local electoral process worthy of closer study.

CONCLUSIONS

We have examined local elections from three perspectives in this chapter, all of which have profound implications for how local democracy is regarded. First, the overall level of contestation for council seats can be used as an important measure of the degree of interest in becoming a local councillor. In this regard local government appears in sound health with the number of unopposed seats falling and the number of candidates contesting each vacancy rising. On the second measure, however, the evidence is less favourable. Women, though making up much larger proportions of local candidates and councillors than found in comparable contests for a seat in the House of Commons, still account for little more than one out of every four councillors. There has been progress since reorganisation but the change has been steady rather than dramatic. The examination of aggregate electoral data suggests little or no discrimination amongst the voting public when choosing between male and female candidates. Local parties, therefore, should have no misgivings about selecting more women candidates. We suspect, however, that part of the problem associated with a gender gap in local elections is structural rather than attitudinal. Women's life styles do not sit comfortably alongside the needs of local elective office. Work, family and other commitments probably mean many able women are currently deterred from pursuing a political career. A similar analysis of the impact and success of ethnic minority candidates in local government awaits the availability of more comprehensive data.

In our third section we considered whether there was an incumbency effect in local elections. Incumbency, of course, is double-edged – if there are too many successful incumbents the system becomes stagnant and resistant to change. If there are too few the rate of turnover becomes destabilising, contributing to discontinuity and uncertainty in decision-making. Where does local government lie on this scale? There was little indication that councillors seeking re-election were in any real sense immune to the wider political currents. If the public mood disapproves of a particular party then there appears little that any single candidate can do to withstand the tide. Moreover, the evidence shows that electoral defeat accounts for only a proportion of total turnover amongst councillors. Many councillors decide, for a variety of reasons, that local council service produces too great a personal strain and voluntarily relinquish office. This picture suggests that far from incumbency being the problem, it is councillor turnover that needs to be highlighted. Again, however, short of instructing voters not to vote out of office those sitting councillors who do seek re-election, the remedy for this problem lies beyond the electoral process itself.

6   Party competition in local elections

INTRODUCTION

The last twenty-five years have witnessed a weakening of the ties between voter and party in Britain. Fewer voters now align themselves very strongly with any political party. Findings from successive British Election Studies, for example, show that the number of respondents who 'strongly identified' with one or other of the two major parties has declined from 40 per cent in 1964 down to just 18 per cent, up slightly on 1987, in 1992 (Denver 1994: 54). This weakening of party ties has been described as a period of dealignment. Changes among the electorate have produced a steady drift away from the once stable two-party system towards a variety of party systems reflecting national, regional and other differences. In local government, however, this process of partisan dealignment has become entangled with an equally powerful process of party politicisation. Local elections, once infrequently contested by the major parties, have been gradually colonised.

Local government, therefore, became exposed to a number of different, some might say divergent, pressures: first, a period of electoral dealignment where voter loyalties grew weaker and where neither Labour nor Conservative parties could any longer guarantee support from a significant proportion of the electorate. Second, a continuing process of party politicisation at the local level which accelerated during and immediately after reorganisation. The electoral process in some parts of the country, principally the more heavily urbanised, had long been dominated by party politics, but for large swathes of rural and suburban Britain parties were still something of a rarity in local elections. Suddenly with reorganisation, Independent councillors who had served under the old system found themselves pressurised by the national parties, principally the Conservatives, to forgo their non-party stance and contest elections under a party banner. In a sense the existence of new authorities with new boundaries and wider powers offered the equivalent of a politically clean slate. Whatever an area's electoral past there was a new present and even in those areas where Conservative and Labour had held sway other parties were determined that the old two-party system was not going to dominate.

Local elections, therefore, became opportunities for an increasingly volatile electorate to express their new freedom from party ties. The old parties not only had to work harder to win electoral support but also to try to fend off the challenge generated by other parties keen to make their mark in the new system. In this chapter we examine, from a number of different perspectives, the nature and extent of party competition in British local elections. Our primary objective will be to highlight the changing structure of party competition, showing in particular how the fight between national parties steadily intruded into the local political arena. To a significant degree the evolution of parties has developed at a different pace and at different times in specific parts of the local government system. Even after more than twenty years of the nationalisation of local party politics significant differences still remain. We have divided our discussion of party competition, therefore, between the London boroughs, metropolitan boroughs, English shire counties and districts, Scotland and Wales. The different electoral cycles operating in these types of local authority plus their often quite different patterns of party system development justify this separate treatment.

PARTY COMPETITION IN THE LONDON BOROUGHS

The high national profile given to competition for political control of London government has meant that these particular elections have long witnessed a wider party struggle than elsewhere. London was reorganised a decade before the rest of the country but even in the 1960s its elections were microcosms of the national political battle. In the very first GLC elections, for example, almost all 32 wards had candidates from the three main parties, a pattern which would continue, with the single exception of 1973, until the authority's abolition in the mid-1980s. In contrast competition for the London boroughs was never quite as fierce, largely due to the Liberal party's difficulty in finding the resources to fight many more contests. In both 1968 and 1971, for example, a majority of wards were still contested by just Labour and Conservative. Defining two-way party contests as those between Conservative and Labour and three-way contests as those at which candidates from the various incarnations of the Liberal party joined them, Table 6.1 demonstrates the extent to which elections in the capital became increasingly competitive. By the mid-1970s even borough elections reflected the growing pressure on two-party politics. In 1974 almost three-quarters of wards saw three-party contests. With the emergence of the SDP in the early 1980s this proportion rose still further and by 1986 only 5 per cent of wards were not three-party competitive.

The level of party competition has, however, been affected by outside events. The 1971 borough elections, for example, saw a reduction in the number of contests with Liberal candidates, down to just 34 per cent, following the party's disappointing showing in the previous year's general election. Similarly, another decline in 1990 reflected the national problems affecting the Liberal party following its split with the SDP after the 1987 general election. Despite such

Table 6.1 Structure of party competition in London 1964–1994

	Conservative v. Labour v. Liberal	Conservative/ Labour	Conservative/ Liberal	Labour/ Liberal	Total wards
GLC					
1964	87.5	12.5	0.0	0.0	32
1967	100.0	0.0	0.0	0.0	32
1970	100.0	0.0	0.0	0.0	32
1973	65.2	34.8	0.0	0.0	92
1977	97.8	2.2	0.0	0.0	92
1981	96.7	3.3	0.0	0.0	92
Boroughs					
1964	58.7	34.1	0.0	4.6	678
1968	42.4	50.5	0.5	1.7	654
1971	34.3	60.9	0.0	0.5	653
1974	72.1	22.4	0.0	1.2	660
1978	59.2	38.5	0.0	0.5	754
1982	91.7	3.8	0.1	3.6	757
1986	95.2	2.0	0.7	2.1	757
1990	70.3	26.9	0.3	1.3	757
1994	86.6	9.9	0.0	3.4	759

Note: Percentages do not total 100; remaining wards had no party contest or featured one major party with minor party or Independent candidates.

fluctuations the overall trend in the capital appears to have been one of extensive and growing three-party competition. The possibility exists, however, that the extent of that competition might be exaggerated. London boroughs have a mix of single and multimember wards. In the latter case a ward would be described as having three-party competition even if parties had not fielded a full slate of candidates. How far, therefore, has there been full three-party competition for seats? Simply by observing the total number of candidates fielded by the main parties we can see that there have indeed been variations in the degree of competition. In some years three-way competition has been relatively complete with parties presenting as many candidates as there are seats available. In 1986, for example, when three-party fights peaked at 95 per cent the range in total number of candidates fielded by each of the three main parties went from Labour's 1,913 to the Conservatives' 1,837 – a gap of just 76. Four years later, however, not only did the number of wards with three-party competition decline but there was also an increased tendency for the Liberal Democrats to field less than a full slate of candidates, often with only a single candidate standing in a three-member ward. No less than 700 fewer Liberal Democrat than Labour candidates contested these elections. By 1994, however, the Liberal Democrats had recovered to field only 284 candidates fewer than Labour. Clearly, the existence of multimember wards does add to the complexity of assessing the overall level of party competition for seats.

The aggregate picture of party competition can also disguise quite significant variations at the individual borough level. While some London authorities experienced virtually uninterrupted rates of three-party competition, in others there were rapid and dramatic developments. In boroughs such as Bromley and Redbridge, for example, the proportion of three-way contests has never fallen below 90 per cent of all wards over a thirty-year period. By contrast in Haringey party competition grew quite gradually. From reorganisation to 1974 less than a third of the borough's 20 wards ever featured Liberal candidates. For the rest of that decade a majority of wards had three-party competition but it was not until the 1982 elections that all wards were similarly contested. A third category of boroughs, however, saw dramatic changes. In 1971 Liberals contested just 3 of Wandsworth's 20 wards but three years later the electorate in all but two wards could choose to vote for a Liberal candidate. Similar events elsewhere meant that by 1994 the Liberal Democrats had majority control in 3 of the 32 boroughs. Yet in those three boroughs, Kingston, Richmond upon Thames and Sutton, at the beginning of the 1970s the Liberals had not even begun to contest all the seats. What this suggests is that although the electoral battle has ostensibly been between national parties those parties have been heavily dependent upon local organisations. In turn those organisations have been shaped by local activists whose presence or not has proved a key factor in establishing and then sustaining a party in a particular locality.

PARTY COMPETITION IN THE METROPOLITAN BOROUGHS

The party politicisation of local government was first and foremost an urban phenomenon. Even before reorganisation Labour and Conservatives had challenged one another for control of cities such as Birmingham, Manchester, Liverpool and Leeds. With reorganisation these cities had now become the centre of large metropolitan boroughs and the established parties were to prove something of a barrier to the further expansion of party competition in them. As Table 6.2 shows, in 1973 less than a third of wards had three-cornered contests with most wards involving a straight fight between Labour and Conservative candidates. It was not until 1980 that in these boroughs the proportion of three-party contests overtook those with candidates from the traditional two parties. The 1981 county and the following year's borough elections marked a sea change in the nature of party competition, with the proportion of three-cornered battles rising by 25 per cent and 39 per cent respectively. This sudden increase came about because of the twin developments of a newly-created SDP anxious to establish a foothold in areas of Labour strength and Liberals spurred on by the prospect of support in their struggle to break the two-party hegemony in the metropolitan boroughs. In time the national fate of the Liberal/SDP Alliance had an impact on competition at the local electoral level. In 1988 the number of three-way contests fell by 15 per cent compared with the previous year and by 1990 just 6 out of 10 wards featured a Liberal Democrat candidate.

Table 6.2 Structure of party competition in metropolitan councils 1973–1995

	Conservative v. Labour v. Liberal	Conservative/ Labour	Conservative/ Liberal	Labour/ Liberal	Total wards
Metropolitan counties					
1973	30.9	59.4	0.5	2.0	547
1977	48.8	48.3	1.1	0.5	547
1981	73.7	22.3	0.5	2.0	547
Metropolitan boroughs					
1973	32.0	55.7	0.7	2.7	822
1975	50.5	36.0	0.6	3.9	822
1976	48.9	41.7	0.5	3.2	822
1978	38.8	55.1	0.7	0.6	822
1979	46.5	47.3	0.5	1.3	822
1980	47.5	43.4	0.4	4.0	830
1982	86.2	4.1	0.2	8.8	827
1983	84.6	5.0	0.4	8.8	827
1984	74.5	15.1	0.0	7.9	827
1986	76.5	10.3	0.0	9.1	827
1987	84.0	6.2	0.5	6.7	827
1988	68.7	25.4	0.1	2.8	827
1990	59.3	28.9	0.1	3.1	827
1991	69.5	22.2	0.0	1.8	827
1992	76.7	16.2	0.0	4.2	827
1994	68.1	19.2	0.0	6.3	827
1995	71.5	16.4	0.1	5.6	827

Note: Percentages do not total 100; remaining wards had no party contest or featured one major party with minor party or Independent candidates.

What we see across the metropolitan boroughs is expanding party competition. Throughout the 1970s the proportion of three-way contests had only once climbed above 50 per cent: by the 1980s they had become the norm and not the exception. Nevertheless, it is also clear that the overall level of three-party competition had been less than that witnessed in the London boroughs. Clearly, in some areas the Liberal Democrats and their predecessors have failed to penetrate the old two-party struggle. Equally, in other areas it is the Conservative party that has failed to establish a competitive presence. In the 1994 elections, for example, the proportion of Labour–Liberal Democrat contests was twice as high in the metropolitan authorities as it was in the London boroughs.

As in London there are marked differences in the pattern of party competition amongst the 36 metropolitan boroughs and the general picture obscures some interesting and important variations. Some authorities, most notably Liverpool and Stockport, already had highly competitive elections by the 1970s. Only for a brief period in the early 1980s were Stockport's elections not all three-party contests and even then that was partly because the Conservatives failed to put up candidates. As an authority, however, few can match the level of party competition seen in elections to Liverpool city council. By the mid-1970s the Liberals had already become a significant force on Merseyside, contesting and winning large numbers of council seats as well as, in a 1979 by-election, the parliamentary constituency of Edge Hill. Because Liverpool was a Liberal stronghold the SDP were never really given an opportunity to establish themselves there and the troubles later affecting the Alliance made no impression on the Liberal ability to make three-party competition universal throughout the city. In sharp contrast were other boroughs, the best two examples of which are Barnsley and Rotherham, which because of Labour's overwhelming electoral strength had, and continue to have, low levels of party competition. Both authorities, based in what was once known as the 'People's Republic of South Yorkshire', have even struggled to maintain two let alone three-party competition. Only in 1982 were all of Barnsley's seats contested by a centre party candidate and even then the Conservatives barely managed to challenge in a majority of wards. In the three years following the Alliance's demise no Liberal candidate was present in Barnsley and never more than six in Rotherham. Such has been Labour's grip that at the 1991 elections 12 of the party's seats in Barnsley and 9 in Rotherham were uncontested.

For other boroughs, however, the birth of the SDP had a dramatic impact on the state of party competition. In Sunderland, Wigan and Walsall the pattern of two-party competition was swept aside overnight as candidates from the fledgling party contested even hopeless seats. In these boroughs, however, party competition was very closely associated with the SDP's national fate. By the late 1980s no more than half their wards enjoyed the luxury of three-party competition. Elsewhere, first the creation and subsequent breakup of the Alliance clearly affected the level of party competition. In Birmingham, for example, before the SDP the Liberals struggled to contest a majority of wards in one of Britain's biggest and most important local authorities. In 1982 that changed with all wards featuring a third-party candidate of some description, a pattern that continued until 1988. With the demise of the SDP competition waned but unlike other boroughs where it never fully recovered Birmingham's electorate by 1991 could once again choose freely among the three main parties. Across the metropolitan boroughs as a whole, therefore, the process of partisan dealignment and increasing party politicisation saw a majority of wards in these authorities with three-party competition by the early 1980s. As we have seen, however, some boroughs resisted this trend while others anticipated it by almost a decade.

PARTY COMPETITION IN THE ENGLISH SHIRE COUNTIES AND DISTRICTS

Thus far we have largely been concerned with the development of party competition in the more densely populated areas of Britain. Among the shires there is considerably more contrast, from cities with electorates greater than most metropolitan boroughs to the most rural districts where the largest centre of population can be a small town with fewer than 5,000 voters on the roll. The overall development of party competition within these shire authorities can be seen in Table 6.3. We have kept contests for the county councils separate from the shire districts for reasons which will become apparent.

If we first examine party competition for the shire counties in England it is clear that the traditional battle between Labour and the Conservatives was the major feature of the first elections in 1973. By the next electoral cycle, however, the number of three-way contests had doubled to over 30 per cent. Less than a decade later it had doubled again and was not unduly affected by the political events of the late 1980s. In 1989 indeed the Liberal Democrats, in the absence of Labour candidates, were to be found in a straight fight with the Conservatives in almost 10 per cent of county divisions. At the 1993 county elections, when the Conservatives lost control of all but one of their councils, Liberal Democrat contestation virtually matched the 1985 peak achieved by the Alliance with party candidates in well over 80 per cent of all English divisions.

In the twenty-year period from 1973, therefore, the county councils had seen almost a five-fold increase in the number of three-party contests. Although the expansion of party competition had been fairly uniform across the 39 English counties some exhibited quite dramatic increases in party competition while for others the break with the traditional two-party system was less noticeable. In Cornwall, for example, the 1973 elections saw just one division contested by a Liberal candidate, nine contested by Conservatives and eleven by Labour. Independent candidates continued to dominate throughout the 1970s as the county firmly resisted the trend toward party politicisation. The following decade, however, saw a rise in party competition but even then Labour's tendency to avoid large areas of the county meant that as late as the 1989 elections just 14 per cent of the divisions had candidates from the three main parties. Nevertheless, once begun, the process of party politicisation tends to be inexorable and with the Liberals openly ambitious for political control the level of three-party competition rose to 32 per cent in 1993 – less than half the overall figure but a clear sign that Cornish politics had entered a new phase. For other counties the great surge in three-party competition coincided with the rise of the Alliance, first noticeable at the 1985 county contests. Lancashire, for example, saw the percentage of divisions with three-party candidacies double to nearly 80 per cent between the 1981 and 1985 elections. In some parts of the country the Liberals have not made such an impact, indeed they have barely managed to alter a pattern of party competition established in the days before reorganisation. In Cumbria, for example, two-party politics has remained dominant with Liberal candidates never contesting above 40 per cent of vacancies.

Such figures both compare and contrast with the pattern of party competition in the lower-tier district authorities. For these particular authorities, however, the figures in Table 6.3 require close scrutiny. It should be recalled that the shire districts have the option of using one of two electoral methods. One method is

Table 6.3 Structure of party competition in English shires 1973–1995

	Conservative v. Labour v. Liberal	Conservative/ Labour	Conservative/ Liberal	Labour/ Liberal	Total wards
Counties					
1973	15.4	52.1	3.6	1.8	2,826
1977	31.4	38.1	8.0	1.7	2,826
1981	53.7	28.1	5.8	3.1	2,938
1985	73.0	12.6	5.5	3.5	3,005
1989	62.7	20.3	9.3	1.7	3,005
1993	71.4	13.9	7.6	2.5	2,998
Districts (whole council)					
1973	7.9	25.3	3.4	3.1	4,118
1976	11.6	30.3	7.0	3.1	4,300
1979	11.2	29.2	6.4	1.5	4,579
1983	30.4	16.0	10.6	4.8	4,649
1987	41.8	11.0	15.1	5.7	4,682
1991	31.0	21.0	12.8	4.0	4,472
1995	40.6	17.8	11.0	8.6	4,678
Districts (partial council)					
1973	18.8	39.9	4.5	3.0	2,111
1976	29.2	34.9	6.5	2.4	2,189
1978	35.5	45.2	5.3	1.4	659
1979	29.8	41.1	4.9	1.3	2,099
1980	45.7	35.0	4.5	2.2	1,542
1982	74.9	4.6	7.1	6.7	1,536
1983	69.4	11.7	6.1	2.9	1,789
1984	65.8	17.2	5.2	3.4	1,852
1986	74.3	10.2	6.0	3.7	1,857
1987	76.3	9.0	5.5	2.9	1,728
1988	60.9	24.8	5.7	1.1	1,752
1990	58.1	27.0	4.3	2.2	1,739
1991	64.8	21.5	4.9	2.0	1,686
1992	71.7	14.7	5.9	2.0	1,723
1994	69.9	14.3	4.6	4.5	1,710
1995	68.2	16.9	3.2	5.5	1,618

Note: Percentages do not total 100; remaining wards had no party contest or featured one major party with minor party or Independent candidates.

for all council seats to come up for election every four years. A second method allows for partial election of the council with approximately one third of all seats being contested at any one election. First, let us examine those authorities in the first category. This particular electoral cycle begins in 1973, runs three-yearly until 1979 when it slips into the familiar pattern of an election every fourth year, concluding in our Table in 1995. These local elections have by no means been completely dominated by the national parties. In 1973, for example, even the level of two-party competition was low with fewer than a third of all contests of this type. Wards with candidates from all three main parties were especially scarce and accounted for barely 8 per cent of all cases. The process of 'nationalisation' had scarcely begun in many shire districts. By the end of the decade the proportion of three-party contests had risen to just 11 per cent while the clash between Conservative and Labour accounted for less than one in three contests. Once again, however, the entrance of the SDP as an electoral force proved significant with a near trebling of three-party fights by the 1983 elections. The proportion rose again in 1987, dropped back from that peak in 1991, and increased again in 1995 as the Liberal Democrats re-established themselves as a potent electoral force. Indeed more than three-quarters of all contests in 1995 were fought out between at least two of the major parties – twice the level of competition in evidence at the inaugural elections in 1973.

Throughout the period since reorganisation authorities with whole council elections compare unfavourably in terms of the level of party competition with those that chose to hold annual elections. That these latter councils, many of them former county boroughs, brought with them a much stronger tradition of partisanship is immediately apparent in Table 6.3. In 1973 three-way contests were more than twice as common as in those authorities which would retain 'whole-council' elections, and in the first year of 'partial' elections, 1978, more than 80 per cent of all wards featured at least two of the major parties. There was a similar contrast between the two types of district in 1979, with the impact of the Alliance in the 1980s prompting an increase in competition from a much higher base point. The importance of the strength of the 'centre' in determining the electoral pattern is clear. At no election since 1982 have more than 10 per cent of wards not experienced at least two-way competition. However, the proportion of three-party contests has varied from a peak of 76 per cent in 1987 to a low of 58 per cent in 1990, almost entirely as a result of the ability of the Liberal Democrats to find candidates.

There appears to be prima facie evidence, therefore, that the nature of party competition varies considerably among shire districts according to which method of election is used by an authority. We took this analysis further by looking at the level of party competition in terms of the proportion of the electorate in each authority which could vote for a candidate from the Conservative, Labour and Liberal parties. Table 6.4 below compares this proportion for the different parties in the two types of district authority. Immediately, we can see a sharp contrast with many more electors able to vote for candidates from each of the parties in the districts with partial elections. In 1973, for example, Conservative and Labour candidates were available to about 20 per cent more of the electorate and Liberal candidates to an extra 10 per cent of it. Such differences have persisted through time even though the presence of party candidates has increased in both types of authority. We can conclude, therefore, that there is a clear difference in overall levels of party competition among the shire districts according to the electoral method utilised. Those authorities which hold annual elections for a part of the council have historically attracted higher rates of competition than those authorities which have whole-council elections every fourth year. However, with all parties beginning to approach saturation coverage in the partial districts in 1995, any further increase in contestation will serve to narrow the gap.

There are a number of possible explanations for the differences detailed in Table 6.4. First, authorities with annual elections tend to be more urban and, as we noted in Chapter 2, the process of party politicisation had extended furthest in such areas by the time of reorganisation. Indeed their pattern of party competition more closely resembles that in the metropolitan boroughs than in the other shire districts. A second, and perhaps associated factor, might be that these authorities are more likely to have compact wards which make it easier for parties to become established in terms of finding candidates and mounting efficient campaigns. Third, there could be a process whereby the more a party fights campaigns the more able it is to repeat that process year after year. In the whole council authorities local parties are less used to fighting elections and many have not had to develop the habit. Finally, we may be guilty of imposing a national perspective of what constitutes party competition which is inappropriate for these authorities. Although non-party or Independent candidates have declined in number they still fought more than one in four wards in 1995, being especially numerous in authorities with whole council elections. In a significant proportion of cases the presence of an Independent candidate might prove sufficient to deter candidates from one of the three main parties from standing. Again this would be most likely to happen in small, rural wards where the qualities of individual local politicians would be known to voters and competitors alike. Such wards are to be found more frequently in the type of authorities where whole council elections are the norm.

Compared with the metropolitan areas the shire districts are socially, economically and geographically relatively heterogeneous. It would be unusual, therefore, if the differences found amongst the larger cities were not also to be found among the shire authorities. Indeed, given the aggregate differences in the level of three-party competition between authorities holding whole council as opposed to partial elections we might expect to find even larger differences in

Table 6.4 Percentage of the electorate able to vote for party candidate

	Whole council districts			*Partial districts*		
	Conservative	Labour	Liberal	Conservative	Labour	Liberal
1973	58.0	64.0	23.4	80.2	82.6	33.5
1979	76.2	58.0	26.8	92.4	82.9	42.2
1983	75.5	66.3	56.9	91.1	88.2	82.8
1987	78.6	71.2	71.9	93.3	91.6	87.1
1991	79.0	71.2	56.7	94.1	92.6	74.3
1995	79.3	85.7	71.9	93.2	97.2	83.0

patterns of party competition. As Table 6.3 demonstrated there has been an erratic development towards greater party contestation, often reflecting the national fortunes of one or other of the main parties. Only two districts, Oxford and Gloucester, have experienced virtually uninterrupted three-party competition throughout the period. Some authorities, such as Brighton and Scunthorpe, underwent a rapid transformation in terms of party competitiveness. Brighton, for example, saw just two of its 19 wards in 1973 with a Liberal candidate but by the end of that decade three-party fights became universal and have remained so. By contrast, however, Scunthorpe saw a sharp rise from 1973, when no Liberals challenged, to 1980 when all but one ward was three-party competitive. With the collapse of the Alliance, however, the centre challenge itself waned and since 1988 the authority has not seen a Liberal candidate contest any of its elections. In some authorities the move towards three-party competition was even more short-lived. Gravesham in Kent saw an extremely vigorous onslaught on its two-party system during the 1980s but once again as the Alliance broke up nationally the enthusiasm of Liberals to continue the fight evaporated. By 1991 Conservative and Labour candidates were virtually untroubled by any other challengers and each emerged from the 1991 elections with 22 councillors apiece. Very few authorities remained locked into a two-party system throughout, although Barrow provides a good example of what such a system might look like. With its practice of partial election this authority has held over 170 contests at 14 elections since 1973 and in that period the Liberals have fielded just 25 candidates leaving Conservative and Labour to fight it out amongst themselves.

PARTY COMPETITION IN SCOTLAND

In both Scotland and, to a lesser extent, Wales the growth of party competition for local council votes and seats has been influenced by the issue of nationalism and nationalist parties. In a later chapter we will examine the specific fate of both the Scottish Nationalist party (SNP) and Plaid Cymru (PC) but suffice to say that their presence has helped to extend the pattern of party competition and led to much more complex party systems both overall and in individual local authorities in each country.

In Scotland Labour has long been electorally dominant, but this hegemony has increasingly been threatened by the greater challenge of other parties at the local level. Both the Liberal Democrats and the SNP have joined the party struggle, helping to make some Scottish local authorities among the most competitive in Britain. As can be seen in Table 6.5, however, this has not always been the case. The first local elections after reorganisation were held a year after those in the remaining parts of Britain and were sandwiched between two general elections. That fact undoubtedly affected the ability of the smaller Liberal and Scottish Nationalist parties to contest seats in any reasonable numbers. During the 1970s fewer than one in twenty seats had four-party competition. In the 1980s party contestation developed at different rates in the regions and districts. Regional divisions, being both fewer in number and electing councillors to the more important tier of government, rapidly reached a position where almost two-thirds of seats were contested by at least three parties. In the districts full party competition also increased but to a lesser extent. By 1988 a seemingly stable pattern had emerged with nearly one half of seats having three- or four-party contests, and about one in six remaining as private battles between Labour and the SNP. The inaugural unitary council elections in 1995 had a pattern of party competition more in keeping with the former districts, on whose wards the intra-council electoral units were based, than with the regions. Four-way contests were only a little more than half the level experienced in the final regional council elections in 1994.

The nature of party competition has been far from uniform across the different local authority types in Scotland. Some regional councils, particularly the more densely populated, were the focus of intense party struggles. Lothian, for example, saw four-way fights in virtually all of its 49 divisions throughout the 1980s. In 1982 the country's largest region, Strathclyde, had the vast majority of its divisions contested by Conservative, Labour and SNP candidates and in three-quarters of these the parties were joined in the fray by a Liberal. Four years later the Alliance stepped up its campaign and fielded even more

Table 6.5 Structure of party competition in Scotland 1974–1994

	4-way	Conservative v. Labour v. SNP	Other 3-way	Conservative/ Labour	Labour/ SNP	Other 2-way	Total wards
Regions							
1974	2.8	12.5	8.5	2.8	8.6	5.0	432
1978	4.2	33.8	2.3	12.3	7.9	6.0	432
1982	30.8	11.1	14.0	4.1	6.1	7.2	441
1986	37.1	8.8	21.3	0.9	11.5	4.4	445
1990	35.7	24.0	8.3	1.6	5.8	10.4	445
1994	44.4	18.5	8.6	1.8	4.0	6.8	453
Districts							
1974	1.5	9.1	7.3	21.8	11.0	4.7	1,116
1977	3.7	18.1	5.3	14.1	12.7	5.9	1,117
1980	3.7	16.1	5.9	15.7	14.2	5.3	1,127
1984	14.4	10.6	13.8	8.2	10.5	7.3	1,152
1988	16.8	22.5	7.0	4.2	16.8	5.9	1,158
1992	18.0	22.9	7.5	2.4	18.0	6.3	1,158
Unitary councils							
1995	24.2	18.1	14.2	1.1	18.0	6.3	1,161

Note: Percentages do not total 100; remaining wards had no party contest or featured one major party with minor party or Independent candidates.

Source: David Denver.

candidates. Although the proportion of four-way contests fell slightly in 1990 it rose again to new heights four years later. In Fife also, the Liberal Democrats were slow to become established. Throughout the 1970s, for example, the region was contested by a solitary Liberal but the advent of the Alliance saw a dramatic increase with more than half the divisions contested. In the final regional elections in 1994 virtually every division featured the four main parties. Three Scottish regions, Borders, Dumfries and Galloway and Highland, have been classified by Bochel and Denver as 'non-partisan' (Bochel and Denver 1974), but even among them there are some interesting variations in patterns of competition. In Borders, for example, there is the genesis of a three-party system which excludes Labour. Always struggling to find candidates Labour did not present a single one to the electorate in either 1986 or 1994. In Dumfries and Galloway, by contrast, Labour has for long contested more seats than any of the other parties, having a candidate in more than half the divisions in 1994.

The same degree of party competition has not been in evidence in the Scottish districts where four-party fights are rare and different permutations of two- or three-party battles more common. In authorities such as West Lothian, Falkirk, Monklands, Midlothian and Clackmannan, for example, voters have most often been presented with a straight choice between Labour and the SNP. In Dundee and Dunfermline those two parties have fielded candidates in nearly every ward since 1984, but the SNP has often had to cede second place on the council to Conservative opponents who fought fewer but won more seats. A still different picture emerges in Kyle and Carrick, where Labour's main opponent has been the Conservative party; in Perth and Kinross where the two-party struggle is between the Conservatives and the SNP; and in North East Fife where it is the Liberal Democrats who have successfully battled for supremacy with the Conservatives since 1984. Other authorities have clearly developed, three-party systems. Cumbernauld and Kilsyth, Kilmarnock and Loudoun, Motherwell and Renfrew have all been well contested in recent years by all main parties with the exception of the Liberal Democrats. Once again, the range and variety of party system across Scottish local authorities reveals sharp differences between localities.

PARTY COMPETITION IN WALES

The overall level of party competition across the Welsh local authorities is much less than anywhere else in Britain. Not only is there less competition between the three main parties, but the nationalist challenge from Plaid Cymru is much less potent than that of the SNP. Although Welsh authorities have the potential to become genuine four-party systems the reality is that very few have realised that potential. Taking the largest set of elections, those for the district councils held in the electoral cycle which features whole council elections, we can see from Table 6.6 that the proportion of wards featuring four-party competition has been consistently small and has lagged some way behind the pattern found in the Scottish districts. Although the unitary elections contested in 1995 appear to have acted as a stimulus to party competition, the comparison with Scotland is again salutary. There, a quarter of seats had four-party competition while in Wales scarcely more than one in twenty wards was contested in this way. This is not, of course, entirely due to the failure of Plaid Cymru to field candidates. As can be seen an average of more than 11 per cent of wards have featured contests between the dominant Labour party and PC candidates. In significant parts of Wales both Conservative and Liberal Democrat candidates are notable by their absence. Overall, the pattern of party competition in Wales suggests that Independents are still a significant force and that various of the parties have been reluctant to become involved in electioneering. During the 1970s only about a third of wards had party competition of any description and even the creation of the Alliance in the 1980s did little to increase that figure. At the unitary council elections in 1995 still more than half the wards in Wales featured either no contest at all or else very limited competition between one party political candidate and one or more Independents or, indeed, Independents fighting each other alone.

Beneath the surface, however, there is a great deal of variation in both the amount and development of party competition, as we found in both England and Scotland. In the eight Welsh counties, for example, there are some authorities such as South Glamorgan and Gwent where party competitiveness was a feature even of the earliest elections and has developed still further in recent years. The 1973 elections saw Conservative and Labour struggle together for political control of South Glamorgan – a race which Labour just won. At the following elections the council swung back to the Conservatives. In the mid-1980s the two were joined by the Alliance parties and the Liberal Democrats have inherited that competitiveness in the area. At the 1993 county elections these three parties were joined by many more PC candidates than before such that 40 per cent of the county's divisions enjoyed four-party competition. The county, of course, covers

Table 6.6 Structure of party competition in Welsh district council elections 1973–1995

	4-way	Conservative v. Labour v. PC	Conservative v. Labour v. LD	Other 3-way	Conservative v. Labour	Labour v. PC	Other 2-way	Total wards
1973	0.9	1.4	1.3	0.4	9.3	10.8	2.9	786
1976	1.4	2.9	1.9	1.6	8.1	13.6	4.2	803
1979	1.3	5.9	0.8	1.1	11.8	12.3	3.3	799
1983	3.9	1.1	6.3	2.1	5.8	10.0	10.0	813
1987	1.7	0.9	9.5	4.1	6.3	8.5	11.2	887
1991	1.6	2.3	6.4	0.9	6.5	10.0	6.0	894
Unitary councils								
1995	5.5	1.6	7.3	2.9	5.0	14.2	9.2	1,272

Note: Percentages do not total 100; remaining wards had no party contest or featured one major party with minor party or Independent candidates.

Cardiff, the capital city, and this pattern reflects that found in Scotland where the major urban centres witness the broadest party competitiveness.

Other parts of Wales have shown a more gradual, even sedate movement towards party competition. In West Glamorgan, for example, the first county elections saw Labour virtually unchallenged by any other party. By 1977, however, the number of candidates fielded by both the Conservatives and Plaid Cymru had doubled. In 1985 the Alliance became Labour's major challenger with both Conservative and PC candidates declining in number. In the last county elections held in 1993 the pattern had changed again with Labour remaining dominant but with the three other parties each contesting around a third of all vacancies.

That leaves a third category of authority where the events of the past twenty years in the rest of Britain appear to have had little impact on local party politics. In the rural counties of Gwynedd and, to an even greater extent Powys, the rise of party has largely been resisted. Gwynedd's early elections saw a few seats featuring Labour and PC candidates but for the most part a range of Independents were the usual choice for electors. Gradually the number of party candidates did increase although even in Labour's peak year for competition in 1985 the party still contested fewer than half the seats. The case of Powys is even more of an anachronism in that the extent of party competition has actually decreased since 1973. The first elections saw Labour contest 15 of the county's 53 divisions, a figure somewhat higher than for any of the other parties. After that the number of party political candidates tended to decline, with just 7 Labour candidates, 5 Liberal Democrat, 4 Plaid Cmyru and a single Conservative at the final county elections in 1993.

The pattern of party competition in the Welsh districts has tended to parallel that in the counties. Cardiff city council elections, for example, have attracted considerable competition. In the 1995 unitary elections 25 out of the city's 28 wards featured candidates from all four main parties. Similarly, in the adjacent district of Vale of Glamorgan the 1995 elections saw four-party contests in 64 per cent of wards. Outside Cardiff, the Vale of Glamorgan and, to a lesser extent, Swansea, three-way, let alone four-way contests are rare. Welsh district authorities can crudely be categorised into those where Labour has candidates in all the seats and wins most of them in most years against infrequent opposition, and those where parties make intermittent appearances in places of known strength and leave the rest to their opponents or Independents. It remains to be seen whether the coming of unitary local authorities to Wales will provide the impetus for an increase in party competition. Their inaugural elections tended to suggest that any such process will be both gradual and patchy.

CONCLUSIONS

Local politics is now largely about party politics. An age when candidates' names were the only description on the ballot paper has long since disappeared

from the majority of local authorities. Local elections have become party
politicised to the extent that a smaller and smaller proportion of contests now
feature only 'Independent' or minor party candidates. A loosening of social ties
and greater mobility has meant that candidates can no longer rely upon a local
reputation for their election but must instead stand under the party umbrella,
particularly in cities and large towns. Critics may argue that this undermines the
real purpose of local government and weakens the relationship between
community and elected representatives. Whatever the merits of the argument
that councillors should represent a community of local interest the reality is that
the majority now represent a political party. Although there are negative aspects
to this, not least councillors voting according to party rather than ward interests,
there have been distinct advantages stemming from the process of party
politicisation. The choices available to most local voters are now greater and a
fair reflection of the nation's wider political choices. Now, when one party or
another does not contest a local election, voters are regarded as somehow
deprived. Greater party competition has arguably stimulated both campaigning
and media interest in local elections.

Although there has been a general movement towards greater party
competition there are still interesting variations between individual local
authorities. In some authorities the development of party politics has proceeded
at a much slower pace. In other parts of the local government system that
evolution has barely taken place at all. In the small and rural Scottish district of
Stewartry, for example, the 12 member council remained solidly Independent
until 1992. None of Scotland's main parties had ever contested local elections in
Stewartry until three Conservative candidates stood in that year and one was
successfully elected. Despite the absence of national parties local voters were by
no means reluctant to participate in the contests that did take place. In other
authorities where the political parties have yet to assume an influential role,
electorates have shown a similar interest in having a say in the outcome. Party
politics has not quite taken over local government, but each cycle of elections
and each structural change increases its grip.

7   Votes, seats and local electoral outcomes

INTRODUCTION

We saw in the previous chapter how party competition intensified in local elections after 1973, spreading outwards from the cities into the suburbs and then into rural Britain throughout the period since reorganisation. In some authorities this development has been resisted but the number of areas where non-partisan candidates dominate proceedings are steadily dwindling. But the degree of party competition is only part of the story; we must also discover the impact on local voting patterns such expansion by the national parties has made. Clearly, other parties have joined the local electoral battle but how much success have they had in breaking the stranglehold exercised jointly by the Conservative and Labour parties? There are a number of ways in which we can answer this question. First, by measuring vote share we can obtain a sense of how far and how quickly voters deserted the traditional two-party system for something different. Interesting though such an analysis might prove it still leaves open the possibility, particularly with Britain's electoral system, that voter support has not translated into greater representation for other parties. A second approach to the question, therefore, will be to examine the extent to which a change in the distribution of the vote has been translated into a change in share of seats for the various parties competing in local elections. This will take the analysis further but, in the end, votes and seats are simply means to an end. For local parties the ultimate goal is to take political control of the local authority. We need, therefore, to describe the impact growing party competition has had both on the overall number of councillors for each party and on the number of authorities under their respective control. Only when we have examined changes in vote share, seat share and council control will we be able to assess the importance of trends in effective party competition in British local government since reorganisation.

This chapter will address the three themes of votes, seats and political control. In keeping with the structure of the previous chapter we have chosen to organise our discussion of votes and seats in terms of the separate areas of the London boroughs, metropolitan boroughs, English shire districts and counties.

Once again we will treat Scotland and Wales separately. In our final section dealing with the impact of seat redistributions on the political control of local authorities, however, we have arranged our discussion so as to look at the overall picture in England, Scotland and Wales respectively.

VOTING IN LONDON

In London structural change was introduced a decade before everywhere else and it is readily apparent from Table 7.1 that changes in the pattern of party competition have affected the combined Conservative/Labour vote. During the 1960s both Labour and Conservative suffered short-term jolts to their vote. In the spring of 1964, for example, Labour was well ahead of the Conservatives in the opinion polls and this lead was reflected in the London vote. By 1968 it was Labour that lagged behind in public support and the party polled its lowest ever vote in the London borough elections of that year. But, although the electoral pendulum swung to and fro the overall two-party vote share hardly altered. Thus, with the advent of the 1970s the votes of Liberals, Independents and fringe parties amounted to less than 10 per cent of the total. Beginning in 1974, shortly after the February general election, the pattern of two-party dominance was dented if not broken although it was not until 1982 that the Conservative/Labour vote fell below 80 per cent. This was largely a function of the Alliance, whose candidates received the support of almost one in four London voters. The 1986 elections brought another good Alliance performance but by 1990 the Liberals had split with the SDP. Despite this, the combined Conservative/Labour vote remained below 80 per cent. Although the centre vote declined from the heights seen in the 1980s the Liberal Democrats alone managed to hang on to a level of support similar to that achieved by the Liberals in the 1974 elections, while the addition of votes for a variety of Greens and Anti-Poll Tax candidates meant a continuing squeeze on the Labour and Conservative vote. In 1994 a slump in Conservative support proved largely beneficial to the Liberal Democrats and the two-party share declined again. Between 1971, when 90 per cent of votes in London were cast for Labour and the Conservatives, and 1994, two decades of growing party competition brought about a fall of nearly 20 per cent in their combined voting strength. In the same period there was a doubling in the number of wards with three-party competition from 34 per cent to 70 per cent. We shall examine later how the expansion of party competition and gradual decline in the two-party vote share affected the distribution of seats in the London boroughs. But before that we examine whether similar changes were taking place in the metropolitan boroughs and the shires.

VOTING IN THE METROPOLITAN BOROUGHS

In the previous chapter we noted how party competition for seats on metropolitan councils underwent a rapid transformation in the early 1980s.

Table 7.1 Overall share of vote in London 1964–1994

	Conservative	Labour	Liberal/Alliance	Independent	Other
GLC					
1964	39.8	44.6	10.4	0.7	4.5
1967	51.9	34.0	9.5	0.4	4.1
1970	50.8	38.8	6.2	0.3	3.9
1973	37.9	47.4	12.5	0.1	2.0
1977	52.5	32.4	7.8	0.0	7.3
1981	39.7	41.8	14.4	0.0	4.1
London boroughs					
1964	38.8	44.5	11.7	0.8	4.3
1968	58.5	28.0	7.7	0.8	5.1
1971	38.5	52.2	4.7	0.5	4.1
1974	40.7	41.8	13.1	0.2	4.2
1978	48.5	39.0	7.0	0.3	5.2
1982	41.5	31.0	24.2	0.5	2.8
1986	35.2	37.3	23.4	0.3	3.8
1990	37.2	39.1	14.2	0.5	9.0
1994	31.3	41.6	22.1	0.1	4.9

Note: In the case of multimember wards the votes for individual parties have been calculated according to the method outlined in Rallings and Thrasher (eds) (1993). Figures shown are the overall vote share for each party.

While this surge began to subside towards the end of the decade there was a more robust increase in the level of three-party competition which in recent elections has averaged over 70 per cent of all wards. Have such changes in the nature of the party struggle been reflected in the distribution of the vote? At the end of the 1970s the situation in the metropolitan authorities was similar to that in London. Indeed, the two-party vote in 1978 in both the metropolitan and London boroughs was identical – 87.5 per cent (see Table 7.2). Four years later both sets of authorities saw the full impact of the Alliance and the two-party vote in the metropolitan areas was only just above 70 per cent. This proved the lowest point for the combined Conservative/Labour vote in these particular authorities. Although the Conservative vote suffered an almost inexorable decline, reaching a low point of just 19.9 per cent in the 1995 elections, the two-party vote was largely held together by a strong showing by Labour. With the exception of 1992, when Labour's defeat in the general election undoubtedly contributed to its lowered vote in the local elections a month later, the party has consistently polled above 40 per cent and four times achieved an absolute majority of votes cast. Examining the two-party vote across the 36 metropolitan boroughs we find a process of fluctuation rather than sustained decline. In 1973, for example, the combined Conservative/Labour vote was 79 per cent, falling to 71 per cent in 1982 only to rise again to 74 per cent in 1987, and then peaking at 81 per cent in

Table 7.2 Overall share of vote in metropolitan councils 1973–1995

	Conservative	Labour	Liberal/Alliance	Independent	Other
Metropolitan counties					
1973	36.2	47.4	12.9	1.1	2.3
1977	52.8	34.8	8.1	0.5	3.7
1981	30.7	50.4	16.5	0.2	2.1
Metropolitan boroughs					
1973	35.4	44.0	12.8	3.2	4.7
1975	45.8	33.7	14.5	0.9	5.1
1976	45.2	37.5	10.8	0.9	5.5
1978	45.0	42.5	7.9	0.8	3.8
1979	39.7	45.9	10.2	0.4	3.8
1980	35.4	48.9	11.5	0.6	3.6
1982	32.5	38.1	27.0	0.6	1.8
1983	33.6	44.6	18.3	0.3	3.2
1984	31.0	48.5	18.8	0.5	1.2
1986	26.5	48.1	23.4	0.7	1.4
1987	31.6	41.9	24.6	0.5	1.5
1988	31.6	50.9	13.9	0.8	2.8
1990	26.4	54.6	13.8	0.7	4.5
1991	31.7	45.0	18.6	0.8	3.9
1992	39.5	39.3	17.1	0.9	3.2
1994	22.7	51.4	22.8	1.0	2.1
1995	19.9	57.1	19.1	0.8	3.1

Note: In the case of multimember wards the votes for individual parties have been calculated according to the method outlined in Rallings and Thrasher (eds) (1993). Figures shown are the overall vote share for each party.

1990. Such figures, and those of the individual parties themselves, suggest that in the metropolitan boroughs as a whole we have a dominant Labour party and two-party competition for the minor placings.

VOTING IN THE ENGLISH SHIRE COUNTIES AND DISTRICTS

In both the London and metropolitan boroughs the two-party system proved to be quite resilient, although different distributions of support were responsible for the Labour and Conservative parties always managing to attract the votes of 7 in 10 electors. Have the shires, with their greater spread of urban, suburban and rural populations shared this experience or has the vote developed differently in these areas? The figures described in Table 7.3 show that the two-party vote in the shires began at a much lower base than in the more densely populated urban authorities. In the early part of the 1970s the explanation for this lay not so much with the prominence of the Liberals but rather with the traditional strength of Independents in the districts. At the 1973 elections the two-party vote stood at just over 63 per cent in the smaller districts though in the counties it was considerably higher, almost 80 per cent. While the counties witnessed a pattern not dissimilar to the London boroughs – a steady though not spectacular decline in the combined Conservative/Labour vote to the advantage of the political centre – the districts were undergoing a quite different development.

If we compare the two-party vote of 1973 (63.3 per cent) with that of 1995 (64.3 per cent) (Table 7.3) we could be forgiven for initially believing there had been virtually no change. However, although the combined two-party vote has hardly strayed outside a range of 10 per cent between these years, an examination of other columns in Table 7.3 suggests that an increase in the third-party vote has been at the expense of Independents. Once again, the position of candidates from these respective groups reversed at the extremes of our time period. In 1973 the Liberal vote was half that of Independents but by 1991 Liberal candidates polled three times better than Independents. In terms of vote

Table 7.3 Overall share of vote in English shires 1973–1995

	Conservative	Labour	Liberal/Alliance	Independent	Other
Counties					
1973	42.1	37.6	9.2	9.1	2.0
1977	58.1	25.9	8.7	4.5	2.9
1981	40.7	34.8	18.3	3.5	2.7
1985	38.4	30.0	27.9	2.5	1.2
1989	42.2	31.1	20.2	2.0	4.5
1993	35.6	31.2	29.3	1.8	2.2
Districts					
1973	32.1	31.2	10.9	21.5	4.2
1976	42.1	26.1	11.9	14.3	5.6
1978	52.5	33.3	9.6	2.8	1.8
1979	41.9	31.4	11.3	11.0	4.4
1980	40.6	39.9	13.7	2.9	3.0
1982	39.5	27.8	28.7	2.2	1.8
1983	40.0	27.0	20.9	7.3	4.8
1984	39.3	34.2	22.5	2.1	1.9
1986	34.6	33.6	28.4	1.6	1.8
1987	39.5	23.5	27.0	7.5	2.5
1988	41.2	35.4	18.6	1.7	3.1
1990	30.7	43.1	18.7	2.4	5.0
1991	35.9	28.5	23.3	8.0	4.2
1992	45.2	29.0	21.4	2.2	2.3
1994	26.6	39.2	29.7	2.5	2.0
1995	26.0	38.3	25.0	8.0	2.7

Note: In the case of multimember wards the votes for individual parties have been calculated according to the method outlined in Rallings and Thrasher (eds) (1993). Figures shown are the overall vote share for each party. Figures for 1995 include the results in 14 new unitary councils which replaced 22 districts and 4 county councils.

distribution, therefore, the districts present an exterior of relative two-party calm but beneath there has been a considerable churning of the waters. Further confirmation of this view is found when we divide the shire districts into those using different electoral methods. The picture is one of remarkable stability for the combined Conservative/Labour vote. In 1973, for example the two-party vote for those authorities with whole-council elections was 52.5 per cent and 68.9 per cent for those using the partial method. This would be expected given the different patterns of party competition identified within these authorities. At the height of the party struggle in the early 1980s these vote shares had risen to just 58.7 per cent and 70.4 per cent respectively. By 1991 whole-council authorities had a two-party vote of 57.8 per cent while those with elections by thirds, 70 per cent. In short, the Conservative/Labour vote had not only remained stable across time but the difference between the two types of authority had also remained. In aggregate terms the rise of the Liberals had not come at the expense of the two main parties. We will examine below whether this replacement of Independents and others by a more organised national party has had consequences for the overall distribution of seats in the shires.

VOTING IN ENGLISH LOCAL AUTHORITIES: AN OVERVIEW

Although there has been a general weakening in support for the two major parties across the different types of local authority, change has not been uniform. In Table 7.4 local authorities have been categorised according to the combined electoral support for the Conservative and Labour parties. Two-party dominance could be said to occur when the combined vote share for Conservative and Labour parties exceeds 90 per cent, while multi-party systems are normally found in areas where this figure has fallen below 75 per cent. Between 1973 and 1979, however, at a time when the national two-party system was under attack, Labour and Conservative gathered strength in local government. The increase from 45 to 74 in the number of two-party dominant authorities can be explained by the collapse of the Independents, which the two established parties were best positioned to exploit, together with the fact that the Independents had not yet been superseded by the Liberals as a significant local electoral force. Since then, however, there has been a steady decline in the number of two-party dominant authorities. By the mid-1980s, Alliance successes, both in terms of expanding party competition and in redistributing the vote, saw the number of two-party systems fall to just 4. Although the number recovered in both 1991 and 1995 the range of party systems has changed substantially since the 1970s. Comparing 1995 with 1979 the number of authorities where the two-party vote share comprises less than 75 per cent has risen by 21 percentage points. This in turn has had important consequences for the administration of local authorities, many of which have no single party with an overall council majority and so some form of coalition or minority government has been established.

Table 7.4 Party systems in English local government

Conservative/ Labour % share	1973		1979		1985		1991		1995	
	N =	%	N =	%	N =	%	N =	%	N =	%
90% >	45	11.0	74	18.0	4	1.0	17	4.2	18	4.6
75%–<90%	131	32.0	156	38.0	126	31.3	124	30.8	119	30.4
60%–<75%	95	23.2	88	21.5	162	40.2	117	29.0	113	28.9
<60%	139	33.9	92	22.4	111	27.5	145	36.0	141	36.1

Note: The figures for 1973 and 1979 include the GLC and six metropolitan counties. The figures for 1995 include the new unitary councils but not the districts and counties they replaced.

VOTING IN SCOTLAND

Labour's dominance in Scotland can be gauged from the fact that even in the party's more difficult electoral years it has still managed to obtain more than 30 per cent of the popular vote in what is effectively a four-party system. Indeed since the 1980s the party has often succeeded in polling more than 40 per cent of the vote at a time when the rate of party competition had actually increased. The weakness of the Conservatives, however, has meant that the combined two-party vote has been lower in Scotland than in England – never more than 70 per cent and as low as 55 per cent in the 1994 regional elections. Table 7.5 shows that the principal agent in this has been not the Liberals as in England but rather the SNP. There have, however, been considerable fluctuations in support between these two parties. In the late 1970s it was the SNP's turn to threaten the two-party system, winning more than a fifth of votes in both regional and district elections. The birth of the SDP and later the Alliance gave the Liberal camp a considerable boost and by 1982 the party system had become even more fragmented with the Alliance edging ahead of the SNP. The post-1987 general election breakup of the Alliance, however, gave the SNP a fresh opportunity which it seized in 1988 when the party almost doubled its vote in the district elections. Since that time the SNP has proved the more dominant and for the moment appears to have won its battle with the Liberal Democrats. Moreover, since 1986 the SNP has out-polled even the Conservative party and certainly in Scottish politics the party does not deserve the label 'minor'.

This complex party struggle has also contributed to a decline of Independents. From obtaining more than 15 per cent of the vote in the 1974 elections, Independent candidates have seen support squeezed as more party candidates have joined the electoral fray. At the 1980 district elections the Independent vote fell below double figures for the first time and by 1994 only one in twenty Scottish voters supported non-party candidates. But such figures only reveal the overall picture and the detail is even more critical for the cause of Independent candidates. Denver (1993) has a three-part categorisation of Scottish District Councils – 'partisan', 'non-partisan' and 'mixed'. In the late

Table 7.5 Overall share of vote in Scotland 1974–1994

	Conservative	Labour	Liberal/Alliance	SNP	Independent/ Other
Regions					
1974	28.6	38.5	5.1	12.6	15.3
1978	30.3	39.6	2.3	20.9	6.8
1982	25.1	37.6	18.1	13.4	5.7
1986	16.9	43.9	15.1	18.2	5.9
1990	19.6	42.7	8.7	21.8	7.2
1994	13.7	41.8	11.9	26.8	5.7
Districts					
1974	26.8	38.4	5.0	12.4	17.5
1977	27.2	31.6	4.0	24.2	13.1
1980	24.1	45.4	6.2	15.5	8.9
1984	21.4	45.7	12.8	11.7	8.4
1988	19.4	42.6	8.4	21.3	8.4
1992	23.2	34.0	9.5	24.3	9.0
Unitary councils					
1995	11.3	43.8	9.7	26.2	9.1

Source: David Denver.

1970s Denver believed 27 districts could be classed as partisan, 17 non-partisan and 9 mixed. By 1992 the number of partisan councils had increased to 34 with just 10 non-partisan districts remaining, largely concentrated in the rural periphery.

VOTING IN WALES

In one respect, that of Labour's dominance, local voting in Wales resembles that in Scotland. The gap between Labour and any other party in the popular vote has never been less than 10 per cent and frequently has been much higher. In recent elections the party's stranglehold has been much in evidence. In the 1993 county elections, for example, Labour polled almost half the votes and had a lead of more than 30 per cent over each of its rivals. In other respects, however, the pattern of voting has been quite different in Wales compared with that in Scotland. The Conservative party, though competing in local elections, has received little electoral encouragement. Even when Labour was unpopular during the mid-1970s only once did the Conservatives manage to poll more than 20 per cent – something the party succeeded in doing in all but one of the six cycles of Scottish district elections. To some extent the stronger tradition of voting for non-party candidates in Welsh local elections may have contributed to the Conservative party's lack of electoral success. Independents have traditionally done well in Wales, never failing to obtain less than a quarter of votes in district council elections. The larger county divisions have proved more problematic, however, and here the drift towards party politics has been more apparent. As Table 7.6 shows, in the first county elections Independents attracted support from more than a third of voters and, although that proportion declined, one in five Welsh electors was still voting for non-party candidates as late as 1989. The 1993 contests, however, saw a significant drop in support for Independent candidates although it was clearly of no help to the Conservative party.

Table 7.6 also shows the extent of the competition between the Liberals and PC for the minor placings. PC candidates clearly benefited from the interest in Welsh nationalism at the end of the 1970s but once devolution dropped down the political agenda the party's candidates were overtaken by those of the Alliance. More recently the battle for votes between the two has been close, but neither has done well enough to break out of the position shared with the Conservatives of being 'also rans' in Welsh local government.

Over the past twenty years local government has seen a significant increase in the rate of party competition and this has had an impact on the distribution of the vote between the parties. In particular, a smaller share of the total is now claimed by the Conservative and Labour parties. In the following section we will focus on the effect of this changing pattern of electoral support on the distribution of

Table 7.6 Overall share of vote in Wales 1973–1993

	Conservative	Labour	Liberal/Alliance	Plaid Cymru	Independent/ Other
Counties					
1973	12.5	37.3	5.3	9.7	35.2
1977	22.0	32.3	3.8	16.1	25.9
1981	17.1	42.4	5.8	11.1	23.6
1985	15.2	45.2	12.9	8.6	18.1
1989	16.5	46.0	7.3	8.8	21.4
1993	12.5	47.1	10.9	13.3	16.2
Districts					
1973	11.0	33.9	4.5	9.1	41.4
1976	15.0	29.1	4.9	14.8	36.1
1979	18.6	37.0	4.2	11.2	29.0
1983	16.3	34.8	12.9	9.9	26.1
1987	14.1	37.0	15.0	8.7	25.1
1991	13.3	38.1	9.4	11.2	28.0
Unitary councils					
1995	8.1	43.6	10.2	12.5	25.5

Note: In the case of multimember wards the votes for individual parties have been calculated according to the method outlined in Rallings and Thrasher (eds) (1993). Figures shown are the overall vote share for each party.

seats. The simple plurality voting system is well known for distorting the vote/ seat ratio and it will be interesting to discover how local authorities with their differences in seat magnitude have experienced these effects.

VOTES AND SEATS IN LONDON

As can be seen from Table 7.7 the operation of the electoral system in London supports the general view that electoral systems in general and 'first past the post' in particular provide a bonus in seats for the leading party. Without exception the party polling the largest share of votes has been rewarded with an even higher share of the seats. In the first elections to the GLC, for example, Labour obtained 64 per cent of the seats on 45 per cent of the vote. In 1968 when Labour polled just 28 per cent they experienced the punishing aspect of the electoral system, obtaining a mere 19 per cent share of seats. Such a fate is well known to small parties, however, and the Liberals have felt the worst aspects of the electoral system. In the initial elections for the London boroughs the Liberals obtained 1 per cent of the seats after polling almost 12 per cent of the vote. During the Liberal revival of the early 1970s the party's vote rose to 13 per cent in the boroughs but this brought just 1.4 per cent of the seats. The early experiences of the Alliance were not much better. Supported by one in four voters in 1982 Alliance councillors won only one in fifteen seats. But then in 1990, frustrated by the process of fielding more candidates, winning more votes but failing to see a payoff in seats, the Liberal Democrats adopted a different strategy. Seats considered by the party to be beyond reach were either ignored completely (the number of three-way contests fell by 25 per cent between 1986 and 1990) or mere 'paper' candidates were fielded and campaigning was negligible. Available resources were channelled into winnable wards. The result was a 9 per cent fall in vote share but a mere 1 per cent decline in seats. In the 1994 elections the Liberal vote was similar to that achieved in the 1980s but their campaigning strategy had played its part in terms of electoral payoffs. While the ratio of seats to votes in 1982 had been 1:3.7 by 1994 it had improved dramatically to 1:1.3.

VOTES AND SEATS IN THE METROPOLITAN BOROUGHS

Labour's polling strength in the metropolitan authorities translates into an even greater share of seats than in London (see Table 7.8). The party seldom obtains less than half of the seats up for election, with the highest share recorded in 1995 when more than 8 out of 10 seats were won with 57 per cent of the vote. The metropolitan boroughs have clearly and consistently rewarded the largest party with a considerable bonus in seats. On the very few occasions when the Conservatives have out-polled Labour in these authorities they too have seen their representation exaggerated by the electoral system. In 1975, for example, the Conservatives won over half the seats on 46 per cent of the borough vote while two years later a similar pattern occurred in the elections for the

Table 7.7 Share of votes and seats in London 1964–1994

	Conservative		Labour		Liberal/Alliance		Total seats
	% vote	% seats	% vote	% seats	% vote	% seats	
GLC							
1964	39.8	36.0	44.6	64.0	10.4	0.0	100
1967	51.9	82.0	34.0	18.0	9.5	0.0	100
1970	50.8	65.0	38.8	35.0	6.2	0.0	100
1973	37.9	33.7	47.4	63.0	12.5	2.2	92
1977	52.5	69.6	32.4	30.4	7.8	0.0	92
1981	39.7	44.6	41.8	52.2	14.4	1.1	92
London boroughs							
1964	38.8	36.4	44.5	59.8	11.7	0.9	1,859
1968	58.5	77.1	28.0	18.8	7.7	0.5	1,864
1971	38.5	32.0	52.2	65.5	4.7	0.5	1,863
1974	40.7	38.2	41.8	58.4	13.1	1.4	1,867
1978	48.5	50.3	39.0	46.2	7.0	1.6	1,908
1982	41.5	51.1	31.0	40.5	24.2	6.6	1,914
1986	35.2	35.7	37.3	49.8	23.4	13.1	1,914
1990	37.2	38.0	39.1	48.4	14.2	12.0	1,914
1994	31.3	27.1	41.6	54.5	22.1	17.1	1,917

metropolitan counties. That said, it appears that Labour has an additional electoral benefit in these particular authorities. For example, a massive gap of 23 points opened up between Labour's vote and seat share in 1986. On most occasions the distorting effects of the electoral system and the configuration of ward boundaries in the metropolitan areas has seen Labour win an absolute majority of seats on a minority vote. This distortion was such that in 1978 Labour was out-polled by the Conservatives but finished 12 per cent ahead in the distribution of seats. Not even a wholesale reorganisation of ward boundaries in the early 1980s solved this anomaly. As recently as 1992 Labour's small deficit in votes materialised into another large advantage in seats. One further problem for the Conservative party has surfaced in recent elections. In both 1994 and 1995 the party polled similarly to the Liberal Democrats but the payoff in seats was significantly lower. This can be explained by a combination of factors, including ward boundaries and campaigning techniques but it does suggest long-term problems for the party in these particular authorities.

With regard to the electoral success of the Liberals the metropolitan boroughs have not behaved as London. Unlike London the electoral system in the metropolitan boroughs has not treated the Liberals badly by always denying them seats for votes but neither has it proved as fruitful as a base for targeting seats. Whereas London saw a considerable gap between Liberal vote and seat shares, the gap in the metropolitan boroughs has rarely been as great. The vote shares for the Liberals in the 1973 metropolitan and following year's London

Table 7.8 Share of votes and seats in metropolitan councils 1973–1995

	Conservative		Labour		Liberal/Alliance		Total seats*
	% vote	% seats	% vote	% seats	% vote	% seats	
Metropolitan counties							
1973	36.2	23.5	47.4	66.9	12.9	8.2	601
1977	52.8	59.9	34.8	35.4	8.1	3.2	601
1981	30.7	20.3	50.4	70.9	16.5	8.3	601
Metropolitan boroughs							
1973	35.4	27.7	44.0	62.4	12.8	7.2	2,518
1975	45.8	53.2	33.7	36.9	14.5	6.1	838
1976	45.2	48.0	37.5	43.9	10.8	4.4	854
1978	45.0	40.5	42.5	52.7	7.9	4.0	875
1979	39.7	32.6	45.9	60.2	10.2	4.4	980
1980	35.4	24.9	48.9	66.6	11.5	6.6	1,364
1982	32.5	31.2	38.1	57.2	27.0	8.1	1,339
1983	33.6	28.3	44.6	63.2	18.3	7.5	845
1984	31.0	22.9	48.5	66.8	18.8	9.0	853
1986	26.5	16.6	48.1	71.1	23.4	11.4	862
1987	31.6	26.8	41.9	60.6	24.6	11.9	873
1988	31.6	20.9	50.9	70.0	13.9	8.2	857
1990	26.4	13.3	54.6	78.6	13.8	7.7	860
1991	31.7	22.1	45.0	62.6	18.6	13.0	840
1992	39.5	32.4	39.3	53.6	17.1	11.6	843
1994	22.7	8.9	51.4	74.7	22.8	15.5	850
1995	19.9	5.8	57.1	81.0	19.1	12.0	842

Note: * The number of seats up for re-election in the metropolitan boroughs varies because of periodic boundary changes and also because of the practice of holding over casual vacancies so that they can be filled at the main May elections.

borough elections were virtually identical (12.8 per cent and 13.1 per cent respectively) but while this gave the Liberals just 1.4 per cent of seats in the capital (due mainly to the considerable seat bonus enjoyed by Labour) in the metropolitan areas they obtained 7.2 per cent of seats. At the other extreme the Liberals have not proved as successful at exploiting the electoral system, although the gap between vote and seat shares has narrowed in recent years. As with London, however, the tactic of fielding many more candidates by the Alliance parties in the early 1980s was not rewarded. In 1982, for example, although Alliance candidates polled more than three times the Liberal vote of four years previously they only managed to double the haul of seats.

VOTES AND SEATS IN THE ENGLISH SHIRES

Just as Labour's lead in the metropolitan authorities gives them an advantage in the distribution of seats, in the English shires it has traditionally been the

Conservatives who have reaped that benefit. In the late 1970s and early 1980s they enjoyed an average 8 per cent lead of seats over votes. As party competition grew, however, and as the Liberals met with some notable successes at both county and district level the Conservative vote/seat ratio began to narrow. As Table 7.9 shows, in 1986 the Conservative share in seats fell below its vote share for the first time in this set of local authorities. Although the party recovered, in recent years it has watched its traditional advantage in the shires evaporate. Beginning with the 1993 county elections the Conservatives have obtained a smaller share of seats than votes in three successive election cycles. In effect the Conservatives have seen their status in the shires decline from the dominant party in the 1970s to a situation in many authorities where they operate more as a third party with the inevitable electoral penalties.

The explanation for this lies in the performances of their main challengers. The shires have not been Labour's favourite territory. In the 1979 local elections,

Table 7.9 Share of votes and seats in English shires 1973–1995

	Conservative		Labour		Liberal/Alliance		Independent		Total seats
	% vote	% seats	% vote	% seats	% vote	% seats	% vote	% seats	
Counties									
1973	42.1	45.2	37.6	35.1	9.2	6.2	9.1	12.3	3,129
1977	58.1	75.3	25.9	14.0	8.7	1.9	4.5	7.6	3,127
1981	40.7	48.2	34.8	35.2	18.3	10.4	3.5	4.7	3,096
1985	38.4	43.6	30.0	32.2	27.9	20.2	2.5	3.3	3,005
1989	42.2	47.3	31.1	33.8	20.2	14.6	2.0	2.7	3,005
1993	35.6	31.2	31.2	37.3	29.3	27.8	1.8	2.4	2,998
Districts									
1973	32.1	32.5	31.2	32.1	10.9	6.8	21.5	25.5	13,535
1976	42.1	50.8	26.1	20.8	11.9	4.3	14.3	20.4	13,589
1978	52.5	59.5	33.3	29.0	9.6	4.0	2.8	4.9	677
1979	41.9	48.8	31.4	23.7	11.3	5.7	11.0	18.5	12,184
1980	40.6	42.8	39.9	39.6	13.7	8.0	2.9	6.7	1,607
1982	39.5	49.3	27.8	28.8	28.7	12.8	2.2	6.3	1,579
1983	40.0	49.2	27.0	22.4	20.9	9.2	7.3	16.7	10,405
1984	39.3	42.9	34.2	35.3	22.5	15.0	2.1	4.8	1,899
1986	34.6	33.3	33.6	37.5	28.4	23.1	1.6	4.4	1,951
1987	39.5	47.9	23.5	20.3	27.0	15.6	7.5	14.0	10,021
1988	41.2	43.8	35.4	37.7	18.6	13.1	1.7	3.8	1,799
1990	30.7	24.6	43.1	49.6	18.7	19.5	2.4	4.6	1,855
1991	35.9	38.4	28.5	26.0	23.3	19.5	8.0	13.6	10,121
1992	45.2	50.8	29.0	29.2	21.4	14.8	2.2	3.5	1,783
1994	26.6	14.5	39.2	47.4	29.7	32.1	2.5	3.1	1,814
1995	26.0	19.6	38.3	42.1	25.0	25.1	8.0	11.3	10,013

Note: Figures for 1995 include the results in 14 new unitary councils which replaced 22 districts and 4 county councils.

for example, the party polled 31 per cent of the vote and received only 24 per cent of the seats. Through the 1980s Labour's vote and seat shares were relatively well matched and it was only in 1990, when the party finally succeeded in out-polling the Conservatives in shire elections, that it received a sizeable seat bonus. That success was repeated in both 1994 and, to a lesser extent, 1995, but we must add another dimension to our analysis in order to understand fully the dynamics of this situation.

The Liberals achieved a dramatic improvement in their vote share in the early 1980s but this was not matched in seats. In 1982 Alliance candidates attracted votes but failed to translate that support into council seats. That pattern continued more or less unabated until 1990 when the Liberal Democrats succeeded in winning more seats than votes. This was despite the fact that the party still polled less than a fifth of all votes – a smaller percentage than at 5 of the 7 district elections in the 1980s. These elections, therefore, saw both Labour and the Liberal Democrats for the first time simultaneously enjoy a bonus in seats. The explanation for this lies in the more effective targeting of Conservative seats by the two opposition parties. In effect, there was a pincer movement as voters switched allegiance to the party perceived as better placed to unseat the incumbent Conservatives. The Liberal Democrats in particular avoided the weakness of gathering votes in areas where the party had little prospect of victory.

If this had remained an isolated incident, a freak occurrence, the Conservative party might have felt more comfortable but that has not proved to be the case. In the 1993 county elections the Conservatives, despite topping the poll, obtained fewer seats than Labour. The maxim that the leading party receives a bonus in seats had been overturned. Again, we need to look at the detail to account for this anomaly. In all the Conservatives lost almost 500 seats. For every two seats lost to Labour, five were lost to the Liberal Democrats. Some areas of the country, for example, Essex, Hertfordshire, Suffolk and Warwickshire saw the Conservatives lose their majorities due to pressure from Labour. Elsewhere, principally in the West Country and along the South Coast, electoral defeat for Conservative candidates came principally at the hands of Liberal Democrats. From experiencing a six-point gap of votes over seats in 1989 the Liberal Democrats moved to one of less than two points. As in 1990 the Conservatives found themselves the victims of a more sophisticated pattern of party competition and campaigning which helped increase and focus the anti-Conservative vote.

Since the 1993 county elections it has been the turn of the shire districts to show how the electoral system can punish parties who fall out of favour with the electorate. In both 1994 and 1995 the district elections saw the Conservatives poll below 30 per cent for the first time in these authorities. The party paid a heavy price for this meagre level of support in what had formerly been regarded as its heartlands. Also for the first time in 1994 the Liberal Democrats out-polled the Conservatives, forcing them into third place. For this the Liberal Democrats received a higher share in seats than votes though the reward was not as great as Labour's. The Conservatives' share of seats was some 12 per cent lower than the party's vote share. In the 1995 elections the Conservatives lost a total of 2,000 seats as they won fewer than a fifth of the seats in exchange for a quarter of the votes. The contrast with earlier stages of this particular electoral cycle are stark. Compared with four years before the Conservative seat share was halved. Compared with the three electoral cycles which marked the years of Conservative general election victories in 1979, 1983 and 1987, the party in 1995 obtained a seat share two and a half times lower. As we shall show later this has had a profound effect upon the political complexion of local government.

VOTES AND SEATS IN SCOTLAND

Interpreting the relationship between votes and seats won in the cases of both Scotland and Wales is made much more difficult by the relatively high proportion of uncontested seats in both countries. The distorting effect of such results means that the seat share for non-party candidates is invariably higher than vote share for the simple reason that it is largely Independent candidates who are returned unopposed. As Tables 7.10 and 7.11 each show the seat share in the Independent and 'others' columns can sometimes be three times as great as vote share. In the 1982 Scottish regional elections, for example, although such candidates attracted support from only just over one in twenty voters, when the councils began their work, one in five of all councillors fitted into this category. The 1993 county council elections in Wales provide another interesting example. Without a ballot cast the number of Independents returned unopposed in Powys was such that it was known well before polling day that the council would continue to be under Independent 'majority' control.

Labour in Scotland has usually been rewarded with a disproportionate number of seats as the most electorally popular party. In every cycle of Scottish regional elections Labour has topped the poll and received a higher share of seats but as can be seen from Table 7.10 the bonus has only been significant since 1986. One explanation for this has to do with the Conservative vote, which proved quite robust until then but subsequently deteriorated badly. In the 1990s the Conservatives have paid a heavy penalty in terms of council representation for their declining popularity. That penalty appears to have become more severe as opposition parties have organised a more effective targeting of Conservative seats. Contrast, for example, the events in 1986 with those of four years later. In 1986 the Conservatives polled just 16.9 per cent and won 14.6 per cent of seats. The 1990 elections saw an improved vote share but the payoff in seats was just 11.7 per cent – a higher vote share, therefore, but a lower share of seats. In 1994 the Conservative seat share was half its vote, as the party suffered not only for being a small party but in addition as the victim of a tactical onslaught by its opponents.

Although the Conservatives in Scotland can now claim that the electoral system is unfair, theirs is not the only cause for grievance. The Liberals, for

Table 7.10 Share of votes and seats in Scotland 1974–1995

	Conservative		Labour		Liberal/ Alliance		SNP		Independent/ Other	
	% vote	% seats	% vote	% seats	% vote	% seats	% vote	% seats	% vote	% seats
Regions										
1974	28.6	25.9	38.5	39.8	5.1	2.5	12.6	4.2	15.3	27.5
1978	30.3	31.5	39.6	41.0	2.3	1.4	20.9	4.2	6.8	22.0
1982	25.1	27.0	37.6	42.2	18.1	5.7	13.4	5.2	5.7	20.0
1986	16.9	14.6	43.9	50.1	15.1	9.0	18.2	8.1	5.9	18.2
1990	19.7	11.7	42.7	52.4	8.7	9.0	21.8	9.4	7.2	17.5
1994	13.7	6.8	41.8	48.6	11.9	13.2	26.8	16.1	5.7	15.2
Districts										
1974	26.8	21.7	38.4	38.6	5.0	1.5	12.4	5.6	17.5	32.6
1977	27.2	24.8	31.6	26.8	4.0	2.8	24.2	15.2	13.1	30.4
1980	24.1	20.4	45.4	44.0	6.2	3.6	15.5	4.8	8.9	27.3
1984	21.4	16.4	45.7	47.4	12.8	6.8	11.7	5.1	8.4	24.2
1988	19.4	14.0	42.6	47.9	8.4	7.3	21.3	9.8	8.4	21.0
1992	23.2	17.6	34.0	40.4	9.5	8.1	24.3	13.0	9.0	20.9
Unitary councils										
1995	11.3	7.1	43.8	53.1	9.7	10.4	26.2	15.6	9.1	13.9

Source: David Denver.

Table 7.11 Share of votes and seats in Wales 1973–1995

	Conservative		Labour		Liberal/ Alliance		Plaid Cymru		Independent/ Other	
	% votes	% seats	% votes	% seats	% votes	% seats	% votes	% seats	% votes	% seats
Counties										
1973	12.5	12.0	37.3	48.1	5.3	3.5	9.7	3.1	35.2	33.3
1977	22.0	24.4	32.3	34.0	3.8	1.9	16.1	6.8	25.9	32.9
1981	17.1	12.8	42.4	49.0	5.8	4.2	11.1	4.3	23.6	29.6
1985	15.2	9.1	45.2	53.3	12.9	6.5	8.6	3.6	18.1	27.5
1989	16.5	7.3	46.0	55.4	7.3	4.4	8.8	5.1	21.4	27.7
1993	12.5	6.4	47.1	54.2	10.9	6.8	13.3	8.2	16.2	24.5
Districts										
1973	11.0	9.1	33.9	42.0	4.5	2.6	9.1	3.2	41.4	43.1
1976	15.0	14.6	29.1	29.0	4.9	2.6	14.8	8.2	36.1	45.6
1979	18.6	12.8	37.0	38.5	4.2	2.6	11.2	4.6	29.0	41.5
1983	16.3	13.0	34.8	41.6	12.9	4.1	9.9	4.7	26.1	36.6
1987	14.1	10.1	37.0	40.2	15.0	6.1	8.7	6.4	25.1	37.2
1991	13.3	7.6	38.1	41.7	9.4	5.5	11.2	8.3	28.0	36.8
Unitary councils										
1995	8.1	3.3	43.6	57.1	10.2	6.2	12.5	8.9	25.5	24.5

example, have often been on the wrong end of the votes/seats distribution. As the Alliance, the party polled 18 per cent in the 1982 regional elections, three times the percentage of seats won. The gap narrowed in subsequent elections but it was not until the Liberal Democrats extended their electoral strategy north of the border that the party repaired its votes/seats deficiency. The SNP have an even greater case for expressing dismay with the electoral system although some critics might argue that its campaigning tactics and decision to contest more seats than any other party is naive. In every single set of elections the party has received fewer seats than it would have done in a more proportional system. The 1978 contests which coincided with the devolution debate saw the party win a fifth of votes but only 4 per cent of seats. Although the ratio has never been as bad it has not been uncommon for the party's vote share to be double that of its seat share. The SNP's fate should be set alongside that of the Liberal Democrats. At the 1994 regional elections the Liberal Democrats won 13.2 per cent of seats in return for 11.9 per cent of votes. The SNP, on the other hand, despite polling more than twice as many votes won just 13 more seats. In the final analysis party strategists must weigh the advantages of fighting a large number of seats against the prospect that many votes will be wasted in terms of winning greater council representation.

VOTES AND SEATS IN WALES

As in Scotland Labour has benefited considerably from being the largest party in Wales. At every election since 1973 the party has received the largest party's winning seat bonus. This bonus has varied from between 1 and 2 per cent upwards to more than 13 per cent at the 1995 unitary council elections as Table 7.11 shows. Almost without exception the other parties have suffered as a consequence, though to varying degrees. The Conservatives, for example, have not suffered in Wales as much as elsewhere, even winning more seats than vote share in the 1977 county contests. Nevertheless in both the 1991 district and 1993 county elections, the party's seat share was virtually half its poll share. In 1995, however, the Conservative party plumbed new depths, winning a mere 3 per cent of seats on the new unitary authorities. Such figures inevitably mean that the Conservatives assume all the characteristics of a minor party in Wales. Similarly, the Liberal Democrats have been disadvantaged by the operation of the electoral system, unable to replicate their recent success in Scotland and elsewhere. Even during the 1990s the party has continued to suffer a four-point gap between its seat and vote shares at a time when that problem appears to have been solved in other parts of the country. For its part PC has performed like the SNP – polling well at times without reward. The final category of Independents and 'others' reflects the fact that large numbers of seats held by Independents in Wales are uncontested. In the 1985 county elections, for example, although Independents and others polled slightly more votes than the Conservative party, their return in seats – many of them unopposed – was three times greater. There was some indication in 1995, however, that this imbalance may now be redressed. The proportion of wards with an uncontested election fell from 37 per cent in 1991 to 23 per cent and the share of seats and votes won by Independents almost exactly matched.

PARTY CONTROL OF LOCAL GOVERNMENT 1973–1995

Political control of a local authority is viewed as an important, if not the most important, prize by local parties. Collective spending by local authorities accounts for broadly a quarter of total government expenditure and running a local administration allows a party to demonstrate its competence and fitness for the national political stage. What have been the overall consequences of changing patterns of party competition and a successful challenge to two-party hegemony in local government over more than two decades?

Table 7.12 summarises those effects in terms of council control. As measures

Table 7.12 Party strength in local government

| | England | | | | | | | |
| | 1973 | | 1979 | | 1987 | | 1995 | |
	seats	councils	seats	councils	seats	councils	seats	councils
Conservative	7,495	92	11,468	231	8,677	144	4,831	13
Labour	8,850	129	6,140	83	6,846	104	9,245	167
Liberal/Alliance	1,363	1	972	1	3,383	12	4,807	51
Independent	4,357	68	3,153	43	1,949	21	1,693	15
NOC	–	120	–	52	–	122	–	149
	Scotland							
	1974		1978		1988		1994	
	seats	councils	seats	councils	seats	councils	seats	councils
Conservative	353	6	413	10	229	3	235	4
Labour	600	18	476	9	777	28	688	23
Liberal/Alliance	28	–	37	1	124	2	155	2
SNP	80	1	188	4	146	1	223	1
Independent	480	22	435	22	326	17	274	14
NOC	–	15	–	16	–	11	–	18
	Wales							
	1973		1979		1987		1993	
	seats	councils	seats	councils	seats	councils	seats	councils
Conservative	214	1	341	3	210	2	146	–
Labour	931	23	794	17	911	22	929	22
Liberal/Alliance	64	–	50	–	139	–	116	–
PC	65	–	113	–	108	–	158	–
Independent	826	19	800	17	666	14	617	14
NOC	–	2	–	8	–	7	–	9

we have used both the number of seats and councils controlled. Each year shown constitutes a snapshot taken immediately after the May elections and includes all authorities, even those without any elections. In the cases of Scotland and Wales we have stopped short of 1995 to avoid confusion stemming from structural changes to local government in those nations. Immediately, it can be seen that the Conservatives appear to have paid a heavy price in local government terms for their domination of Westminster. To some extent the figures for 1973/4 are misleading because of the number of successful candidates who chose to stand as Independents rather than under a party label. Nevertheless, what is not in doubt is the relatively weak position of the Liberals. With few councillors and even fewer councils they were marginal to the administration of local government.

Labour was in office from 1974–79 and in that time the party locally suffered for bouts of governmental unpopularity. Equally, the Liberals, who for a time gave parliamentary support to the minority Labour government, suffered in a range of local elections. During this period the Nationalist parties in both Wales and Scotland improved their positions. Adding more than a hundred councillors to its tally the SNP also gained control of an extra three authorities. Although Plaid Cymru's performance was less spectacular it is likely that both parties won additional seats because of voters' frustration over the devolution issue. In England, the Conservatives benefited greatly from the losses incurred by the Labour and Liberal partners. The number of Conservative councillors increased by over 50 per cent and by 1979 the party controlled more than half of all councils. In a very real sense such developments were of considerable help to the party in its bid to win back power at Westminster.

By 1987, however, the Conservatives had been in power long enough for the inevitable anti-government backlash to begin to express itself. What should not be overlooked, of course, is that despite losing more than 3,000 council seats and political control of 95 councils since first returning to power in 1979, the party was still in a position to win the 1987 general election and it was still the major player in local government. A further decade on, however, there has been a virtually unrelenting erosion of local Conservative strength. In the last ten years their numbers have fallen dramatically to the point where they have become the third party of local government. During the same time the number of Conservative controlled councils has collapsed to little more than a handful. An important consequence of changing patterns of party competition and electoral support, however, has meant that the principal beneficiaries of this decline have been the Liberal Democrats rather than Labour. In the 1970s the electoral pendulum, certainly in England, would have swung between Conservative and Labour but over the past two decades it has behaved rather differently. While Labour can currently claim to be the major party of local government in terms of seats and councils controlled it has had to share the political windfall of a declining Conservative party with the Liberal Democrats. Moreover, the number of hung councils has increased as both votes and seats have become more widely dispersed. The consequences of this for the administration of local government will be taken up in Chapter 12.

CONCLUSIONS

In itself greater party competition need not result in a significant lowering of the vote share for established parties. In the case of local government elections two virtually parallel processes have been at work. First, as both the absolute number and electoral success of Independent candidates has fallen, so too has their vote share. On its own this could have meant the two main parties enjoying a higher proportion of the local vote. A second factor, increasing contestation from other parties, has, however, served to limit the two-party share to virtually what it had been when Independents were much more of an electoral force. Thus, in the 1973 shire district elections the combined vote share for Conservative and Labour candidates was 63.3 per cent. In the 1995 elections it was 64.3 per cent. The net effect in terms of Conservative/Labour share looks small, but beneath the surface enormous changes have taken place.

Such movements in party competition and transfers of voter support will ultimately feed through to council seats and control. In recent years there have been some dramatic changes, most notably a collapse in local electoral support for the Conservatives. Each year since 1993 has seen a major attrition of the party's local electoral base to the point where it now has fewer councillors and controls many fewer councils than even the Liberal Democrats. The next chapter will examine in more detail the experiences of the main parties in local government but for the moment it is important to note how far political power has become fragmented. At the peak of Conservative/Labour domination in 1979 almost three in four councils were either blue or red. Currently, less than half fit that description. While national politics is still characterised as a battle only between two parties the reality in local government is considerably different. Often, administrative control is shared between parties. National politicians may well be emphasising party differences at precisely the same time as their local counterparts are working closely with the supposed 'enemy'. The nationalisation of local party politics has frequently been regarded as a damaging process. It has been inferred that when national parties fight local elections the system becomes homogenised and the part played by local issues is devalued. The evidence, however, points to something different. Greater party competition has brought a new impetus to the conduct of local elections, has helped loosen the stranglehold exerted by the two main parties in many authorities and has resulted in new ways of administering local authority business. Party politicisation of local government, therefore, has often brought variety and not drab uniformity to local electoral outcomes.

8 Major parties and local elections

INTRODUCTION

When the electoral pendulum swung between just two parties the fate of one tended to be a mirror image of the other: when Conservative fortunes rose those of Labour fell and when the electoral mood swung against the Conservatives, Labour was the beneficiary. As a third major political force entered the electoral fray, and met with some partial successes, this certainty started to evaporate. Given more choices the electorate has expressed its preferences or its protests in different ways in different places at different times. The erosion of Conservative support has neither been uniform nor in one direction. In some areas the party has resisted electoral hostility better than in others. Where it has lost ground Labour has sometimes been the prime beneficiary, elsewhere it has been the Liberal Democrats or the Scottish Nationalists. The outcome of local elections, therefore, has often been unpredictable.

In this chapter we wish to chart the ebb and flow of electoral fortune for each of three main political parties – Conservative, Labour and the Liberal Democrats and their various previous incarnations. In the following chapter we turn our attention to the performance of the Nationalist parties and other political groups which have played a greater or lesser role in local electoral politics during the past two decades. Specifically, our concern is to describe the successes and failures for each party, the areas and type of local authority where it has made the biggest impact and what factors appear relevant in its local electoral development.

The Conservative party will be discussed first since for many years it was the most dominant. For that reason its recent failures have been dramatic and have had a profound effect upon the map of local authority control. Next, the focus switches to Labour, which has seen its fortunes ebb and flow, but is currently enjoying perhaps its best phase in terms of local government representation. For each of these parties local electoral performance has frequently been related to its control or not of national government. The fact that there is regularly a local protest vote against the party in power at Westminster is well known, though in recent years even this picture has altered as more and more voters appear attracted to the idea of 'contextual voting' (Rallings and Thrasher 1993a). The Liberal Democrats, preceded by the Liberals, have had an increasing impact in local government elections. In the early years of local government reorganisation the Liberal Party had problems simply contesting local elections and met with little success. In the early 1980s, however, the creation of the SDP, followed by the forging of the Liberal/SDP Alliance, helped to catapult this 'third force' into greater prominence. Although the headlines concentrated on Alliance victories in parliamentary by-elections and leads in the opinion polls it was at the local level where the most significant advances were made. Eventually, the Alliance was replaced by the Liberal Democrats whose successes have far surpassed its predecessors in terms of establishing a strong local government presence. In many parts of Britain any claim about the continued existence of a two-party system at local level would now necessarily include the Liberal Democrats and exclude one or other of Labour or the Conservatives.

CONSERVATIVES

Whatever party wins control at Westminster there are inevitably occasions when voters' frustration with its stewardship of national government will express itself in adverse local election results. Despite protestations that local elections should be about local issues many councillors through the years have lost their seats because of their own party's failures at the national level. The Conservative party is no exception to this general rule: indeed since its fourth consecutive general election victory in 1992 the party has paid a very heavy price in council seats for its success in dominating national government. Following the 1995 local elections the Conservative party was left with fewer than 5,000 councillors throughout Great Britain. In large areas of the country, particularly in Wales, Scotland and the more urbanised parts of England, the party had experienced an almost continuous decline in its support since the early 1980s. By the mid-1990s, however, support had evaporated even in its former heartlands in the shires. The Conservative party's fall from grace has been one of the most dramatic in recent years and it will be some years before it can hope to recover the position it once occupied as the dominant party of local government.

In order to assess the local electoral damage sustained by the Conservatives over the period from 1979 onwards we need first to examine how the party fared when it was last in opposition at Westminster. During the five-year period from February 1974 Labour struggled along first as a minority government, then with a wafer-thin majority and finally retained power only with support from the Liberals. Throughout this period the Conservative party enjoyed considerable success in local elections. In 1977, for example, the party recaptured control of the Greater London Council and in the following year won half the seats across the London boroughs. Outside the capital there was a similar story of Conservative triumph. Beginning in 1975 the party obtained more than 45 per cent of the vote in four successive elections across the metropolitan counties and boroughs. By 1979 the party controlled fifteen metropolitan councils including four counties: Greater Manchester, Merseyside, West Midlands and West Yorkshire. The party's dominance in the shires was even greater. Conservatives won three-quarters of the more than 3,000 English county councillors elected in 1977 and majority control in 34 of the 39 counties in England. Out of more than 13,000 district councillors elected on the same day as Mrs Thatcher's first general election win in 1979 almost half were Conservative.

During this period the party clearly benefited first from Labour's problems at Westminster and second from the decision by many former Independents to stand under the Tory banner. The party's grip on power both national and local was formidable and provided the foundation for the Thatcherite revolution. By the close of the first chapter in that process of change the Conservatives' dominance in local government matched the party's majority of 144 won at the 1983 general election. Across England and Wales the party had more than 10,000 councillors and control of half the councils in England and Wales. Even in Scotland, where resistance to Conservative control from Westminster had been fiercest, the party was still able to win roughly a quarter of the vote and control of seven councils at the beginning of the 1980s. Throughout Great Britain the party had majority control in almost 200 local authorities, or four in ten councils. During the middle and later 1980s the Conservatives did suffer reversals at local level, but these were relatively modest thanks to a helpful coincidence of circumstances. Until 1987 Labour was weak and divided and then, just as Labour began to recover as an electoral force, controversy over the SDP/Liberal merger in 1988 allowed the Conservatives to recover ground which they had lost to the centre parties in so-called 'middle England' (see the data on the changing electoral fortunes of the parties in Chapter 7). Conservatives themselves would of course argue that their fortunes were more positively enhanced by a buoyant economy and popular policies. Although local opposition to some of central government's policy initiatives was aired, the extent of Conservative representation ensured that that voice was necessarily muted.

Ironically, therefore, it was arguably the government's reluctance to listen to local opinion that prompted the beginning of its rapid electoral decline. The poll tax was introduced first in Scotland in 1989 and then in England and Wales a year later despite the near-unanimous view of commentators that it would prove both politically unpopular and difficult to implement. The 1990 elections gave the voting public their first opportunity to express an opinion about a policy that had not been foreshadowed in the Conservatives' general election manifesto. Apart from in a handful of London boroughs the overwhelming reaction was one of rejection as the party recorded its then worst ever local election result. In the short term, criticism of the Conservative performance was counteracted by their successes in places like Ealing, won from Labour, and Westminster and Wandsworth. Overall the party sustained about 200 net losses but had they not gained 80 seats from Labour across London the figures would have been much worse. In the shires, however, and especially in the south of England, the disastrous effects of the poll tax on the Conservative party were more in evidence. In traditional areas of strength like Bath, Gillingham, Gosport and Torbay, Conservative councillors paid with their seats for the government's failure to persuade many of its supporters of the efficacy of the poll tax.

The 1990 elections have since proved to be but the first of a series of local election setbacks for the Conservatives. Judged in terms of the local electoral cycle the party's performance in recent years has established a new record low, the sole exception being 1992 when the local elections followed closely on John Major's general election victory. The 1991 shire district elections saw the Conservatives incur net losses of 900 seats. A regional analysis of the Conservative vote in the shires since the party had come to power in 1979 shows some interesting variations. In the north the average vote share for Conservative candidates rose by 0.5 per cent between 1979 and 1991. Everywhere else it fell back, though the decline was not uniform. In the Midlands the mean Conservative share fell by just 2 per cent in this period. In the Conservative heartlands in the South and South East, however, their vote declined by 5 per cent and 8 per cent respectively.

Further signs that the formerly solid Conservative vote in the south was under threat came at the 1993 county council elections. The party lost almost 500 councillors as counties such as Kent, which had been under Conservative control for more than a century, were lost. Out of 47 counties in England and Wales the party now controlled just Buckinghamshire. In some areas the fall from grace was truly dramatic. Along the South Coast, from Cornwall to Kent the Conservative vote declined by an average of 9 per cent, peaking in West Sussex with a drop of more than 12 per cent. In the Home Counties too traditionally loyal Conservative voters departed the party. Surrey, Berkshire, and Buckinghamshire all witnessed a more than 9 per cent decline in support. Even Essex, which only the year before had played an important symbolic role in the general election victory, turned its back on the Conservatives. Across the county the Conservative vote fell by 9 per cent, with Brentwood (15 per cent), Castle Point (26 per cent), and Colchester (12 per cent) registering much larger swings against the government party.

The following year saw a re-run of the 1990 local electoral cycle and an even worse set of results for the Conservatives. Some within the Conservative party, including the party chairman, believed that the party could make gains in 1994 simply because the results four years before had been so awful. One hint of the carnage to come, however, was the attempt by some local Conservative associations to distance themselves from the national party. Significantly Conservatives in the party's two flagship councils of Westminster and Wandsworth did not encourage government ministers to become involved in their election campaigns. Their fears proved justified. The Conservative vote collapsed as the party lost 430 seats and control of 21 councils, including 9 London boroughs. In the space of a year the Conservatives had seen their political control of the main spending local authorities in Britain reduced to just six – one county (Buckinghamshire), one metropolitan borough (Trafford) and four London boroughs (Bromley, Kensington and Chelsea, Wandsworth and Westminster).

The Conservatives were now in uncharted waters as their decline in local government accelerated apace. The reorganisation of Scottish local government meant that elections for the 29 unitary authorities which would replace the regional and district councils were held in April 1995. Despite the fact that the new system had, according to many commentators, been designed to maximise Conservative representation, the outcome was disastrous. In only one authority, Edinburgh, did the party's council membership reach double figures and across Scotland as a whole just 81 Conservative councillors were elected, fewer than not only Labour but also the SNP, the Liberal Democrats and even Independents. When these new authorities assumed full responsibility for Scottish local government in 1996 the Conservative party did not control a single authority. The result produced shock waves amongst Conservatives south of the border.

In some ways the Conservative councillors seeking re-election in May 1995 had been amongst the most fortunate in electoral terms. Beneficiaries of an electoral cycle which had coincided on three of the previous four occasions with an imminent Conservative general election victory, this time they faced the prospect of widespread defeat. For the third consecutive year the party recorded its lowest ever local election vote resulting, on this occasion, in the loss of more than 2,000 council seats and political control of no fewer than 61 councils. The contrast between when the Conservatives had come to national power in the late 1970s and 1995 was stark. Then, the party had more than 10,000 councillors responsible for the administration of almost 200 local authorities throughout Britain. Following the 1995 elections the party was reduced to majority control in just 13 local authorities covering less than 4 per cent of the British population and, with fewer than 5,000 councillors, now lagged behind even the Liberal Democrats. Quite simply, the Conservative party which had registered four straight general election victories had paid dearly for this success in terms of its strength in local government. Thousands of Conservative controlled seats had fallen. Councils which, in many cases, had been perceived as permanently within the party's domain had been lost.

No party before had seen its local electoral base destroyed in quite the same way as the Conservatives during the 1990s. The one bright spot in this period had been 1992 when the party made widespread gains as the local elections followed within a month of the general election. Many of the Conservative councillors elected then might have believed that the general election cycle, with a contest almost due by 1996 and with the governing party likely to have begun its recovery from any mid-term blues, would guarantee the preservation of their seats. They would not have foreseen that the party nationally would still be so unpopular so close to a general election. Trailing badly in the polls and losing a parliamentary by-election to Labour in Staffordshire South East at the beginning of April, the Conservatives entered the 1996 local election campaign in poor shape. Although the party was defending merely 1,166 seats the scale of earlier losses was such that these seats now represented almost a quarter of the party's total councillor strength. One significant measure of that decline was that out of 150 councils with elections the Conservative party exercised majority control in a mere four. Forecasts of further heavy losses proved accurate and although the party's 'national equivalent vote', by which we mean an estimate of the share of the vote which each party would have obtained *if* elections had been held throughout Great Britain, rose by three points compared with the previous year, it still lost a net total of 663 seats. By the mid-1990s councils that had once been synonymous with Conservatism had new political identities. Tunbridge Wells, for example, often characterised as populated by those resistant to all forms of change now had a Liberal Democrat administration. In no less than 50 local authorities across Great Britain, more than a tenth of the total and containing more than six million electors, the Conservative party had no council representatives whatsoever.

LABOUR

The major beneficiary of the Conservative decline in local government in the 1990s has been the Labour party, which performed particularly well in the 1995 local elections. Success brought the party's total number of councillors to more than 10,000 throughout Britain – more than the combined total of the Conservatives and Liberal Democrats – and gave it political control in more than 200 local authorities. An important component of such strength was its electoral breakthrough in many district councils normally dominated by the Conservative party. Despite Labour's almost unrelenting grip in the metropolitan boroughs – it won more than seven out of every ten seats in those authorities in 1986 and two years later polled an absolute majority of votes cast – the shires had largely resisted the party's blandishments in previous periods of Conservative unpopularity. In 1995, however, the Labour vote in such unlikely places as Blackpool, Dover, Gloucester and Luton rose above 50 per cent and the party took majority control of these councils where no Labour MP has been elected for over twenty years. But how fragile is that position? Labour's local government triumphs were largely a reflection of growing voter disenchantment with a Conservative party in power at Westminster since 1979. While the Conservatives have been hit hard by the now traditional backlash against the governing party, it has taken four terms of office for its effects to produce the current nadir. History shows that Labour in government is perhaps even more vulnerable to a withdrawal of support locally.

Labour's periods in government from 1964–70 and again from 1974–1979 were both accompanied by heavy losses at local elections. In 1967 Labour lost control of Britain's largest local authority, the Greater London Council, in spectacular fashion winning just 18 of the capital's 100 seats. In 1968 further heavy losses were sustained in the London borough elections as Labour lost control in 16 of its 20 councils. More than 700 Labour seats were lost in London in a year that also saw the party lose political control in cities such as Sheffield. By the end of the decade Labour had been driven out of many of its urban heartlands. The scale of these losses was to have a profound impact on the party's subsequent development. In effect a political vacuum was established where Labour councillors had once held power, both on the council and within the party itself. Their defeat meant that local parties proved vulnerable to take-over by new elements, many of whom espoused the view that Labour must reposition itself further to the left of British politics. Such groups were particularly energetic in London which saw some of the bloodiest battles between what remained of the old guard and the new, more left-wing members (Lansley *et al.* 1989).

Labour's return to power in February 1974 followed a further erosion of its long-term councillor base as local government reorganisation took hold. As Gyford (1985) notes, fewer councillors were required to serve on the new local authorities and many of Labour's survivors from the party's devastating setbacks of the 1967 and 1968 local elections decided to retire rather than serve on the new councils. Those first elections, held in 1973, saw Labour perform particularly well. In the English shire counties and districts Labour won a third of new council seats while in the metropolitan boroughs and the GLC almost two-thirds of seats were captured by the party. By 1976, however, when the time for re-election came round, Labour in office was facing a different set of political circumstances. In the shire districts the party won just a quarter of the vote and a fifth of the seats, with a proportionate decline in the metropolitan areas. By the autumn of that year the party had lost its Commons' majority prompting a pact with David Steel's Liberal party the following spring. As a prelude to the 1977 local contests a Labour majority of 23,000 was overturned in a parliamentary by-election at Ashfield, and at the elections themselves the party's share of seats won halved compared with four years previously. In such a short space of time the Conservatives, as we noted above, had become the dominant party of local government. Labour's decline in its strongest areas, whilst not as dramatic as that in the late 1960s, proved sufficient for those wanting radical change within the party to gain the upper hand. This internecine struggle took place in many towns and cities throughout the country and severely damaged the party. A long political exile was about to begin.

Though Labour achieved some successes in the early 1980s, most notably in the metropolitan boroughs, they were by no means of the scale normally registered by the opposition party. Indeed, the creation of the Social Democratic party in March 1981 helped to split the anti-Conservative vote and gave fresh heart to the Liberals, who captured a tenth of county council seats contested that year. Though Labour too made advances at those elections, including recapturing the GLC, the signs were already in place that electoral politics would not run in Labour's favour. In the summer of 1981 the SDP and Liberals agreed upon the principle of their Alliance and by the autumn Labour found itself trailing in third place in the polls. The Alliance threat to Labour's national electoral prospects was rehearsed at the 1983 council contests. With the Conservative vote little changed from four years before, Mrs Thatcher understood that with a divided opposition her passage towards a second administration was assured. In a pattern to be repeated in 1987 the local elections, having confirmed the government's pre-eminence, were followed a month later by a general election and another Conservative victory. Though the Alliance failed to break Labour, the emergence of a third force in local politics meant that opportunities for advance were minimal. Indeed, at the 1985 county council elections, when the anti-government protest vote was at its highest, Labour's vote and seat share actually fell compared with 1981 while that of the Alliance almost doubled.

Throughout this period the Labour leadership struggled to free itself from its left-wing image. While the party leadership attempted to broaden Labour's electoral appeal the media highlighted the party's local government activities. The *Sun*, for example, labelled the London borough of Brent as Britain's 'looniest council' and what became known as the 'London effect' began to create problems for Labour nationally. Ironically, Labour had performed well in the 1986 London borough elections, boosting its support from 31 per cent to 37 per cent as well as regaining control of Ealing. Almost immediately large rate increases were imposed in many Labour-controlled boroughs, partly to offset cutbacks made by Mrs Thatcher's government and partly as a result of ambitious spending plans proposed by the new administrations. An early manifestation of the voters' dislike for Labour's London image came with its loss of Greenwich to the SDP at a parliamentary by-election in February 1987, and the party continued to underperform in the capital right through to the 1990 elections. Despite widespread hostility towards the Conservatives over the poll tax, in some London boroughs voters could not bring themselves to support Labour. In Ealing, for example, where rate increases had been considerable, there was a 6 per cent swing from Labour to Conservative and one of 7 per cent in Brent. Labour discovered that bad publicity acquired at the local level could remain in voters' memories for some substantial time.

Arguably Labour has only recently rediscovered its ability to fight and win local elections. The party had some success in the 1980s but, throughout, its 'national equivalent' share of the vote was stubbornly stuck below 40 per cent. National reaction to the poll tax, allied with a difficult period for the newly emerging Liberal Democrats, substantially boosted Labour in 1990, the party winning eight out of ten seats in the metropolitan boroughs and half of those contested in the shire districts. Despite an increased vote share the party failed to make as many gains as anticipated at the 1991 elections and was obliged to cede the limelight to the greater successes of the Liberal Democrats in rural and suburban England. There was similar frustration again in 1993 and 1994 when Labour comfortably out-polled both its rivals but made many fewer seat gains than the Liberal Democrats. In 1995 however, the first local elections following

Tony Blair's assumption of the leadership, the pattern was broken. By securing a national equivalent vote of 47 per cent, more than 20 points better than either the Conservatives or Liberal Democrats, Labour at last won the battle for seats as well – making 1,800 gains compared to 500 by the Liberal Democrats. More significant, perhaps, was the party's performances in authorities which a decade before had shown little or no electoral support for Labour. In Bracknell Forest, for example, where Labour had not even had a single councillor between 1983 and 1991, and in Castle Point where the party's representation had been no more than one since 1979, Labour now won overall control and, in Castle Point, also an absolute majority of votes. Similar occurrences took place in other parts of England long considered virtual no-go areas for the party, with the capture of Hove borough council even proving sufficient to entice the party Deputy Leader for a celebratory visit. In 1996 Labour once more gained three times as many seats as the Liberal Democrats, further underlining its current hegemony in British local government.

LIBERALS, ALLIANCE AND LIBERAL DEMOCRATS

A famous victory in the Orpington parliamentary by-election in 1962 provided the perfect platform for the Liberal party then to make more than 500 gains in that year's local elections and take political control in twenty local authorities (Wallace 1983). Gains on such a scale were unusual, however, as the party struggled to come to terms with the penalties imposed by the electoral system. In the inaugural 1964 elections for the newly constituted London boroughs and GLC, for example, Liberal candidates saw a 10 per cent vote share translate into less than 1 per cent of seats on the borough councils and not a single one on the 100-member GLC. When the rest of British local government was reorganised in the early 1970s Liberal candidates failed to make an impression. Indeed, the party had majority control in just one council (Eastbourne) out of more than 500 new authorities and only one out of every twenty-four councillors across Britain was a Liberal. Two decades later the Liberal's successor party, the Liberal Democrats, has transformed that situation. Following the 1995 local elections the party had over 5,000 councillors, controlled 51 local authorities and had a pivotal role in scores of hung councils. But this advance has been far from uniform. In this section we will examine how the Liberals were eventually joined in an electoral Alliance by the SDP and the effect of this on the local electoral process. The Alliance was ended amidst much acrimony before the Liberal Democrat party emerged from the ashes.

One of the biggest difficulties facing the Liberal party in the early years after local government reorganisation was the sheer scale of the electoral challenge. For a small struggling party merely contesting local elections proved a formidable challenge. In 1973 alone almost 20,000 local council seats were eligible for election. The Liberals' best effort was to contest one in five seats in the shire counties. As the electoral cycle became less frenetic Liberal candidates did come forward in greater numbers. By 1977 the party was able to contest 40 per cent of county seats but resources, in terms of both finance and personnel, were severely stretched two years later when local elections coincided with the general election. The coincidence of these elections, however, also demonstrated voters' greater willingness to cast a ballot for the Liberals at the local as opposed to national level. Steed (1979) calculated that as many as one million more people voted Liberal locally than did so nationally on general election day 1979. Analysis of the mean share achieved by Liberal candidates in both forms of contest supports this view. At the general election the average share of the vote obtained by Liberal candidates was 15 per cent; in wards in the English shire districts it was as high as 30 per cent.

What the Liberals needed was some sort of critical mass. There were too many wards where voters had no opportunity to express their putative support for the Liberals in the context of local government. This position changed, virtually overnight, with the creation of the SDP in 1981 followed closely by a formal Alliance between the new party and the Liberals. The impact on electoral competition was dramatic. In 1982, for example, Alliance candidates in contesting nine in ten district council seats outnumbered those from the two main parties. Even in the following year's 'all-out' district contests Alliance candidates challenged in half of the more than 10,000 seats. This expansion in candidates brought benefits in both vote and seat share. The Alliance vote in the shire districts in 1982 (28.7 per cent) was more than double what the Liberals had achieved in 1980 (13.7 per cent). At the 1983 local elections more than 1,000 Alliance councillors were elected and a month later Alliance candidates had a quarter of the general election vote and twenty-three Members of Parliament elected.

Superficially, the arrival of the SDP had had the effect of reinforcing the Liberal presence in local government elections. For a new party the SDP looked to have developed an effective electoral machine in a remarkably short space of time. The reality, however, was that although there were two parties in the Alliance the marriage was certainly not one of equals in terms of local electoral success. Although analyses of the respective parties at the 1983 general election concluded that neither party did significantly better than the other (Butler and Waller 1983; Crewe 1983; Curtice and Steed 1984), the evidence from local elections told a different story. In local by-elections held between 1983 and 1985, for example, Liberal candidates performed better than those from the SDP. Liberal and SDP candidates contested those by-elections in the ratio of 6:4 but Liberal candidates won four times as many contests as did their partners within the Alliance. In county council elections there was a similar story. In the 1985 elections, for example, the mean vote share for Liberal candidates was 34.7 per cent while that for SDP candidates was eight points lower at 26.8 per cent (Rallings and Thrasher 1986c). Defenders of the SDP might well argue that in many cases the seats allocated to the SDP were precisely those which the Liberals had chosen to ignore and that a poorer performance could be expected.

Although there is some merit in this argument the crucial fact remained that far from extending the appeal of the Liberals by exploring and colonising new electoral territory, the SDP was often content to harvest local election pickings by following in the wake of its older and better organised partner.

Following the slump in Alliance fortunes in the 1987 general election the strains between the two party leaders, David Steel and David Owen, became clearer. Steel urged the two parties formally to merge and a majority of members of both voted for this in January 1988. Owen, however, continued to lead a rump SDP and although for a year the opinion polls suggested it remained almost as popular as the new Social and Liberal Democrats, local election results proved otherwise. Across England and Wales the SDP fielded just 282 candidates in the 1988 contests – six times fewer than the Liberal Democrats. A mere four SDP councillors were elected compared with over 300 Liberal Democrats. The average vote share for Liberal Democrat candidates in the shire districts was 25.7 per cent, for the SDP just 11.7 per cent. In wards where candidates from the two parties competed the Liberal Democrats were twice as popular as the SDP in the shires and six times more popular in the metropolitan boroughs. The SDP were no match for the Liberal Democrats at local elections. Indeed, the Liberal Democrats' national equivalent vote share in the 1988 elections was 17 per cent – three times the party's average opinion poll rating. Thus began a pattern of a sizeable gap between the Liberal Democrats' popularity as suggested by opinion polls and their support in local elections.

While the SDP eventually disappeared without trace the Liberal Democrats had to meet the challenge of maintaining the local electoral success enjoyed by the Alliance. On the last occasion the county councils had held elections in 1985, for example, the Alliance had won one in five seats and finished just 2 per cent behind Labour in the popular vote. It seemed inevitable that the Liberal Democrats would lose perhaps two-thirds of those seats in 1989. Although the party did falter, its losses were small. In total the party lost 193 seats in England, but these were partially offset by more than 80 gains. These elections established a process which saw Liberal Democrats repeatedly do less well than had the Alliance in terms of vote share but as well if not better in terms of seat share. In the 1990 London borough elections, for example, the party polled just 14 per cent – 10 per cent lower than the Alliance four years before but its share of seats (229 seats, 12 per cent) was virtually identical (249 seats, 13 per cent). So successful was this approach that the party added the London boroughs of Tower Hamlets and Sutton to the growing number of authorities under its control. Much of this electoral terrain was not, on the face of it, to their liking – inner city wards where Labour was strong. Moreover, the poll tax which so dominated the elections was an issue suited to Labour's national campaigning style. Despite these circumstances the Liberal Democrats emerged from the elections in far better shape than might have been expected for a party whose opinion poll rating was still not in double figures.

The 1991 local elections presented the Liberal Democrats with possibly their biggest test to date. Across England and Wales there were contests for over 11,000 council seats and finding sufficient candidates stretched the party's slender resources to the limit. In many wards with multiple vacancies the party fielded only a single candidate and in large areas of the country potential Liberal Democrat voters were left with a choice of abstention, using less than their full quota of votes, or of dividing their support amongst other parties. However the results seemed to justify the Liberal Democrats' strategy of targeting wards. Despite a decline in vote share from 27 per cent in 1987 to 23 per cent in 1991 the party enjoyed a net gain of almost 500 seats. Overall, in 128 out of 332 local authorities the Liberal Democrat vote fell at the same time as its share of seats either remained static or increased.

A yet more impressive demonstration of the party's new found ability to use the electoral system to its advantage came in the 1993 county elections. In winning 800 seats the Liberal Democrats effectively doubled their representation. In the far South West, long talked of as a centre of Liberal Democrat core support, they won majority control in Cornwall and Somerset and fell only narrowly short in both Devon and Dorset. Across the country their 27 per cent share of the vote matched what the Alliance had achieved in 1985. On that occasion, however, the reward was just one fifth of the seats. In 1993 the Liberal Democrats' seat share was virtually identical to its share of the poll. How had this feat been achieved? Closer analysis of the voting figures reveals little evidence of tactical voting but some remarkable swings towards the party. In the more than 200 seats gained from the Conservatives, for example, the Liberal Democrat vote rose by an average of 20 per cent compared with 1989. In no fewer than 49 cases the Liberal Democrat candidate came from third place to overtake both the incumbent Conservative and the Labour challenger. In these particular seats the party's vote rose by an average of 31 per cent. Swings of this magnitude, far larger than the national equivalent vote shares would have suggested, help provide an important insight into Liberal Democrat success enjoyed in recent local elections. Our preliminary analysis suggests that there appears to be a sort of electoral contagion effect, whereby Liberal Democrats do better in wards which share boundaries with wards where it already enjoys representation (Dorling, Rallings and Thrasher forthcoming). Such an explanation fits well with the Liberal Democrats' own campaigning strategy which emphasises the importance of 'pavement politics' and a focus on specifically local issues. Again in both 1995 and 1996 the party received a full reward in seats for the votes that had been cast in its favour.

Since the party's establishment in 1988 the Liberal Democrats have developed a strong local electoral base. The party now has more seats and controls more councils than either the Liberals or the Alliance. Following the 1996 elections the party had amassed a total of more than 5,000 councillors and majority control in more than 50 councils. Without question it is the second party of local government. In sharp contrast to the Liberals and the Alliance, Liberal Democrat candidates do not fail to translate votes into seats. The Liberal

Democrats appear to possess much more acute electoral antennae, avoiding seats where the party has little chance and instead focusing on those where support can be more easily established. The consequence of this strategy has been that the party's vote is now much less widely dispersed than before and that what was once a sizeable gap between vote and seat share has narrowed considerably.

CONCLUSIONS

Much has changed in the local party system since reorganisation in the 1970s. In the first years of the new local authorities two-party politics was the norm with the Liberals having only sporadic successes. The fortunes of the Conservative and Labour parties were dominated by the electoral effect produced by the national political scene. The pattern was more or less uniform; the party in power at Westminster would suffer when local voters felt this was the only mechanism available to express their concerns. Thus, Labour were able to win control in the first elections to the Greater London Council in 1964 as the electoral tide turned in its favour, only to lose control spectacularly three years later when it was its turn to suffer from the 'mid-term blues'. How well the party had run London in the interim was almost beside the point. The Conservative party in government suffered in much the same way. Although the construction of the new local authorities had been interpreted by many as a means of protecting the Conservative power base in the shires, there was no withstanding the degree of protest registered against the party in the 1973 elections. So poorly did the party perform in those elections that it was unable to win a majority in southern counties like Berkshire, Hampshire, Hertfordshire and Wiltshire. Four years later however, and this time in opposition, the Conservatives stormed to power winning all but five of the English counties. In metropolitan England only South Yorkshire and Tyne and Wear resisted the Conservative onslaught. In the 1970s, then, the electoral pendulum swung rapidly, but it did so in a fairly regular and predictable manner.

That pattern was disrupted by the emergence of the SDP in the early 1980s and the subsequent electoral agreement with the Liberals. The Liberal/SDP Alliance might not have broken the parliamentary mould but it certainly had a dramatic effect in the distribution of power in local government. Although the Alliance gained majority control of just one county in the 1985 elections its impact was such that in 23 others the council became hung. A similar outcome followed the 1987 shire district elections. While the Alliance gained control in just two districts its electoral presence was sufficient to deprive the two major parties of majority control in almost a third of district councils. The effect would have been even greater had the Alliance pursued a more efficient campaigning strategy. Driven by the public's apparent dislike of both major parties Alliance candidates stood for election even in areas where their prospects of victory were slim. As a consequence the Alliance's vote share flattered to deceive. Only 2 per cent behind Labour in the 1985 county vote the Alliance received 12 per cent

fewer seats; 4 per cent ahead of Labour in the 1987 shire district vote the SDP/
Liberals won 5 per cent fewer seats. The Alliance's entry into the local electoral
scene was spectacular but it was not sophisticated.

The 1987 general election proved one election too far for the Alliance. Inter-
party rivalries surfaced when the electoral allies failed to make the breakthrough.
A new centre party was formed in 1988, but it took the Liberal Democrats until
1991 to become properly organised as a local electoral fighting force. Those
elections, however, served notice that the relationship amongst Britain's main
parties had altered. The Liberal Democrats successfully targeted council seats,
abandoning the practice of fighting everywhere without too much consideration
of the effectiveness of such a strategy. As a result the number of hung councils
rose to almost 100 and the combined Conservative and Labour tally of shire
districts fell from 179 to 149 authorities. Such events were but a modest foretaste
of what was to come. By the 1993 county elections the two main parties ran just
10 of the 39 English counties, with the Conservatives retaining control in just
one. In the majority of hung counties it was the Liberal Democrats who held the
balance of power. This pattern was repeated two years later in the shire district
elections with the proportion of these authorities controlled by one or other of
the two main parties falling to just over 40 per cent. Across large parts of Britain
the concept of a 'two-party system' took on a new meaning as the Liberal
Democrats consolidated their place as one of those two parties.

The major losers from this movement have been the Conservatives who have,
in effect, become trapped in a pincer movement, with Labour and the Liberal
Democrats proving a credible local threat in different councils and parts of the
country. We have discussed some of the impact of this above, but we need also to
address its longer-term consequences. In one sense the strategy of the Liberal
Democrats in local elections can be viewed as part of the party's attempt to
secure greater parliamentary representation. That said, even if that goal were to
remain unfulfilled, it is unlikely that the Liberal Democrats will suffer dramatic
reversals in local government. Their success has come in spite of the party's poor
opinion poll ratings and has more to do with campaigning efforts on the ground
than national personalities and policies. The Conservative party cannot therefore
guarantee that those local voters who have deserted it at this critical moment will
necessarily return when its fortunes improve. Labour too has demonstrated that a
change of image and style in the national party has enabled it to compete more
effectively in local elections. Moreover, there is some evidence that local
elections may provide a better context for Labour in attracting support than
general elections in as much as voters are swayed more by public service than
pocket book issues – see Chapter 10. Both opposition parties, therefore, are
currently enjoying a level of success never seen before. To an extent, of course,
the Conservative party's local government recovery will be a function of what
happens at the national level. Should the party find itself out of government then,
if history repeats itself, it is likely to achieve more success in local elections. But
the decline in Conservative fortunes has been such that it would take enormous

swings against both Labour and the Liberal Democrats over a number of elections for the party to recover its former position. Structural changes now taking place, especially the creation of new unitary authorities, mean that the relationship between the national and local electoral cycles has been altered. The scope for the Conservative party to bounce back quickly and easily has been much reduced.

9 Minor parties and local elections

INTRODUCTION

Any division of parties into 'major' and 'minor' categories is both arbitrary and certain to cause offence to the supporters of those parties relegated to the lesser status. Political scientists have struggled for many years to arrive at an acceptable system of classification. For some the critical factor has been whether the party in question succeeds in winning legislative representation (Lijphart 1984). Others seem to imply that minor parties are those which defy cross-national 'family' analysis (Gallagher *et al.* 1995; Muller-Rommel and Pridham 1991). What most of these studies have in common, however, is that the discussion centres on national, not local electoral politics. Naturally, the threshold for minor parties to succeed at the national level is different to that for achieving local representation. In one sense this confuses the picture still further. By suggesting that small parties are not after all so insignificant when local rather than national elections are being discussed we appear to be calling into question the distinction between major and minor parties. We are not about to resolve this issue here but it is hoped that what follows will at least provide a greater insight into the nature and extent of electoral competition provided by parties outside the national mainstream.

Although the main parties have dominated local elections there have been others whose contributions have been significant. In both Scotland and to a lesser extent Wales, local elections have been important platforms for the development of nationalist parties. Fluctuations in support for some form of devolution or independence have been reflected in the council ballot box. The Scottish National party (SNP) in particular has proved successful in winning seats and council control. Beyond the nationalist parties there has been a wide variety of party groupings but the most numerous candidates have been those who, strictly speaking, have eschewed a party description altogether. The label 'Independent' refers not to a party but rather announces the candidate's conscious rejection of a formal party description on the ballot paper. Nevertheless, a book on local elections in Britain could not be written without taking into account the important role played by Independent candidates and councillors. This discussion is followed by a number of brief profiles of parties that have made some impression on the local electoral scene. These include the Green party, Ratepayer and Residents' Associations from around the country, as well as parties and groupings of the Far Right and Far Left.

THE SCOTTISH AND WELSH NATIONALISTS

In November 1967 the SNP captured the safe Labour seat of Hamilton at a parliamentary by-election. The victory came a year after the Welsh nationalists, Plaid Cymru, had made their own by-election breakthrough in Carmarthen. Such events gave a great boost to the nationalist cause, which saw each party at the 1970 general election more than double its previous vote. Four years later Scotland had a bumper election year, with local elections for both the new district and the regional and islands councils sandwiched between two general elections. Though the resources of the party were stretched there was no better moment to place the question of Scottish independence firmly on the electoral agenda. Local voters in Wales had voted for their new local authorities just a year earlier in 1973 so this period marks a suitable point at which to begin our evaluation of local electoral support for the two nationalist parties. Though much has been written about the nationalist movement and its impact in general elections relatively little has been published in relation to local elections. Readers wishing for more detail about the SNP in Scottish local elections should refer to the biennial volumes of results published by Bochel and Denver since 1974. For an excellent summary of local election trends in Scotland, Denver (1993) should be consulted.

Certainly, the coincidence of so many elections in 1974 was a spur to Scottish nationalism. Campaigning for the new local authorities came soon after the February general election which had seen the SNP win more than a fifth of votes and have seven MPs elected. Although that momentum proved important for the party, the pressure of fighting all but one of Scotland's 71 constituencies appeared to have taken its toll. In the districts SNP candidates contested only a quarter of seats, winning fractionally over 12 per cent of the total vote. The elections for the larger regional councils attracted more party competition in general, but still the SNP fought fewer than three in ten seats for a similar vote share to that achieved in the districts. Although the results showed that the electoral system had clearly penalised the party – its share of the seats being less than half its share of the vote – it did have some successes. In the Central Region nine SNP councillors were a significant factor in depriving the Labour party of overall control while in Clackmannan district the SNP became the largest party in a hung council. The SNP's greatest symbolic success, however, was in gaining control of the ten-member Cumbernauld and Kilsyth council. Although the local elections were clearly not as important to the party as the struggle for parliamentary representation they did serve to sustain electors' interest in the nationalist message. In the October 1974 general election the SNP captured 30.4 per cent of the vote and added four new MPs to its tally.

Compared with their nationalist colleagues in Scotland those in Wales were less successful. In one sense the timing of the 1973 local elections, coming a year earlier, might have been a disadvantage to Plaid Cymru. Without the media interest of a general election campaign to carry it forward the party struggled first to find candidates and then to win votes. In the 8 Welsh counties less than 17 per cent of vacancies were fought by PC candidates and slightly over 14 per cent of the district seats. In both types of authority the party's vote share was less than 10 per cent and with 3 per cent of council seats across the country Plaid Cymru was in no position to control any council. Nevertheless, there were some successes in individual authorities. In Mid Glamorgan county, for example, PC candidates captured more than a fifth of the vote and with 10 councillors became the second largest party. Much of that nationalist challenge had been focused in Cynon Valley where the party obtained more than a third of votes cast and 12 district council seats. Plaid candidates also performed quite well in nearby Merthyr Tydfil and Rhymney Valley, setting the foundations for future electoral forays.

One test of a political party's ability to sustain itself is how well it performs when the initial surge of enthusiasm for its electoral message begins to wane. The Labour government elected in 1974 had committed itself to a policy of devolution for both Scotland and Wales. The reality, of course, was that a slender Commons' majority vanished with by-election losses and the government was forced to accept amendments to its legislation placing conditions on how the results of the March 1979 Scottish and Welsh referendums on devolution would be judged. In the event Wales rejected devolution by a margin of four to one, while the small majority in Scotland voting in favour comprised an insufficient proportion of the electorate to allow the policy to proceed. The impact on the nationalist parties was immediately felt in a general election which followed just two months later. Both parties saw their vote share decline and the number of nationalist MPs in the House of Commons fell from 14 to just 4. Without a nationwide campaign to nourish their development could the nationalist parties now find sustenance from local election activity?

In Scotland SNP candidates increased in number for both district and regional council elections. By the mid-1980s the party had overtaken the Liberal/SDP Alliance in terms of contestation levels in both types of authority. In 1988 the SNP fielded more candidates than the Conservatives in the district elections and four years later were to eclipse even the Labour party. There was, perhaps, a sense of bravado about this practice of contesting more seats than any other party. While it certainly fulfilled a symbolic purpose in elevating the party to the status of a truly 'national' organisation, did it have an effect on its share of the vote and, more importantly, its control of seats? From achieving around one in eight votes in the first local elections the SNP gradually built up support, attracting the votes of more than one in five electors in 1990. Crucially, the party was able to achieve a similar vote at the 1992 general election, an increase of a third on its 1987 performance. To an important degree, therefore, the party's policy of mass candidature at local elections had helped both to keep it visible and to allow potential supporters to get into the habit of voting for it.

Despite the fact that the SNP had pushed the Conservatives back into third place in terms of the popular vote the reward in seats was disappointing. In the 1992 district elections, for example, the Conservatives polled fewer votes than the SNP but won 200 seats to the nationalists' 150. That deficit, however, was dramatically overturned in the 1994 regional elections when the SNP vote reached the critical mass necessary for it to reap a more appropriate reward from the electoral system. Its 26.8 per cent share of the vote against a paltry 13.7 per cent for the Conservatives won it 73 of the 453 regional council seats (16 per cent) while the Conservatives, now in the position of a third party, could manage just 31 seats. These were the last elections under the old structure and in 1995 elections for shadow authorities for Scotland's 29 new unitary councils took place. These confirmed the SNP as the second party of Scottish local government as it won more than twice as many votes and seats as the Conservatives and majority control of three councils. One of these, Angus, had been under SNP control since 1984, but Moray and Perthshire and Kinross were new additions in 1995. The last named authority encompassed the parliamentary constituency of Perth and Kinross where a parliamentary by-election was pending and the following month the SNP were successful in that too. This example serves to illustrate the more general point about the nature of the SNP challenge. Since the early 1970s the party has apparently succeeded in withstanding the lower electoral salience of the devolution issue and steadily developed its local government base. Though the party has yet to challenge Labour's hegemony that situation may change were Labour to win a general election and face the prospect of local elections held at times of national unpopularity. The next local elections are due in 1999 and the SNP appears strategically placed to make further gains in votes and seats.

Although the SNP has been successful in local elections Plaid Cymru has not performed as well in Wales. Certainly, the party has had some success but it has never matched the SNP in the vital areas of contestation, vote and seat share, and council control. The peak of activity for PC came in the 1977 county elections when the party fought in more than 40 per cent of seats but since then its activity at local elections has declined. By 1989 only 23 per cent of county seats featured a PC candidate and in the district elections two years later only 18 per cent of the more than 1,300 wards had a Plaid candidate. As with Scotland, however, local government reorganisation appears to have stimulated the nationalists' interest in fighting local elections. In the 1995 unitary elections PC candidates were present in more than 300 (35 per cent) wards. We must await the next elections, scheduled for 1999, to see whether this initial enthusiasm is maintained.

The relatively low level of contestation would not lead us to expect PC to have performed particularly well in terms of either vote or seat share across Wales as a whole. Since 1973 PC's highest local vote share has been the 16 per cent won in the 1977 county council elections when the devolution issue was salient. Apart from that year the party has achieved a vote share in double figures on only two other occasions. The most recent of these was, in fact, the 1995 unitary elections and clearly stems from the party's decision to contest more wards than usual. With such small proportions of the vote Plaid Cymru has been unable to break free of the penalties imposed by the electoral system on small parties. Even in 1977 the party won only 39 out of 577 county seats (7 per cent) as its reward for a share of the vote more than twice as large.

In elections for district councils PC has fared a little better for a variety of reasons. First, ward sizes are smaller than in the counties, making campaigning by smaller parties easier. Second, the party is able to concentrate its campaign in a number of particular authorities, ignoring areas where there is little prospect of advancement. Third, at the district level there is a greater chance of one of its candidates being returned unopposed than in the more competitive county contests. Plaid Cymru's best showings have been in 1991 when it won 8.3 per cent of district council seats and in the 1995 unitary authority elections when it contested more seats than either the Conservatives or the Liberal Democrats, winning an eighth of the vote and 113 of the 1,272 seats (9 per cent). A more detailed analysis reveals pockets of PC strength in individual local authorities. Merthyr Tydfil, for example, where the party had one of its better results in 1973, became the first Welsh local authority to have a PC majority administration following the 1976 elections when Plaid benefited from Labour's national unpopularity. Although unable to defend its majority successfully three years later, Plaid Cymru has regularly won local election seats in other district councils in the Mid Glamorgan valleys like Cynon Valley and Taff Ely. When the boundaries of the new unitary councils were announced PC was hopeful of its electoral prospects in the inelegantly named Rhondda/Cynon/Taff authority. The party did poll a third of the vote in this authority in 1995, but was overwhelmed in seat share at least by Labour. Plaid Cymru won 14 of the 75 seats (19 per cent) while Labour picked up no fewer than 57 (76 per cent) for its share of just over half of the total vote.

In the very different environment of North Wales it is noticeable that in many areas where Plaid Cymru has achieved parliamentary success it has made little attempt to gain local representation. Part of the explanation for this lies in the fact that rural Wales has remained one of the last bastions of non-political local government in Britain, but even here there are exceptions. The small district of Arfon in Gwynedd, for example, with an electorate of approximately 40,000, has seen a sustained nationalist presence in local elections ever since 1973. In the first elections five PC councillors were elected and the party gradually increased its representation until in 1979 it occupied a pivotal position in a hung council. Neighbouring Meirionnydd elected its first PC councillors in 1976 and by 1991 almost a third of the 41-strong council were nationalists. The merger of the bulk of these two councils into the new Caernarfonshire and Merionethshire unitary authority in 1995 (subsequently renamed Gwynedd like the old county) gave Plaid Cymru a significant opportunity to stamp its mark on Welsh local government. The area had elected two nationalist MPs continuously for more than twenty years and the party believed the time had come to emulate the Liberal Democrats in England by providing them with a strong local power base. In the 1995 elections the party contested 58 of the 83 seats and immediately found itself returned unopposed in 21 of them. It won 24 more by conventional means with 43 per cent of the total vote and gained overall control of the new council. Although Plaid Cymru has not enjoyed the same measure of success as the SNP, it is clear that the two parties have pursued, to a limited extent, similar electoral strategies. Those strategies have been to build support in a relatively small number of local authorities and then to use that power base to mount more effective parliamentary campaigns. Unlike the SNP, however, Plaid Cymru has not tried to mount as wide a challenge as possible, fighting virtually all available vacancies, and have instead adopted a more cautious approach in local elections.

INDEPENDENTS

The local government system created at the beginning of the 1970s inherited a tradition whereby in some parts of the country elections were largely contested by candidates without party labels. In some people's eyes this characteristic made local democracy special, as it involved individuals appealing to an electorate directly and without party politics intervening. As we noted in Chapter 2, the emergence of parties in local elections had largely been an urban phenomenon and had failed to penetrate more rural areas. This was amply demonstrated in the inaugural elections held in 1973. Whilst Independent candidates hardly featured in elections for the London and metropolitan boroughs, in the English shire counties and districts they accounted for 28 per cent and 48 per cent of all candidatures respectively. Independents also enjoyed a strong presence in Scotland and Wales. In Scotland one in four candidates in the 1974 district and regional elections stood as Independents, while in Wales they contested fully three-quarters of both county and district council seats in 1973. The outcome of those early elections demonstrated that although the structure and functions of local government had been altered, some electoral traditions survived. In the English shire districts Independents obtained a fifth of the vote and some 3,500 Independent councillors were elected. In over half of the new district authorities Independent candidates polled more than 30 per cent of the vote.

Already, however, overall levels of party competition had begun to increase following reorganisation and it could be questioned whether Independents would continue to play such a prominent part in future local elections and whether they would have as much success. Answers to such questions were not long in coming. By the end of the decade both the number and the vote share of Independent candidates were in decline. From contesting almost half the seats in the shire districts Independents now challenged in less than a third. In county elections the rate of contestation halved between 1973 and 1981. The story was similar in terms of votes, with Independents obtaining just 11 per cent of the district vote in 1979 and a meagre 4 per cent in the county elections two years later. The number of Independent councillors elected in the 1979 shire district elections was little over 2,000, representing a fall of some 1,300 seats from the high point of 1973.

During this period there were a number of simultaneous processes which contributed to the dramatic decline of Independents in local government. First, growing party politicisation saw areas which formerly had been party-free brought under a more rigorous party regime. In some cases this was because the new local government structure amalgamated rural areas which had been non-partisan with traditionally partisan urban authorities. Policy was now more likely to be determined in party caucus meetings rather than within the formal committee structure or the full council. Furthermore, the increased size of the new authorities meant that many Independents could no longer enjoy the face-to-face relationship with voters that had contributed to their electoral prosperity. Second, party politicisation contributed to an increasing level of party competition, particularly with the Liberal resurgence and the creation of the SDP. A third factor, directly related to the previous two, was the practice of national parties, especially the Conservative party, of actively encouraging or even compelling Independents with a known party sympathy to display it on the ballot paper. Thus, while the number of Independents fell steadily from 1973 onwards that decline was not entirely a function of electoral defeat but was, in some cases, simply the result of an individual who might once have stood as an Independent now openly declaring a party allegiance.

The impact of these pressures meant that the Independent decline in British local government became inexorable. In 1989, for example, Independents contested just 8 per cent of the 3,000 English county divisions, winning 2 per cent of the vote and being elected in just three in every hundred seats. To some extent the larger sized county divisions worked against Independents appealing for a personal vote, but even in the smaller shire district wards the outlook was grim. There were Independent candidates for a quarter of the more than 12,000 seats across the 296 English districts contested in 1991, but they were successful in only half those cases. The Independents who were still elected tended to be geographically concentrated in the far South West, where ten councils were under Independent rule, in parts of East Anglia and in Shropshire. Significantly, while one fifth of all Independents elected in 1991 were from the South West, only one tenth were from the South and just one in twenty represented a ward in the South East – both areas with much larger populations and thus many more seats at stake. An analysis of ward level census data shows that Independents were indeed much more likely to be elected in rural wards with a below average electorate size. The mean electorate in wards represented by an Independent in 1992 was less than half that in those represented by one of the main political parties. Nor are there signs that the Independent cause can withstand the pattern of change of the past twenty years. Following the 1995 elections Independents could claim overall control in only 15 councils, four of which were in Shropshire but now none in the South West.

Marginalised in English local government the Independents have faced challenges in Scotland and Wales too. In both countries, of course, the pattern of party competition has been different because candidates from the SNP and Plaid Cymru have contested local elections. Even so Independents have fared better over the years in both countries than in England. Elections were held in 1974 for the Scottish district and regional councils where Independents received only 14 per cent and 12 per cent of the vote respectively. Despite such vote shares Independents nonetheless comprised 31 per cent of all district councillors and 26 per cent of those in the regions. The reason for this disparity between vote and seat share was quite simply that many Independents were returned unopposed. A fifth of district and a tenth of regional seats were uncontested and Independents were the main beneficiaries of this lack of contestation. In Scotland as in England, however, the number of Independents seeking political office has declined over time. From comprising a quarter of all candidates for Scottish district council seats in 1974, Independent contestation fell to a fifth in 1977, a sixth by 1980 and by 1992 only one in nine candidates had no party label. Nevertheless, and partly as a result of continuing unopposed returns allowing the survival of the stronger Independent tradition in rural Scotland, a fifth of all district and a sixth of all regional councillors were still Independents in the early 1990s. Even following the 1995 unitary elections Independents emerged with 154 seats (13 per cent of the total) and control of three councils, Argyll and Bute, Borders and Highland. Those three councils, of course, are very small in population terms.

Wales has followed a similar pattern to Scotland with the Independent cause resisting the pressure from the main parties. The survival of the Independent in Welsh local government should be viewed in context. At the first elections held in 1973 three-quarters of the seats in the 8 counties and 37 districts were contested by Independent candidates, a larger proportion than any political party. In terms of vote share the strength of the Independents in Wales can be seen by comparing their electoral support with that of their English counterparts. In England the Independent vote declined from 22 per cent in the 1973 district elections to 8 per cent in the 1991 equivalents. Over the same period, however, support for Welsh Independent candidates went from 24 per cent to 18 per cent – a 6-point rather than 14-point fall. As in Scotland seat share has exceeded vote share, simply because so many Independents are returned unopposed. In 1989, for example, 29 per cent of Welsh county divisions saw no contest and in half it was an Independent who benefited. At the 1995 unitary elections almost a quarter of the more than 1,200 councillors were elected as Independents. Although many Welsh councillors will continue to have no party allegiance, the Independents' grip on power shows signs of weakening. While direct comparisons between the old and new authorities proved difficult, in at least four unitary authorities where Independents were expected to do well the new administration will be run by a political party or has become a hung council.

While some may yearn for a return to those times when party politics played an insignificant role in the conduct and management of local government, the days of the Independent must surely be numbered. Elections since 1973 show an overall decline in their numbers although the rate of that decline has varied. In the more rural areas Independents have proved rather more successful at surviving than in urban authorities, but even there they are now increasingly subject to challenge from party candidates where once they might have survived by being spared a contest. By 1996 fewer than one tenth of all councillors were Independents and just 24 councils across Great Britain had Independent-run administrations. It is difficult to envisage circumstances under which this process of decline could be reversed. As the profile of local elections rises and as parties invest more resources in their campaigns, the fate of individuals without similar resources appears to be sealed. At successive stages in the local electoral cycle the gains/losses column for Independents has always been negative. We will soon reach a point where there are virtually no Independent seats still to be lost.

THE GREENS

In 1989 the Green party threatened to make a spectacular entrance into British politics. In that year's European Parliament elections the party captured 15 per cent of the national vote. Although they failed to win any seats Green candidates came second in six and altogether the party attracted more than two million votes. After years of fruitless battles to win support in local and parliamentary elections the Greens appeared poised to transform the electoral agenda. Behind this success, however, lay problems which ensured that the party could not capitalise on this wave of support. A decision had been made that the party would not elect a leader but would instead have a number of individuals operating as some form of collective leadership. Policy was determined, in theory at least, from the bottom-up. In practice it emerged, if at all, out of a series of almost random utterances from different sections of the party. Organisationally, therefore, the party consisted of an extremely loose federation of local groups and individuals with no clear sense of purpose or direction. Some of these groups were able to build a serious party organisation and proved relatively successful in a number of local elections. Many others, however, were extremely transitory, and disbanded following electoral failure. Overall, the record of the Greens in local government elections has been poor although there have been a small number of authorities where they have met with some measure of success.

The Ecology party, as the Green party was known formerly, began contesting local elections in the mid-1970s. At first a very small number of candidates appeared. In 1978, for example, there were just two Ecology candidates out of almost 6,000 contesting the London borough elections. During the late 1980s, however, the number of Green candidates rose considerably as support for the party increased nationally. In the 1989 county council elections the Greens contested more than 600 divisions, almost one in five of the total across England and Wales. Although the party won just two seats their mean vote share in seats contested was a respectable 9.3 per cent. The foundations for the Greens successful campaign in the European elections had clearly been set a month earlier in the county elections. This momentum continued through to the 1990 elections when Green candidates fought a quarter of all vacancies, despite the fact that many were in inner city wards which in the past had not proved fruitful for the party. Such interest needed electoral success to sustain it, however, and the party were finding it difficult to break the domination of the three main parties.

Even at the height of their success the Greens made little more than a dent in the three-party vote. In London their average vote struggled into double figures, but in other cities Green candidates had only a token presence, barely averaging more than a 5 per cent vote share. Perhaps more fertile ground lay in the shire districts, particularly in parts of the south of England. In the 1991 district elections, for example, the Greens averaged 10 per cent of the vote in the fewer than one in ten seats which they contested overall. Despite this relative success, however, the party failed to make a breakthrough in terms of council membership, winning just 14 seats across the English shires. Two of those successes came in East Devon district which also saw a candidate from the Raving Loony Green Giant party elected at the same time. This proved to be the pinnacle of the Green achievement in local government elections. In recent years Green candidates have become even more of an endangered species. In the 1995 local elections, although still receiving an average 9 per cent of the vote where they stood, there were Green candidates for only 5 per cent of the seats and they were victorious in just 12 wards.

With a more developed electoral strategy could the Greens have achieved more? In the absence of any clear analysis of where the party's voting strength lay Green candidates were left free to fight any ward of their own choosing. This produced a certain degree of clustering of Green party activity. In London, for example, the inner boroughs of Camden, Haringey and Islington saw large numbers of wards contested by the Greens while suburbs like Bromley, Harrow and Havering saw virtually none. It may be a coincidence, but those boroughs with high levels of Green contestation also happen to include or be close to the railway line along which nuclear waste is conveyed (Fothergill and Vincent 1985: 82–3). Outside the capital the Greens appeared active in some cities such as Manchester, Birmingham and Leeds, but not in Liverpool or Sheffield. The variable pattern of both contestation and electoral success by the Greens reflected the party's absence of a proper national organisation and the consequent reliance on individuals on the ground to make the difference between a moribund and an active local group. Not that such an approach to electoral politics should be dismissed out of hand, for as we have seen, much of the local success of the Liberal Democrats has stemmed from similarly modest roots.

When the shire districts and counties are examined in more detail it appears that the Greens have been most active in those authorities containing a university. Thus, places like Bristol, Reading, Milton Keynes, Exeter, Canterbury, Norwich, York and Oxford have had large numbers of wards sporadically contested by Green candidates and they have tended to do comparatively well. In one district, however, Green councillors have been a regular feature at local elections. Stroud district council saw its first Green elected in 1986 for the Trinity ward and since then the party has safely defended this ward and added others to its strength. Stroud, of course, has featured prominently in the media as an area with a higher than average incidence of meningitis and there is a clear association between this and the Greens' electoral activity.

From this evidence it is apparent that the Greens might have proved more successful if they had analysed their own electoral performance. An analysis of the socio-economic characteristics of those wards where Green candidates performed well showed that they were more likely to do better in areas with higher than average numbers of young people, particularly students in further and higher education. In London their vote was also stronger in wards with high levels of multiple-occupancy housing and immigrant populations. This potential support among students in higher education or electors concerned by disease or the pollution brought about by proximity to power stations or the transport of toxic waste might have been better exploited by targeted campaigning. Instead, the party either failed to notice this phenomenon or was powerless to co-ordinate an electoral strategy to capitalise on it. If it continues to be left to local groups to mount their own future campaigns the Greens can look forward to future moments of success in authorities such as Oxford and Stroud but have little prospect of becoming a serious force in local government.

RATEPAYERS' AND RESIDENTS' ASSOCIATIONS

There is a long tradition in British local government of Ratepayers' and Residents' Associations taking their concerns about the finance and management of local services to the point of contesting elections (Young 1975). Since reorganisation these candidates have suffered, like many other fringe parties and groups, from the increase in party politics. Despite the formidable challenges presented by the main parties, however, some vestiges of ratepayer power still remain, though increasingly electoral success is restricted to a handful of local authorities.

Unfortunately reliable data are unavailable relating to the performance of ratepayer candidates prior to reorganisation. The 1973 elections, therefore, provide us with our earliest opportunity to describe in detail where such candidates stood and with what success. In fact, judging from the geography of contestation, the ratepayer movement was still healthy – candidates contested at least one ward in a quarter of English shire districts. Among the local authorities still with a sizeable ratepayer movement at this time were Kingswood, Chiltern, Basildon, Fareham, Havant, Rushmoor, East Hertfordshire, Elmbridge, Epsom and Ewell, and Worthing. Those candidates who did stand met with a considerable level of success. Their average share of the vote was an impressive 38 per cent and 275 out of more than 400 candidates were elected as councillors. In Epsom and Ewell not a single one of the 34 Residents' Association candidates was defeated as they took council control.

With each successive electoral cycle, however, ratepayer councillors appear to have succumbed to either time or the advance of modern party campaigning. The 1995 elections provided an opportunity to gauge the current health of ratepayer groups throughout the country, both in terms of candidacy and electoral performance. The number of candidates had fallen by half to less than 200 compared with 1973, but, remarkably, more than half of those were still elected. In the metropolitan areas ratepayer candidates were even rarer, contesting just six out of more than 800 wards with just two elected. The previous year in London, where once the ratepayer movement was particularly strong in some areas, ratepayer or residents' candidates challenged in just 23 out of 759 wards. A third of those challenges came in a single borough, Havering.

Certainly ratepayer candidates are now fewer in number and those that survive are restricted to a relatively small number of authorities. In Havering, for example, success for residents' candidates has contributed to that authority having a hung council since 1986. Elsewhere in London there are pockets of support in authorities such as Merton and Islington. On the outer fringes of London, residual ratepayer strength can be found. In Surrey, for example, electors in Elmbridge and Epsom and Ewell still consistently return councillors for residents' groups. Such is their strength in the latter authority that they have run the council continually since 1973 with the major parties seldom able to win more than a single ward in any one election year. Though other groups have not met with similar success candidates still do regularly contest and win wards in authorities such as Eden in Cumbria, Epping Forest, Fylde, South Buckinghamshire, Staffordshire Moorlands and Windsor and Maidenhead. Where they do survive to continue the electoral struggle such candidates perform quite well. In 1995, for example, the average vote for ratepayer and residents' candidates was 38 per cent – precisely what it had been more than twenty years before. How long such groups can survive against more developed local party systems is open to question, however. In Epsom and Ewell, for example, residents' candidates have only rarely been challenged by the Conservatives. There can be no guarantee that local, let alone national, Conservatives will always be prepared to accept a commonality of interest between themselves and a group beyond the reach of party policy and discipline.

THE FAR RIGHT

Britain has no tradition of electoral support for parties representing opinion at the extreme left or right wings of the political spectrum. An electoral system which penalises small parties and a political culture that frowns upon extremism have served to relegate such parties to the fringe. In September 1993, for example, there was considerable media attention given to a local by-election in the Millwall ward of Tower Hamlets. The reason was simple: racial tensions were high in the area and the British National party (BNP) announced its decision to contest the vacancy. Media coverage rose still further when the BNP were successful, relegating Labour into second place by just seven votes. The BNP, however, had not contested the ward at the previous elections in 1990 and Labour recaptured the seat in the subsequent elections in 1994. In a sense Millwall was a typical, if unusually spectacular, example of the Far Right's sporadic and largely unsuccessful forays into electoral politics in Britain.

Both the National Front (NF) and BNP contested local elections in London during the 1960s but met with little success. By the early 1970s, however, their rate of contestation had increased marginally and support for the Far Right began to spread out from the capital. In 1973 NF candidates contested 68 (0.6 per cent of the total) shire district wards, averaged 15 per cent of the vote and polled well in Blackburn and Leicester. By 1976 the number of National Front candidates had increased to more than 80 and, although average vote shares fell, there were areas, particularly in Lancashire, where NF candidates contested a high proportion of vacancies. The party proved especially active in the 1978 London borough elections, fighting more than a third of wards and winning an average 6 per cent of the vote. Although the 1979 elections coincided with the general election with NF candidates challenging in almost half of the parliamentary constituencies, the party also fought 159 wards in the shire districts, concentrated still in the North West but now spreading to cities as far south as Plymouth. In the metropolitan boroughs NF candidates steadily increased in number during the 1970s culminating in 164 candidates at the 1978 elections. These candidates were concentrated in the West Midlands and across parts of West Yorkshire. The increase in contestation was not matched in votes, however, and their average share fell to 4 per cent in the shires and just 2.6 per cent in the metropolitan authorities. By the end of the 1970s both the NF and BNP had experienced a loss of momentum as candidates became fewer and in 1983 the National Front fought less than one tenth of 1 per cent of wards.

Although BNP and NF candidates had rarely challenged one another in local elections, at the national level rivalry between the two parties proved damaging. By the early 1980s the BNP had largely replaced the NF as the chosen vehicle for those very few candidates openly espousing extreme right wing views, but they too made no impact. In the 1995 elections just 13 wards in the shire districts and 10 in the metropolitan boroughs had avowed Far Right candidates and none came anywhere close to being elected. Despite media interest in the Millwall by-election, therefore, it is clear that the British local electorate has given little succour to such parties.

THE FAR LEFT

Candidates from Far Left parties have been rather more plentiful and have met with more success than those from the Far Right. There are examples from a variety of parties and groups, ranging from traditional Far Left parties like the Communists and the Socialist Workers' party through to newer political groupings like Militant Labour and the Anti-Poll Tax Federation. Arguably, these newer Far Left groups have proved more successful than the older parties. Since reorganisation, for example, there have been fewer than 100 challenges by Communist candidates in literally tens of thousands of shire ward elections. Only in some Welsh authorities, notably Rhondda and Merthyr Tydfil, have Communist candidates consistently fought local elections, though they contested a mere six seats at the elections for the new Welsh unitary authorities in 1995. In even fewer cases have Communist candidates succeeded in breaking the hold of the main parties. One success story was that of John Peck who repeatedly contested elections in Nottingham for city and county wards from 1973 onwards. In 1987 he was finally elected for the Bulwell East ward and for a time held the balance of power in the hung Nottingham city council. He continued to serve as a Communist councillor until 1991 when he stood and was re-elected on a Green party ticket. In Scotland there has been a similar success for the Communists who have held a seat in Kirkcaldy, Fife continuously since 1974.

The Anti-Poll Tax Federation was particularly active in trying to persuade its supporters to contest the 1990 local elections. It was only partially successful. In the London boroughs, for example, just three candidates stood on this specific issue and made little impact. In the shires, however, there were twenty such candidates in 1990 and although none were elected, some did poll a respectable share of the vote. The group's greatest successes came in Scotland where both the imposition of and opposition to the tax had pre-dated that south of the border. In May 1992 an anti-poll tax activist, Tommy Sheridan, was elected to Glasgow city council despite the fact that he was at the time incarcerated in Barlinnie prison. In September of the same year another candidate associated with Sheridan's protest was successful in winning a by-election for a seat on Strathclyde regional council. By this time such candidates were choosing to fight elections under the label of 'Scottish Militant Labour' and another by-election success in the month following suggested that a considerable momentum had begun to develop. The pattern of such protests, however, suggests that once the initial, single issue enthusiasm begins to wane it is very difficult to sustain electoral pressure. At the regional elections in 1994 Scottish Militant Labour was unable to defend its by-election victories on Strathclyde council and a year later, and despite contesting a large proportion of the seats on the new Glasgow unitary council in 1995, Tommy Sheridan himself was the party's sole victor.

It was Neil Kinnock, of course, who famously denounced Militant in his speech to the Labour conference in October 1985. The principal target in this onslaught was Liverpool city council and its deputy leader Derek Hatton. The council had earlier in the year fixed an illegal rate in open defiance of the government's rate-capping legislation. Kinnock's action made it inadmissable for any member of the Labour party also to be a member of Militant. Since that time there have been a growing number of local elections where candidates have stood as 'Militant Labour' or plain 'Militant'. In Liverpool, where the 'Militant Tendency' first came to prominence, candidates have contested local elections but have not proved successful in winning any seats. Elsewhere, Militant candidates have stood in a haphazard way, contesting one or two wards in an authority but showing little sign of widespread support. In Coventry, for example, Dave Nellist, once one of the city's Labour MPs but subsequently expelled for his connections with Militant, contested the 1995 elections but could not defeat the official Labour candidate. At the time of writing not a single Militant Labour candidate has been successful in any form of local election in England and Wales.

Developments within the Labour party since the expulsion of Militant supporters have helped promote a number of left-wing movements, many of which signify some form of ideological split with the official party. Normally, such candidates have been deselected by the local party and then stand as 'Independent Labour' (and the same phenomenon applies, of course, to many 'Independent Conservative' candidates too), but in recent years we have noted increasing use of such descriptions as 'Real Labour' or, alternatively, the name of the local ward is used as a prefix to signify separation from the official ward Labour party. Again, elections in Liverpool present many examples of this practice but in recent years it has spread to other authorities too. In the 1996 elections, for example, the suspension of Labour councillors in Walsall led to divisions within the local party and four wards featured contests between the rival factions. A year previously a similar dispute stemming from left-wing opposition to reforms proposed by Tony Blair saw a group calling themselves 'Corby First Labour' challenge official Labour candidates in that district's elections. In neither case did the break-away group win any seats. Normally such disputes are short-lived, either because the controversy dies away or because the lack of electoral success deprives the group of the necessary oxygen of publicity.

CONCLUSIONS

Local elections in Britain provide a rich source of data about minor parties and the part they play in our electoral system. While the 'first past the post' system has served largely to exclude such parties from parliamentary representation the threshold for success is much lower in local election contests. This has allowed a wide variety of individuals from outside the party mainstream to stand and sometimes be elected to local authorities. Since 1973, however, minor parties have been faced with a process of increased party politicisation, an expansion in competition and a more vigorous pattern of election campaigning. The dice are loaded against success for minor parties and Independents alike.

The nationalist parties have fared a little better largely because they have become organised along similar lines to the three main parties. The SNP in particular has learned to mount co-ordinated campaigns although arguably the party still fights too many seats where there is little prospect of victory. In Wales Plaid Cymru has met with less success but continues to do well in those areas where it is also strong in parliamentary elections. Both parties, though strongly identified with a single issue, have also succeeded in broadening their appeal. That has not been true for other minor parties and to some extent explains their failure to break through in local elections. The Greens, for example, while championing environmental issues in local campaigns have not made a wider appeal amongst the local electorate on matters associated with education, social services and the like. Similarly, parties of the Far Left and Far Right have been largely single issue parties where success, if at all, has been temporary. Such parties are highly dependent upon the organising skills of a handful of individuals and as such are highly unstable. Successes, few and far between, have rarely been sustained.

In parts of the country, however, old voting habits die hard and Independents and various types of Ratepayers' and Residents' Associations survive. But, unlike an endangered species in the animal kingdom, such groups have no one to champion their cause, no one to protect them from the domination of the main parties. Critics might argue that without the discipline brought by political parties the process of policy making in local government would be more uncertain and erratic. Yet surveys of public opinion repeatedly show that politicians, and by this is meant party politicians, are held in considerable contempt. One day, perhaps, the circumstances might be right for individuals to return to the local electoral fray without the shackles imposed by membership of one or other of the main parties. At present, however, the major parties set the agenda of local politics throughout the country and, even when they are opposed by other groups, attract the votes of the vast majority of those who choose to participate.

10 Local elections and national politics

INTRODUCTION

The increasing importance attached by the media to local elections in Britain should not be interpreted as a revival of interest in local government *per se*. As a general rule it treats local elections as little more than a dress rehearsal for what it regards as 'the real thing', the general election, and its analyses focus on what the results might portend for that event. This attitude is so pronounced that when local results run counter to the perceived national trend they are regarded as an aberration. In the BBC Local Elections results programme in 1989, for example, the presenter, David Dimbleby, used the word 'shambles' to summarise his disappointment that the national picture was being blurred by a host of seemingly contradictory local outcomes. Similarly, when national newspapers cover local elections, either before or after the event, there is a bias towards unidimensional interpretations. These focus more on how many seat losses represent a bad result for the government, rather than on how such losses translate into changes of council control and on their impact on policies followed by local authorities. Naturally, this style of presentation upsets those who firmly believe that local elections should be about local issues and personalities. Councillors defeated following a national swing against their party are often quoted arguing, with some justification, that their seat was lost due to circumstances beyond their control and that the result says little about the electorate's judgement of their own stewardship of the local authority. Some academics have also raised objections to this style of media presentation. As Jones and Stewart remark, 'It is so readily accepted in the media that local elections are about national issues that the possibility that local issues influence, and are increasingly influencing, the results goes virtually unexamined' (Jones and Stewart 1983: 16). Dunleavy (1990: 463) believes that this treatment of sub-national elections in Britain is a product of 'system bias' – because governmental power is centralised, the dominant concerns of political punditry and psephology are with those parties which are likely to gain that power and with the support they need in order to achieve it.

Are such critics justified in their view? Certainly survey data report that a substantial proportion of the electorate now changes its party allegiances over quite short periods of time, suggesting that extrapolation from one set of elections to another is fraught with danger (Miller *et al.* 1990). Although such individual volatility is often disguised by an overt picture of aggregate stability, its significance as an indicator of dealignment cannot be underestimated. In theory, a dealigned voter will be one willing to tailor his or her vote in order to achieve the desired electoral outcome. One of the few systematic studies of national/local voting patterns followed the 1979 elections when general and local elections occurred simultaneously (Waller 1980). In a study of the two types of election in 100 constituencies, Waller concluded that whereas in urban constituencies few differences emerged 'in rural areas there can be no doubt that the correlation between . . . [the] results is much less close' (Waller 1980: 145). Such divergences in behaviour, according to Waller, seemed to be a function of the personal popularity of individual candidates, the existence of salient local issues, and a greater willingness to cast a vote for other than the Conservative and Labour parties in a local as opposed to a general election. A more limited study by Game (1981) of 4 highly politically competitive towns – Cambridge, Gillingham, Gloucester and Watford – similarly showed that thousands of electors split their parliamentary and local votes between different parties.

In this chapter our purpose is to explore the extent to which there are significant differences between local and national voting. In the first section we take a broad view and examine differences between local voting and the findings from national opinion polls. Our purpose is to identify and account for any systematic differences between how people say they will vote and how they actually do vote in local elections. The second section narrows the focus and looks specifically at the 1990 local elections to see what variations, if any, existed between local authorities in a set of elections widely acknowledged as primarily influenced by nation-wide hostility to the implementation of the 'poll tax'. Finally the focus is narrowed still further as we examine a number of cases where local factors do appear to have had a significant impact on results. Some of our examples of local voting display characteristics which suggest deep-rooted attitudes amongst voters prepared consistently to make different choices in local as opposed to national elections. Other examples show that local events at certain times do appear capable of triggering a form of voting contrary to the perceived national pattern, but that such divergences are contingent and temporary.

NATIONAL AND LOCAL VOTING: THE AGGREGATE PICTURE

It used to be believed that it was reasonable to characterise local elections as little more than referenda on the current standing of the national parties (Newton 1976; Schofield 1977). Yet, there is growing evidence that a significant minority of voters do not behave the same way in a local as in a general election, and that there can be wide variations in party support even in socially similar or geographically adjacent areas. Any proposition which now sought to describe local elections purely as a form of national referendum would need to explain away some clearly contrary findings. Labour, for example, appears to record higher levels of support in the opinion polls than it is able to translate into the ballot box at local elections. The Liberal Democrats, by contrast, have managed to restore their share of the local vote in the wake of the break up of the Alliance to a level far in excess of their opinion poll rating at the time of local elections. The Greens may once have excited the pollsters, even attracted healthy support in European elections, but they have thus far only intermittently made an impression with some local voters.

In recent years, national opinion polls have asked respondents in mid and late April not only how they would vote 'if there were a general election tomorrow', but also how they intended to vote in the forthcoming local elections. The answers to these two questions never seem to be quite the same and, albeit on the basis of data almost wholly gathered during a period of Conservative government, the Labour party tends to perform better in terms of local as opposed to national support. In 1988, for example, Gallup found an 11 per cent Labour lead in local voting intention as against a mere 1 per cent 'general election' margin (Gallup 1988). In 1989, the same organisation asked respondents whether they were more likely to vote Conservative at a local or at a general election. Of those who said it made a difference, 13 per cent were more likely to support the Tories at a general election and only 5 per cent more likely to do so at a local contest (Gallup 1989). In 1991 MORI discovered that a 2 per cent Conservative lead in terms of national voting intention was translated into a 2 per cent Labour advantage at local level. Moreover, both parties seemed likely to lose local votes to the Liberal Democrats whose support jumped from 15 per cent at a putative general election to 21 per cent for the locals (*Sunday Times*, 28 April 1991). Again, in 1995, MORI reported a 30 per cent gap between Labour and the Conservatives in national voting intention widening to one of 33 per cent when respondents were asked how they intended to vote at the following week's local contests (*The Times*, 28 April 1995).

These differences may not in themselves be dramatic, but they do exist and could reflect greater volatility in choice at the individual as opposed to the aggregate level. Miller has conducted two discrete pieces of survey research which help to throw light on what may be happening. In May 1986 he found that '80 per cent of respondents had local choices for Conservative, Labour or Alliance that were exactly in accord with their party identification – and 83 per cent in accord with their current parliamentary preference' (Miller 1988). Looked at from the perspective of wanting to interpret local results for national purposes this finding appears impressive and reassuring. From another perspective, however, it says something quite different. Approximately one in five voters are admitting that they make different choices for national as opposed to local elections. Moreover, whilst there was little direct exchange between Conservative and Labour preferences at the two levels, according to Miller, 'the

Alliance gains more than it loses in local elections from the willingness of people to desert their national political choice' (Miller 1988: 166).

In a later study, this time during the 1987 general election campaign, Miller and his colleagues (Miller *et al.* 1990) were able to compare directly how their respondents had voted in the May local elections with their parliamentary vote five weeks later. The degree of correspondence between the parties varies, but once again the analysis depicts a sizeable level of voter fluidity. Some 87 per cent of 'local' Conservatives stayed with the party at the general election as did 80 per cent of Labour supporters and 63 per cent of those of the Alliance. It appears that there were, 'substantial shifts from voting Labour in the local elections to voting Alliance in the parliamentary election; and from voting Alliance in the local elections to voting both Labour and Conservative in the parliamentary' (Miller *et al.* 1990: 28). A survey conducted by National Opinion Polls (NOP) in March 1994 showed similar differences of support for the parties according to whether the question concerned national or local voting preferences. Of respondents who had signalled their intention of voting Conservative in the forthcoming local elections only two-thirds had made a similar commitment to vote for the party at a subsequent general election. Amongst those with local voting sympathies towards the Liberal Democrats, one in eight intended to vote Labour at the next general election, while more than one in five voiced their intention to switch to the Conservative party. Such findings do not, of course, accord with an image of local voting being synonymous with national voting.

This finding has been confirmed by a recent analysis of British Election Study Panel data which compared the reported behaviour of voters at the 1992 general and 1994 local elections. Nearly half the sample – including a majority of Conservative and Liberal Democrat supporters – said they had voted in 1994 with local rather than national considerations uppermost in their minds. The Liberal Democrats particularly appeared to benefit from being seen as a 'localist' party and reaped an especial advantage in the few cases where they were perceived to be in control of the council (McLean *et al.* 1995).

Nor is the evidence of movement in party support confined to opinion poll answers or the traced behaviour of individual electors. We compare in Table 10.1 the average score received by the parties in all opinion polls conducted and published in the month prior to the May local elections with the actual national equivalent result of the election. Although the polls and local election results are in broad agreement for the Conservative party in recent years that has not been the case for either Labour or the Liberal Democrats. Since 1990 Labour's support in the polls has overstated its achieved vote in local elections by an average of more than 6 per cent. The experience of the post-merger Liberal Democrats has been the reverse. Since 1988 they have been able to consolidate their support in local elections to a point that has never been less than 3 per cent higher than the average of their most recent opinion poll scores. Some commentators suggest that this discrepancy poses a problem for the parties, particularly for Labour and its ability to persuade all putative supporters to the polls. Others see evidence of a methodological problem for the opinion pollsters. In 1995, for example, MORI's question about local voting intention found 55 per cent of respondents who claimed to be intending to vote Labour and just 18 per cent Liberal Democrat. Our argument here is a different one. The discrepancy between the two measures is supportive of the proposition that voters appear increasingly sensitive to electoral context. A weakening of party identification, a more volatile electorate, a greater propensity towards 'gesture' voting all help muddy the waters. Moreover, the electorate appear at ease with identifying with one party at one type of election only to switch to its rival for a different sort of election. Those who wish to extrapolate local voting trends from national opinion poll data must realise that voters make important distinctions between the two. By the same token, making statements about national trends from local election results is something now to be approached with extreme caution.

The dangers of extrapolation are highlighted by the considerable variation between councils in the same tier of local government in each party's best and worst performances. In Table 10.2 we present the results for three pairs of elections, together with similar statistics for the rather lower level of aggregation of the parliamentary constituency at the 1987 general election. The a priori expectation that the standard deviation would increase with the number of units of analysis is not met. In fact only the English counties (N = 39) show levels of standard deviation in changes in party shares of the vote less than that for the constituencies (N = 633). Such differences would seem to be too large to be explained solely by reference to changing socio-economic trends in different

Table 10.1 Comparision of party shares as calculated by April opinion polls with 'national equivalent result' of the May local elections, 1985–1995

	Conservative			Labour			Liberal		
	Polls %	Local elections %	Poll Lead	Polls %	Local elections %	Poll Lead	Polls %	Local elections %	Poll Lead
1985	35	32	+3	38	37	+1	26	27	−1
1986	32	34	−2	38	38	0	28	26	+2
1987	41	39	+2	30	31	−1	26	28	−2
1988	43	40	+3	41	42	−1	14	18	−4
1989	41	37.5	3.5	40	41.5	−1.5	15	18	−3
1990	31	32	−1	53	43	+10	9	16	−7
1991	41	37	+4	41	39	+2	14	21	−7
1992	43	47	−4	38	32	+6	16	19	−3
1993	32	31	+1	46	41	+5	20	24	−4
1994	26	28	−2	47	40	+7	23	27	−4
1995	26	25	+1	56	47	+9	15	23	−8

Note: The concept and calculation of the 'national equivalent' vote is explained in Chapter 8, p. 126.

geographical areas, but identification of these differences leads naturally to the next section.

LOCAL 'GENERAL' ELECTIONS

One possible explanation for the variation in party performance among local authorities is that the electorate make a judgement about the record of their own council when deciding how to vote. The extent of accountability, an essential requirement of democratic local government, has been at the forefront of recent investigations, particularly relating to the matter of local finance. Although the consensus view among political scientists seems to be that increases in rates (the property tax which existed until 1990) are 'only rarely an important factor in determining local election results', Gibson presents some data and claims that rate increases were related to changes in party vote shares and that 'the effect of rate changes appeared to be large enough to explain why local councillors anticipate detrimental electoral effects from rate increases' (Gibson 1988: 205). However, whilst councils facing election may moderate their taxation demands

Table 10.2 Council level comparisons of change in party share of the vote between pairs of elections

	Mean	Maximum	Minimum	Standard deviation
Metropolitan boroughs 1986–90 (N = 36)				
Conservative	−0.0	9.4	−6.7	4.3
Labour	6.6	17.1	−1.0	4.6
Alliance/Liberal Democrat	−9.3	1.1	−18.3	4.2
London boroughs 1986–90 (N = 32)				
Conservative	2.0	11.2	−6.8	4.2
Labour	1.4	11.8	−6.8	4.8
Alliance/Liberal Democrat	−9.3	0.9	−26.4	5.2
English counties 1985–89 (N = 39)				
Conservative	3.9	8.4	−0.5	2.2
Labour	1.0	6.6	−7.3	2.5
Alliance/Liberal Democrat	−7.3	2.9	−18.0	3.7
English shire districts 1987–91 (N = 296)				
Conservative	−4.3	16.8	−29.5	5.5
Labour	5.3	19.3	−13.5	5.1
Alliance/Liberal Democrat	−4.0	14.9	−27.8	8.0
General election 1983–87 (N = 633)				
Conservative	−0.6	10.9	−17.1	3.6
Labour	+3.7	13.9	−9.6	3.9
Alliance	−3.2	17.5	−15.9	4.2

in the face of anticipated public hostility, it has been argued that 'it would be totally wrong to equate variations in local government election results with reactions to rates policy or even with reactions to local government policy outputs generally' (Miller 1988: 148).

A belief that this was the case was certainly one factor encouraging the Conservative government in the 1980s to introduce their per capita tax, the community charge or 'poll tax'. It was the government's aim to draw every adult's attention to exactly how much their local services were costing and to encourage them to assess whether they were receiving value for money from their local authority. However, an intensive examination of electoral and fiscal data for the first 'poll tax' election led us to conclude 'that the election results in individual local authorities in 1990 were at most only marginally affected by absolute or relative poll tax levels' (Rallings and Thrasher 1991a: 183). Rather, and ironically, the tax was so generally unpopular that local authorities managed to avoid being called to account because the elections were used as a stick with which to beat the government. This interpretation fits quite neatly with one of Miller's observations from his survey analysis of public opinion at the time of the 1986 local elections. He notes that the local elections made respondents, 'more aware of the restrictions placed upon local government; they became more favourable to local autonomy; and they became more favourable towards higher levels of taxes and services – a policy position that was generally supported by local authorities and opposed by central government' (Miller 1988: 202).

Such survey evidence clarifies why Labour and the Liberal Democrats have done relatively well in local government elections since the advent of Conservative government in 1979. What it does not explain is why inter-council variations persist. Some clues about this may, however, be gleaned from the London borough elections of 1990. On average Labour did much less well in London than in the rest of the country at those elections. Although in part this reflected problems of both policy and image that the party had suffered in the capital going back to before the 1987 general election, it was also the product of distinct patterns of behaviour in certain boroughs. Within the context of a swing from Labour to the Conservatives of 0.5 per cent in London as a whole since 1986, five boroughs swung to the Conservatives by more than 5 per cent and six swung to Labour by more than 3 per cent.

With the exception of Wandsworth and Westminster where incumbent Conservative councils, aided by very generous block grant settlements, were able to impose a very small poll tax, there is no evidence that it was the level of the tax itself which had an impact on the performance of the parties. Rather, Labour-controlled councils which had received adverse publicity about their conduct were noticeably more inclined to register large swings to the Conservatives. Conversely, where Labour councils appeared successfully to have changed public perceptions of their competence and efficiency and where Conservative councils had been unable to levy poll tax in keeping with that in Wandsworth and Westminster, then a swing to Labour more in line with the national trend was common (Rallings and Thrasher, 1991a). Gibson and Stewart (1992), in their own study of the 1990 London borough elections, argue that both Labour and Conservative incumbents were harmed by the issue of local taxation and similarly point to systematic variation in the results between authorities.

Localised patterns of support were also found in the case of the Liberal Democrats. The party easily retained the three London boroughs which it effectively controlled prior to the elections and, despite its overall share of the vote in the capital falling from 24 per cent to 14 per cent, won the same proportion of the total number of seats – one in eight – as it had in 1986. Borough-specific patterns of electoral behaviour are perhaps not surprising in an area like London. On the one hand, large wards and a relatively mobile population make voting on the basis of candidates' characteristics less feasible, whereas the intense national media coverage accorded to local government in what is for most outlets their own home territory means that levels of information about and hostility towards some individual councils may be higher than normal. In 1990 the 'goodies' and 'baddies' were clearly and repeatedly identified and the overall tenor of the analysis was never likely to advantage Labour.

London, however, is not the only place where such authority-wide effects have been noted. Since 1979 the idea that the 'context' in which the election is being held can affect voters' behaviour has received somewhat wider currency. In a detailed examination of the parliamentary and local elections in Liverpool, Cox and Laver (1979) show that voting for the Liberals in the city as a whole was twice as high at the local than at the general election, with two votes being taken from Labour for every one lost by the Conservatives. Subsequent voting in Liverpool has seen this pattern persisting, at least as far as the relationship between the Liberals (and their successors) and the Conservatives is concerned. As Figure 10.1 demonstrates, the Conservative vote has shown a long-term tendency to decline at local elections, only to pick up – albeit to a decreasing level – at general elections. Although party politics in Liverpool over recent years appears to have been a two-party battle between Labour and the Liberal Democrats the continuing ability of both 'major' parties to command a greater level of support when a national government is being chosen deprived the Alliance in 1987 of victory in two constituencies where the local results just five weeks previously had given them every cause for optimism. Similarly, at the 1992 general election, the Liberal Democrats polled just 21 per cent across the city yet saw their share of the vote almost double to 41 per cent at the local contests a month later.

But local and national voting in Liverpool has become more than just a simple oscillation in support amongst the three main parties. In recent years, particularly following the expulsion of Militant in the late 1980s, local elections have been contested by a range of candidates representing different factions amongst the city's left-wing activists. In the 1991 local elections, for example,

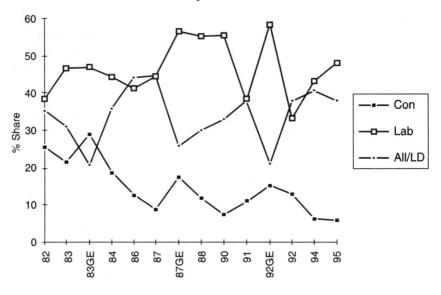

Figure 10.1 Local and national voting in Liverpool 1982–1995

candidates from the Far Left won the support of one in nine voters across the city. At the following year's general election, however, with the exception of the Liverpool Broadgreen constituency, which the expelled Labour MP Terry Fields contested, no Far Left candidates stood. In the local elections which followed a month later there were no fewer than 22 Far Left candidates contesting 34 seats and winning 13 per cent of the vote. As Figure 10.1 shows, the Labour local vote dropped dramatically at the 1992 local elections although in the two following sets of contests it has risen back towards the long-term mean.

The complexity of local/national voting in Liverpool has not been restricted to the Left. When the Liberals and SDP announced their electoral Alliance in 1981 there were some members in each party who were unhappy with the arrangement. In Liverpool this antagonism became clear when the two parties could not agree on a common candidate in the Broadgreen constituency at the 1983 general election and fought one another. These tensions were ultimately resolved at the parliamentary level but they remained visible in local elections. Contests between Liberal and SDP candidates were a familiar feature in Liverpool elections throughout the 1980s. Following the breakup of the Alliance after the 1987 general election and the subsequent merger between the SDP and Liberal parties, the situation became even more complicated. Liberal Democrat candidates now found themselves fighting on two fronts. In the 1992 local elections Liberal Democrats fought SDP candidates in seven wards while in another five they were challenged by the Liberals.

Liverpool, then, clearly has its own brand of local politics, unlike that in any other city in Britain. The nature of party competition is both more complex and more unstable than elsewhere. Whether this was the cause or effect of tendencies within the electorate to vote differently in local and national elections is a difficult question to answer. However, there can be no denying that to draw conclusions about national voting from the results of local elections in Liverpool is more than usually hazardous.

Consistent differences between national and local voting patterns are evident, albeit in less stark form than in Liverpool, in other local authorities. A clutch of councils in the south of England, many of them situated in former new towns, record more support for Labour at local than at general elections. The best evidence for this comes from 1992, when the Conservatives' general election victory was followed four weeks later by their attracting an even larger share of the vote at the district council contests. Making allowances for the difference between constituency and local authority boundaries, it appears that Labour did better and the Conservatives worse in Crawley, Harlow, Slough and Thamesdown (Swindon) than at the general election. We can only hypothesise that many electors in these authorities desire different policy outcomes from the two types of election and adjust their vote accordingly.

LOCAL VOTING AND LOCAL ISSUES

In 1982 Labour lost control of the Lothian region in Scotland while making advances elsewhere. Labour's vote share fell by 10 per cent across the region compared with the elections four years earlier, in direct contrast to Strathclyde where it rose by 3 per cent. Lothian had, in fact, been at the forefront of a campaign protesting against government spending reductions and in 1980 the council had raised local rates by 41 per cent (Lansley *et al.* 1989: 32–3). To judge from the fall in Labour's vote in the 1982 regional elections some voters were not impressed by the campaign and withdrew support from the party. Similar variations in party performance between authorities in England in the same year led Jones and Stewart (1983: 16) to observe that 'the actions of a local authority can affect the election even when a Falklands factor is at work'. In the London borough of Islington, for example, the Conservative vote fell by 13 per cent but in Merton it declined by just 2 per cent. In Islington the Labour share increased by less than 1 per cent while in Merton it fell by more than 9 per cent. Given that the pattern of party competition in the two boroughs was virtually identical the clue to these divergent fortunes must be sought in the performance of the new SDP/Liberal Alliance. In Islington their share was 20 per cent higher than the Liberal party had won in 1978; almost wholly at the expense of the Conservatives. In Merton the Alliance polled 13 per cent more than the Liberals and drew the bulk of this from Labour. In each authority it was the party running the council – Labour in Islington and the Conservatives in Merton – who fared best. Such an example shows that although there are national trends running for or against a particular party, at the local authority level other influences can be at work.

Sometimes the explanation for such differences in electoral behaviour is readily apparent from local events and policies. In the 1989 county council elections, for example, the change in the combined votes of the Liberal Democrats and the SDP compared with those of the Alliance four years previously varied across all the counties in England, from an increase of 2.9 per cent in Cornwall to a decrease of 18 per cent in neighbouring Devon. The increase in Cornwall was an artefact of the new party contesting more seats and thus enabling more of its supporters actually to vote for it; the decrease in Devon demands a more complex explanation. First, it could be argued that in the previous elections Alliance candidates had benefited from a disproportionately large swing against the Conservatives brought about by a number of policy issues, notably threats to the future of the Royal Naval Dockyard in Plymouth. An adjustment in the form of a larger than expected fall in the 'centre' vote was, therefore, unsurprising. Beyond that, however, it seems likely that there was a direct and disillusioned public response to the perceived inadequacies of the two parties in running the county council following the acrimonious events surrounding the merger of the greater part of each in March 1988 (Temple 1993).

There are plenty of other examples of parties falling into or out of electoral favour as a consequence of specifically local concerns. In recent years, for instance, it has been noticeable that the national swing to Labour at successive local elections has been absent or even reversed in Sheffield. The Labour-controlled council had proved controversial with its proposals to cut the local authority workforce as a way of reducing the council's budgetary deficit. In a city renowned for its support for public sector services, local trade unions and other groups actively campaigned against such a solution. The council's reputation for economic efficiency was further dented by the massive over-spend on the World Student Games. These tensions surfaced at the 1994 local elections with Labour's vote share declining by 20 per cent compared with 1990 despite a national decrease of less than 3 per cent over the same electoral cycle. The controversy continued to dog Labour in Sheffield at the 1995 elections. Although the local party polled 6 per cent better than in 1994, it was still underperfoming by at least 10 per cent in terms of its long-term relationship to Labour's national vote (see Table 10.3). As with some London boroughs, Sheffield's recent elections show that once an electorate's traditional party loyalty has been damaged the recovery can be painfully slow and weakly affected by national trends.

No party appears immune to such variations in support, though the fluctuations do not always have a negative influence. In nearby Bradford, for example, the Conservative party, under its leader Eric Pickles, successfully increased support at a higher rate than the party nationally in the late 1980s. Conservative control of national government inevitably led to the mid-term attrition of its local government base but Bradford, for a time at least, proved an exception. Following two by-election gains in 1988 the Conservatives took control of the council and introduced policies which led to it being dubbed the 'Westminster of the North'. At the poll tax elections of 1990 Bradford's

Table 10.3 Labour's local election performance in Sheffield, 1988–1995

	% Share in Sheffield	National equivalent % share	% Difference
1987	51.1	31.0	+20.1
1988	59.0	40.0	+19.0
1990	62.2	43.0	+19.2
1991	49.9	39.0	+10.9
1992	38.3	32.0	+6.3
1994	41.2	40.0	+1.2
1995	47.4	47.0	+0.4

Conservatives believed that while the national trend was against them they would benefit locally from actions taken to curb the budget. Although the party lost its wafer-thin majority its vote share actually rose in Bradford at the same time as declining nationally compared with four years previously. Pickles himself went on to fight and win a parliamentary seat at the 1992 general election and Bradford's time under the spotlight was virtually over. The local Conservatives' fall from grace was precipitous. In 1992 they won nineteen of the authority's thirty wards; in 1995 just four.

One final example has been chosen to reinforce our argument about the importance of local issues because it involves a party, the Liberal Democrats, which normally thrives under conditions where protest voting is strong. In 1994 the party nationally gained almost 400 council seats and secured a national equivalent share of the vote (27 per cent) on a par with anything achieved during the halcyon days of the Alliance. In London the party easily retained two of the boroughs it controlled, Richmond upon Thames and Sutton, and added Kingston upon Thames to its tally. In east London, however, a quite different story was unfolding in Tower Hamlets. First the Alliance and then the Liberal Democrats had benefited from Labour's unpopularity in the borough during the 1980s. At the 1990 elections the Liberal Democrats matched Labour in the popular vote and, thanks to a favourable distribution of that vote, established a comfortable ten-seat majority on the council. Accusations then surfaced that the ruling local party had pursued a racist agenda in its housing policies and the national party ordered an inquiry. Controversy grew still further when the BNP won the Millwall by-election in September 1993 and when, shortly before the 1994 elections, a number of local councillors were expelled from the party by the Liberal Democrats' national executive. A divided and battered local party was punished by the electorate and saw its representation dramatically reduced. The Liberal Democrat vote fell by 13 per cent in 1994 compared with 1990, not helped by rival candidates from disaffected elements in the party competing against each other in some wards, and it managed to win just seven seats.

These examples serve to show that at different times and for different reasons some local authorities defy the national political trend. Some local electorates resolutely refuse to follow the pattern set elsewhere because for them the saliency of a local issue overshadows all other considerations. In some ways the task of identifying such opportunities for local voting are aided by the media. As coverage of the issue graduates from the local to the national level so many more people begin to follow the story. To some extent the local electorate may well feel themselves to be in the media spotlight and begin to take their local voting responsibilities more seriously. In many cases electoral participation increases as controversy rises. That situation in itself raises a problem, however. What if the media coverage was the cause of the subsequent variation in voting patterns? In short, we may be confusing cause with effect. Is there a way in which we can investigate the existence or not of variations in local voting which may or may not have been affected by previous national media exposure? One method might be to analyse voting on an even smaller scale, the ward level. If we are able to discern differences across wards in the same local authority then we might truly claim that local voting does exist and does matter.

VARIATIONS BY WARD – A TRULY 'LOCAL' ELECTION

The marginalisation of Independents, and the increasing intensity of party competition at ward level should not necessarily imply that each ward acts as a mirror of the national party battle. A substantial proportion of the electorate (39 per cent) at least claims to vote for the candidate, and among this group there is, unsurprisingly, a greater inclination to make a different party choice at the local than at the national level (Miller 1988: 170). Candidates who are not formally Independents and who hope to capitalise on such a vote, must ensure that they are not weighed down by the baggage of their party label. Either they need to work in harmony with their party and become its personal manifestation in a particular ward, or they must attempt to transcend their party label by a record of service and commitment to their constituents. At the parliamentary level in Britain the 'personal vote' for MPs usually refers to the latter case, but in local government there is some evidence that the campaigning activity of the party in a ward can itself establish the qualities of candidates in the voters' minds (Bruce and Lee 1982). It has also been argued that it is possible to identify ward level reaction to tax and service issues and that these too can have an impact on individual results (Gibson and Stewart 1992; Bristow 1982). Our earlier analysis in Chapter 5 provided little evidence that voters in wards discriminate between candidates on the basis of their gender, nor could we make a convincing case that incumbency always bestowed an electoral advantage on candidates seeking re-election. In some cases incumbents do better than their party as a whole; in others it is clear that the kind of 'personal vote' referred to above simply does not exist. Overall it appears that incumbents are almost as prone to be swept aside by an adverse swing against their party as any other of their colleagues, their own longevity in office and record of service notwithstanding.

Apart from the question of incumbency, one of the few systematic studies of ward level political behaviour has concluded that social class, in terms both of the relationship between an individual's class position and his/her vote and of the overall socio-economic composition of the ward, 'remains the most important predictor of election results' (Warde *et al.* 1988: 339). However, the same research also acknowledges that distinctly local processes – at both ward and town level – are present, and Johnston (1986: 52) has argued that parties, 'will seek to become part of the local culture, participating in the socialisation of individuals . . . and creating a base that can be mobilised and drawn upon at election time'. In local elections in England such a strategy would seem most appropriate and necessary for those parties which are unable to rely on the certainty of a core of class-derived support. Our contention is that the Liberal party and its various successors and allies, to the statistical explanation of whose share of the vote 'class variables contribute nothing' (Warde *et al.* 1988: 345), have successfully followed just such a path (Dorling *et al.* forthcoming).

Building support from the grassroots has been the main goal of the long-established organisation now known as the Association of Liberal Democrat Councillors. This body is located away from London and has a separate administrative, financial and campaigning structure from that of the national party: neither of the other major parties sustain anything similar. The ALDC has become a sort of clearing house for the techniques and propaganda of 'community politics', and it has made a major contribution to the disproportionate success of the party in local elections noted above. The regular local newsletter, used to identify both issues and personalities to electors, has become something of a totem of this style of campaign and it is a device increasingly adopted by other parties too. That at least must be an expression of a belief that localism does matter. However, can we produce any statistical evidence of the impact of such activity? It has been claimed that the 'third' party in England has been frustrated in its efforts to 'break the mould' by the existence of a ceiling or plateau in its potential electoral support (Curtice *et al.* 1983). Our data suggest, however, that the Liberal Democrats have been relatively successful both in retaining in lean years those council seats they won at boom elections for the party and, contrary to the 'plateau theory', in achieving an above average increase or below average decrease in their share of the vote in seats they retain. Table 10.4 shows the mean change in share of the vote for each party in seats they did and did not hold at a range of elections and it demonstrates a consistent pattern whereby all parties seem to perform better where they were the incumbent.

Two other aspects of the Liberal Democrat performance are worth noting. First, we have clearly shown elsewhere that a strong Liberal Democrat (Alliance) vote is correlated with greater turnout (Rallings and Thrasher 1990). Liberal Democrats would appear, thus, directly to benefit from campaigning strategies which encourage more people to go the polls *and vote for them*. Second, much of

Table 10.4 Mean percentage change in share of the vote controlling for party incumbency

	Conservative	Labour	Liberal Democrat
English shire counties 1985–89			
Seat held	4.2	4.3	−5.4
Other seats contested	3.0	0.8	−8.4
Metropolitan boroughs 1990–94			
Seat held	−2.7	−1.7	9.1
Other seats contested	−3.6	−3.2	4.3
English shire districts 1991–95			
Seat held	−3.5	13.9	3.1
Other seats contested	−8.3	2.5	−0.7

their success at the local just as at the parliamentary level has been in by-elections (see Chapter 11). These contests, which take place every week throughout the country, were once regarded as rather insignificant political events. However, because of Liberal Democrat attempts to capitalise on their achievements by claiming a connection between their local by-election record and their national electoral standing, the other parties too are now keen to maximise their own contestation and performance. Between the 1983 and 1992 general elections the Liberal Democrats, in their various incarnations, made 340 net gains from all other parties in local by-elections, compared with 75 net gains for Labour and more than 270 net losses for the Conservatives. Although their average share of the vote in by-election contests over this period (26.7 per cent) leaves them in third place, it is significantly above their average opinion poll rating of 16.3 per cent. Whether Liberal Democrat by-election success is attributed to their ability to catch the protest vote from both sides, or to their investing more effort into the election, the fact remains that the record of the party is a good example of how electors in individual wards can be persuaded to cast their ballots in a way that is specific to both time and circumstance. The results thus confirm Miller's survey findings on the greater likelihood of voting for the (then) Alliance at the local level.

Patterns of contestation are also important in determining ward results. Within a general pattern of increased party competition in local government, both Labour and the Conservatives do concentrate their resources to a limited extent. Labour either cannot find the candidates or does not bother to field them in many rural authorities, whereas Conservatives are thin on the ground in parts of industrial England. The Liberal Democrats are more likely to concentrate their electoral efforts in carefully targeted seats. In the 1995 local elections they contested fewer wards (about 5,700, compared with 7,400 contested by Labour and 6,400 by the Conservatives) than either of the other major parties; in local by-elections since the creation of the new party in 1988 they have had candidates in about 10 per cent fewer contests than either Labour or the Conservatives. The fact that they do not compete in so many seats immediately gives rise to one sort of dispute about how their performance is to be measured. Is it more relevant to look at their share of the total vote, or should their share of the vote in seats contested be the relevant benchmark? Understandably, partisanship plays its part in this argument, but the difference between the two indicators can be quite large as Table 10.5 shows. The Liberal Democrats' rational, or as some would have it cynical, approach means not only do they not stand where the position is hopeless, but also often give a free run to an incumbent Independent or even 'other party' candidate whom they know has a strong personal vote. The availability of choice is perhaps the prime determinant of the 'context' of any election. Where the choice is restricted, so a party's performance can become distorted.

Finally, it should be noted that voting in a ward is the local equivalent of voting in a constituency. Candidates, campaign activity, local issues and the choice provided the elector are all important, and examples of each of them having a decisive impact on the result are too numerous and perhaps by definition too idiosyncratic to subject to systematic analysis. The concept of tactical voting is also relevant at the ward level in local elections. One explanation for Labour's seeming ability to do better in local than in general elections in the South of England precisely revolves round this point (Burnham 1990). Electors who are Labour supporters living in wards where the party has a history of either winning or challenging strongly in local elections will express their loyalty in the ballot box. If, however, that ward is in a constituency where Labour is a poor third in general elections, then they may desert their 'natural' party in that form of contest for the one most able to defeat their least preferred alternative. Ironically, therefore, Labour supporters may vote 'nationally' at local level, but tactically in general elections. Here the electoral system may be said to provide the context for the vote and it has worked to the Conservatives' very considerable disadvantage in the two most recent local elections. In 1995 Labour's vote rose by 13 per cent and the Liberal Democrats' by just 2 per cent compared with 1991 in those Conservative-held wards in which Labour began the contest in second place. Where the Liberal Democrats were second, the Labour vote rose by 9 per cent and the Liberal Democrat share by 7 per cent (*Sunday Times*, 7 May 1995). In 1996, Labour's vote rose by 17 points in

Table 10.5 Liberal Democrat vote share overall and in seats contested

	1990 London boroughs	1993 English counties	1994 Metropolitan boroughs	1995 English districts
Overall	14.1	29.3	22.8	25.0
Seats contested	19.6	33.8	25.9	31.6

Conservative seats where it was the main challenger and by only 9 per cent where the party started in third place. The Liberal Democrats, by contrast, saw their vote share increase by 8 per cent where they were second and by 5 per cent where they were third (*Guardian*, 4 May 1996).

CONCLUSION

Local elections provide opportunities for movements away from any national pattern or trend. Behaviour and outcomes vary among and even within local authorities. Local issues and concerns can influence the vote over either the entire area of a council or in individual wards. Similarly, party campaigns and the personality of the candidates can have a clear impact on the result. Everything that has been written about the 'denationalisation' of British politics in recent general elections applies, except even more so, to the local electoral arena (Cain *et al.* 1987; Curtice and Steed 1988). The identification of such potential sources of variation is important. For whilst, on the one hand, they do seem neither so crucial nor so universal to mean that local elections in Britain cannot be dissected for their underlying message, equally, the possibility that aggregate national trends are at least in part the product of the smoothing out of contradictory local forces must not be neglected.

Local voters do apparently respond to local issues. However, the influence of those issues varies from place to place and from time to time and certainly none of the factors we have considered is an adequate or sufficient explanation of such variation on its own. More than two decades ago Green (1972) tried statistically to account for the proportion of variance in local electoral behaviour explained at each of the different levels of analysis we have examined. Basing his study on local elections over a fifteen-year period between 1951 and 1966 in Leeds and Sheffield, he attributed 73 per cent of the swing in party support to factors common to both cities (the 'national' explanation); 6 per cent to city-wide, but also city-specific factors; and the remaining 21 per cent to ward level influences. However, when we replicated his analysis for the same two cities for the period 1983–1991 (Rallings and Thrasher 1993a), we found that the 'national' explanation could only account for 42 per cent of the variance in annual ward by ward swings. The prima facie implication was that the ability of national level influences to explain local electoral outcomes had declined markedly since Green undertook his analysis. We put this to the test by conducting a similar comparative examination of ward level swings in two other metropolitan borough councils of widely differing social and political complexions, Manchester and Solihull. In those cases the 'national' explanation once more came to the fore, accounting for a full three-quarters of the changes in the pattern of party support. In other words, results in Manchester and Solihull had more in common with each other during this period than did those in Leeds and Sheffield. Such findings are entirely consistent with the point we have been making throughout this chapter. Some authorities appear to have results in keeping with the national trend; in others there are distinct patterns of behaviour across council territory; in yet others ward level effects, whether of a spatial, political or personal kind are important. Moreover, it is a plausible hypothesis that the relative influence of each of these factors will vary across authorities between cycles of elections.

The evidence from local elections demonstrates that local voting can become a matter of 'horses for courses'. Such factors as the nature of party competition, the conduct of canvassing and campaigning, and the characteristics of the candidates themselves, either real or as portrayed by the local media, would all appear to have a bearing upon voters' perceptions of electoral context. For the political parties the possibility that a proportion of the electorate have already identified particular parties as suitable or unsuitable for a particular electoral context is of enormous consequence. The Liberal Democrats' emphasis on 'pavement politics' could appear appropriate for local government, but their policies and their presence might be deemed irrelevant when voting takes place within a European context. Similarly Labour, regarded as the party more sympathetic to public services and social welfare, does relatively better than the Conservatives in the context of elections to local authorities entrusted with the administration of education, social services and housing. Although we have shown that local voting does exist that is not the same as denying the influence of national factors. Precisely how those local results may be used to say something about national electoral trends will be one of the subjects of the following chapter.

11   Local by-elections – parochial contests or national electoral indicators?

INTRODUCTION

Our purpose in this chapter is two-fold. One objective follows on from the theme of the last chapter and it is to examine whether and how local voting can be used to make observations about the national electoral mood. As we saw, there are many instances where local voting is dominated by local issues and local responses to national influences. That still leaves a great deal of behaviour which is national in orientation, with local voters using local elections as a vehicle to express their views about the wider political situation (Curtice and Payne 1991). The largest number of local elections occur, of course, in the first week in May but though these are plentiful they are only partly suited to our purpose. Although these election results can be used to note annual rises and falls in the performance of the parties, they offer few clues for election forecasting unless, as in 1983, 1987 and, perhaps 1991, a general election is thought to be imminent. Moreover, because they only take place once a year, they cannot help in the frequent mapping of trends in behaviour in a manner similar to that undertaken by opinion polls. What we require for this task is local votes which are cast throughout the year. That, in effect, means using the results from local government by-elections.

That brings us to our second purpose. Before we can test the usefulness of local by-elections as surrogate indicators of wider political change more needs to be discovered about them. First, some of the circumstances giving rise to local by-elections need to be assessed. In most instances they are caused by much the same events as are parliamentary by-elections, primarily death and resignation. In some cases, however, local by-elections can occur for reasons which have no parliamentary equivalent and the circumstances of the contest can sometimes have a direct bearing on the outcome. A second consideration is when and how frequently by-elections occur. This is critical because if they are to be used as the basis of a model of electoral behaviour they need to be distributed fairly randomly throughout the year. If they were concentrated in time then they would suffer the same sorts of weakness as do the May elections. A third issue has to do with the spatial distribution of local by-elections. By-elections concentrated in one part of the country, or in one type of local authority, would tell us a great deal about behaviour in that specific area but would be less useful for drawing conclusions about the national picture. On each of these three points, therefore, we need to satisfy ourselves that local by-elections are both frequent and fairly random political events. If those conditions are met, then what remains is to develop a method whereby the results can be translated into surrogate indicators of the national electoral climate. This discussion will be in two parts. First, we address the value of by-election data as a means for monitoring the state of party competition. This entails collecting data about gains and losses and using that information to make more general comments about the strength of the various national parties. The second approach is more ambitious and seeks to develop a model of electoral behaviour which uses by-election data to forecast electoral events, such as the main May elections and, more ambitiously, a general election outcome. Depending upon the success of that model we can then begin to draw conclusions about the possible relationship between local and national voting.

WHY DO LOCAL BY-ELECTIONS OCCUR?

There are a number of reasons why casual vacancies occur on local councils. The Widdicombe inquiry found that the majority of councillors were aged 45 or over with the oldest aged 85 (Widdicombe 1986b: 20). It is unsurprising, therefore, that one of the main causes of by-elections is the death of a councillor. However, although neither MPs nor councillors can cheat the grim reaper, by-elections caused by resignations are much more frequent at local level. Unpaid councillors are often forced by sheer pressure of work or personal circumstances or by having to move following a change of job, to resign. Salaried MPs are not only protected from many such pressures, but also find that their party whips are unwilling to sanction by-elections being caused by such 'voluntary' action. Indeed while both MPs and councillors are legally obliged to resign if declared bankrupt, the consequences of such a resignation are likely to be so much more acute at Westminster that parties do everything in their power to avoid individuals being placed in that position. Bankrupt local councillors are usually less fortunate. Councillors – like MPs – can be forced from office because of scandal, political and otherwise, and they run the further, unique risk of being obliged to stand down simply as a consequence of failing to turn up at council meetings for a period of six months. The financial constraints on local councillors, exercised via the legal concept of *ultra vires*, are also far more severe than those on MPs and breaches of these regulations have resulted in by-elections. The most celebrated of such by-elections in recent times were those in Liverpool when left-wing councillors protesting against central government spending targets were removed from office, and disqualified from standing, after failing to set a legal rate on time. As with the fifteen parliamentary by-elections forced by the resignation of Northern Ireland Unionist MPs in 1986 to protest at the Hillsborough accord, there have been instances of local by-elections similarly provoked to make a political point. In September 1984 Ken Livingstone and three other Labour councillors resigned their seats on the Greater London Council. Their purpose was to galvanise opposition to the plans to abolish the GLC along with the other six metropolitan county councils. Although they were all safely re-elected, their strategy was partially undermined when no Conservative stood against them in the by-elections. In the event, of course, the government ignored the protest and the councils were eventually abolished in 1986.

WHEN DO THEY OCCUR?

On average there are about thirty local by-elections every month throughout Great Britain. We have been compiling local by-election data since 1983, recording the results of over 4,500 by-elections to date. In terms of frequency, therefore, there appear to be enough of them to draw sensible conclusions about the prevailing state of party competition and electoral preferences. Although the timing of some by-elections cannot be avoided, for example when the councillor dies in office, many can be called at times which are convenient, either administratively or politically. For this reason by-elections are rare during August and January. The busiest month is May when contests are often timed to coincide with the annual round of local elections even if the authority itself has a fallow year. Local authorities are permitted the option of delaying the by-election if a member leaves office after September and there are elections planned for the following May. While this can save on administrative costs there are occasions when this option is ignored by the local parties who wish to fill the vacancy. The early autumn has also proved popular for by-elections. As Table 11.1 shows the months of September and October together account for almost a quarter of all by-elections. One explanation for this lies with the timing of summer holidays – for administrators and party activists alike – while there may also be a sense in which this period represents the beginning of the political season, marked by the different party conferences held at this time. It is not unknown for local parties in Brighton and Blackpool to call by-elections for their councils to coincide with a party conference so as to receive maximum publicity rewards for winning or retaining a seat.

Over time there does appear to be a pattern in the occurrence of local by-elections which is related to the wider local electoral cycle. Table 11.1 also reveals that years with the highest volume of by-elections are coincident with shire county election years, viz., 1985, 1989 and 1993. The explanation for this is that in these years shire district, metropolitan and London borough councils, which have no May elections, find it difficult to avoid holding by-elections when casual vacancies occur. Confirmation of this view comes with its opposite effect. By-elections are rarest in those years which contain 'all-out' elections for the shire district councils, viz., 1987, 1991 and 1995. For the remaining years the incidence of by-elections has been relatively uniform.

Table 11.1 The cycle of local by-elections

Year	Total in year	Month	% Yearly total in month
1984	375	Jan	3.5
1985	451	Feb	6.3
1986	363	Mar	9.7
1987	261	Apr	5.5
1988	391	May	15.0
1989	507	Jun	8.8
1990	360	Jul	8.2
1991	264	Aug	3.5
1992	355	Sep	12.0
1993	447	Oct	12.0
1994	311	Nov	9.2
1995	224	Dec	6.1

WHERE DO THEY OCCUR?

By-elections are most frequent in district authorities, with almost 60 per cent of our cases coming from this level of local government. The shire counties account for the next largest share of by-elections followed by the more urban authorities in London and the metropolitan districts. Instead of examining the overall number of by-elections from the different types of authority it is more interesting to focus upon the propensity of by-elections to occur in one type of authority rather than another. Without doubt the district authorities account for the largest number of councillors – their more than 14,000 members are four times as many as the next most populous category, the county councils. As Table 11.2 demonstrates, however, the proportion of by-elections to total number of seats in the counties and district is exactly the same. We arrived at these proportions by comparing the total number of by-elections for each sector of local government over a ten-year period with the total number of councillors for the same sector. This has to be something of an approximate exercise since the number of councillors at any one time is a function of the current ward boundaries in existence, with the periodic redrawing of boundaries leading to fluctuations in the number of councillors.

At first glance there appears to be a considerable disparity between the likelihood of a by-election in a London borough compared with the comparable authorities in the metropolitan authorities. In both cases these authorities cover relatively densely populated areas and have similar patterns of socio-economic composition, yet by-elections appear to have occurred in more than one in five seats in London but only in one in eight seats in the metropolitan boroughs. It would be a mistake, however, to conclude that councillor turnover was higher in London than in the metropolitan authorities. As we outlined in Chapter 3 these two types of local authority run to an entirely different electoral cycle. The

Table 11.2 Frequency of by-elections by type of local authority 1983–1993

	Number of by-elections	% of all by-elections	By-elections as % of all seats in type of authority
Shire counties (England and Wales)	548	14.0	15.6
Shire districts (England and Wales)	2,362	60.2	15.6
London boroughs	403	10.2	21.0
Metropolitan boroughs	316	8.1	12.7
Scottish regions	200	2.3	20.6
Scottish districts	92	5.2	17.3

metropolitan boroughs hold annual elections by thirds while the London councils hold whole council elections every four years. This has a critical impact upon the calling of by-elections. In the metropolitan areas councils attempt to reduce costs, and parties to reduce the pressure on their activists, by postponing elections for casual vacancies until the main diet of elections in May. The figures reveal that in 1992 there were 16 vacancies filled in this manner, 13 the year previously and no less than 33 in 1990. In London, however, a similar option does not exist and when members resign or die, mid-term by-elections are largely inevitable. We should conclude, therefore, that there are no significant differences in the frequency of by-elections between the various types of local authority which cannot be explained by the nature of the electoral cycle.

TURNOUT IN LOCAL BY-ELECTIONS

The pattern of turnout in local by-elections is broadly similar to that for local elections as a whole discussed in Chapter 4. Although average turnout levels are smaller, in part reflecting the very low key nature of many campaigns, the data in Table 11.3 do not support claims of a clear year-on-year reduction in participation in these elections. Having said that, such a position may have to be revised if the figure for 1995 turns out to be other than a one-off aberration. Examples of very high and very low turnouts have been infrequent over the years. In just 4 cases have there been local by-elections held on days which did not correspond with a general or parliamentary by-election in the area where turnout exceeded 70 per cent. The record, 73.2 per cent, is held by the Hemingford Abbots ward in Huntingdonshire at a by-election held on European Parliament election day in 1994 when turnout in the Cambridgeshire Euro-constituency of which it was a part was just 35.9 per cent. At the other extreme, six by-elections have attracted fewer than one in ten electors to the polls – the lowest recorded turnout being 8.9 per cent in the Cowper ward of Blyth Valley district in September 1995.

Table 11.3 Average turnout in local by-elections by year and by month 1984–1995

Year	Mean % turnout	N =	Month	Mean % turnout	N =
1984	34.9	310	Jan	32.7	144
1985	36.7	435	Feb	34.8	256
1986	38.9	357	Mar	38.3	397
1987	35.0	261	Apr	40.8	208
1988	34.9	385	May	41.9	603
1989	36.9	491	Jun	39.3	398
1990	38.6	354	Jul	35.8	343
1991	36.8	259	Aug	36.1	140
1992	36.3	346	Sep	33.9	483
1993	35.0	440	Oct	33.0	506
1994	35.2	305	Nov	32.6	421
1995	31.9	224	Dec	30.0	268

LOCAL BY-ELECTIONS AND THE STATE OF PARTY COMPETITION

Parliamentary by-elections have earned a reputation for being unique political events; of interest as a spectacle but, perhaps, too idiosyncratic to be worthy of serious study by academic political scientists. By-elections can have an enormous political impact, however. For some they serve as a quasi-referendum on the performance of the government (Butler 1973). For others by-election outcomes are directly related to time- or situation-specific factors, only some of which continue to exert influence in later elections (Norris 1990). In general, electoral volatility is seen at its greatest at by-elections, which makes generalisations all but impossible. An added problem is that for a variety of reasons, not least the fact that this very electoral volatility makes results unpredictable and unforced contests too much of a risk for the parties, the actual number of parliamentary by-elections has decreased (Norris 1990). This has the effect of their attracting even more media attention and reduces still further the wider political relevance these occasions might once have enjoyed. It is significant that all the seats which changed hands at by-elections during the 1987–92 parliament were subsequently regained by the original party at the general election. The political parties have become so concerned about the media focus given to their by-election candidates that they now intervene in the selection process to ensure that they have 'suitable' representatives and then provide them with campaign minders whose tasks range from answering awkward questions on behalf of the candidate to monitoring photo-opportunities. For all these reasons the study of parliamentary by-elections would seem to be off-limits to those who would draw conclusions about the state of party competition and evolving political behaviour from their results.

How far is the study of local by-elections prone to fall into similar traps? In general the competition to fill casual vacancies in local government is good. Less than 1 per cent of contests result in a single candidate being returned unopposed, with an average of three candidates fighting for each seat. This is considerably fewer, of course, than in parliamentary by-elections where the number of fringe candidates and publicity-seekers has grown almost out of control despite the deposit level having been raised from £150 to £500. The steady demise of Independent candidates in local by-elections ('Independents' have stood in fewer than one in five contests since 1984) has been accompanied by a gradual though not uniform increase in party competition. As Table 11.4 indicates, contests involving candidates from each of the three main parties (Labour, Conservative and the various incarnations of the Liberal Democrats) constitute nearly two-thirds of all by-elections since 1983. But just as there are seasonal fluctuations in the number of by-elections, so also are there external political fluctuations which appear to affect patterns of party competition. The Conservatives, for example, experienced a troubled year in 1986 starting in January with the crisis over Westland helicopters and Michael Heseltine's dramatic departure from the Cabinet, followed by damaging parliamentary by-election losses in Fulham and Ryedale. In 1984, 1985 and again in 1986 it was the Liberal/SDP Alliance which fought more by-elections that either of the more established parties. Alliance candidates, buoyed by the unlikely victories achieved by their respective parties, appeared ready to fight the most difficult of seats. The political strategy was often long-term. While there were risks in fielding candidates who were badly beaten, the Liberals in particular felt it was important to campaign vigorously at the grass-roots and to build support gradually over a number of years (Greaves 1982). Overall, three-party competition reached a peak in 1987, when the political temperature was heightened by the general election and when all three parties had reason to take every possible opportunity to demonstrate their strength.

Table 11.4 Percentage of by-elections fought by three main parties

	Conservative	*Labour*	*Liberal*	*3-Party contests*
1984	86.7	84.5	87.2	68.0
1985	86.3	84.5	91.4	69.6
1986	79.9	87.9	88.7	68.0
1987	92.7	91.6	86.2	76.6
1988	92.6	81.6	79.8	55.5
1989	87.0	80.1	73.0	56.4
1990	85.8	85.6	67.8	56.4
1991	87.9	85.2	75.4	64.4
1992	89.7	82.6	82.0	64.5
1993	87.7	85.6	87.1	70.9
1994	80.7	81.4	87.1	63.0
1995	84.8	96.4	88.8	73.7
Mean	87.5	84.9	82.9	65.6

The result of the general election had its own impact on contestation. The Conservatives were now to be found fighting more than nine in ten of all vacancies, while electoral defeat dented Labour's ability to field candidates in the following two years. However, its decline was overshadowed by the consequences of the breakup of the Liberal/SDP Alliance. A prolonged phase of internal party recriminations and realignments and the subsequent merger between the Liberals and parts of the former SDP severely reduced the 'centre's' visibility in local contests. The two factors together meant that the proportion of by-elections featuring all three parties dipped by 20 per cent in 1988 and remained at little more than half of all contests until 1991. It took four years for the single party which emerged from the ashes, now the Liberal Democrats, to rebuild its level of contestation to match that achieved in the heyday of the Alliance. By 1995, with both Labour and the Liberal Democrats registering participation in local by-elections at or close to historic highs, it was the turn of the Conservatives to suffer the translation of national unpopularity into an inability to find candidates for all local government casual vacancies.

Increasing party competition and a volatile electorate has had an impact too on the outcome of local by-elections. In her study of parliamentary contests Norris (1990), defining a volatile election as one where any party saw its share of the vote change by 15 per cent or more, noted that whereas only one in ten by-elections met this criterion in the post-war decade, by 1980 the proportion had risen to nearer six in ten. Although we are unable to replicate these statistics we can highlight the proportion of seats which were held, gained or lost during a particular period as a means of estimating overall levels of electoral volatility. In Table 11.5 we have examined by-elections on a yearly basis, noting overall figures for seats gained, held and lost. The final column calculates the seats lost or gained in each year as a percentage of all contests. Over the period an average of 34 per cent of local by-elections resulted in a gain or loss – a figure very similar to the eight out of twenty-four parliamentary by-elections which changed hands during the 1987–92 parliament. The number of local by-elections permits us, however, to make observations about changes in the rate at which seats are transferred between parties. The most volatile years throughout this period were 1985 and 1986 when the Conservatives were under severe pressure from the Alliance during their mid-term, and again in 1994 when Labour mounted a huge challenge to the Conservatives following Tony Blair's election as party leader. Two of the lowest rates of seat transfer occurred in 1987 and 1992 – both general election years. This pattern suggests that to some extent local government by-elections conform to the usual electoral trends within a parliament. Seats, and especially seats held by the party in power at Westminster, are vulnerable at the mid-point of a parliament.

There is, however, another long-term trend which may undermine this relationship. We noted in Chapter 8 the steady erosion in the Conservative base in local government. This would suggest that the number of casual vacancies caused by retiring Conservatives would decline along with their total

Table 11.5 Turnover of seats in local by-elections 1984–1995

	Held	Gains/Losses	Seats with change of party control as % of all contests
1984	244	125	33.9
1985	257	186	42.0
1986	202	157	43.7
1987	199	68	25.5
1988	271	129	32.3
1989	354	161	31.3
1990	232	128	35.6
1991	179	92	33.9
1992	257	106	29.2
1993	310	142	31.4
1994	179	145	44.8
1995	175	65	27.1

representation in local government as a whole. Comparing the frequency of by-elections in Conservative-held seats at the same point in different electoral cycles shows a consistent pattern of decrease. In 1985, 1989 and 1993 the percentages of by-elections in Conservative-held seats were 42.1, 38.5 and 35.3 per cent respectively. The comparable figures for 1983, 1987 and 1991 were 40.9, 31.8 and 25.8 per cent. In 1995, when few by-elections took place prior to the May contests which themselves saw Conservative losses of more than 2,000 seats, only 25.3 per cent of by-elections throughout the year were in Conservative seats. The steady erosion of Conservative local government representation has meant those seats that do remain form a significant part of the party's bedrock support. By-election losses, therefore, are less frequent but arguably more significant.

Which of the two main opposition parties have represented the greatest threat to the Conservatives in local by-elections? Table 11.6 shows the direction of seat gains and losses across three parliaments: June 1983 to June 1987; June 1987 to April 1992; April 1992 to May 1996. Dividing local by-elections in this way allows us to set their results in the wider context of national party competition. As can be seen the Conservatives suffered no less than 274 losses in the 1983–87 parliament, largely at the hands of Liberal/SDP Alliance candidates. The performance of Labour was indifferent. Although the party made 80 gains (including a net advance of 35 against the Conservatives), it incurred 92 losses of its own. An interesting feature of this parliament was the way in which Labour was forced to fight on two fronts simultaneously. Victories in Conservative seats were often counterbalanced by defeats by Alliance candidates. Interestingly, Labour's deficit with the SDP was consistently less than that with the Liberals and contains a clue to the Alliance's failure to replace Labour as the main party of opposition (Rallings and Thrasher 1986c). Nevertheless, the outcome of the

Table 11.6 Transfer of seats between major parties in local government by-elections

July 1983–June 1987

	Conservative	Labour	Liberal	SDP	Total losses
Conservative	–	53	155	66	274
Labour	18	–	42	32	92
Liberal	17	18	–	–	35
SDP	4	9	–	–	13
Total gains	39	80	197	98	
Net gains/losses	−235	−12	+162	+85	

June 1987–April 1992

	Conservative	Labour	Liberal Democrat	Total losses
Conservative	–	87	93	180
Labour	48	–	35	83
Liberal Democrat	59	41	–	100
Total gains	107	128	128	
Net gains/losses	−73	+45	+28	

April 1992–May 1996

	Conservative	Labour	Liberal Democrat	Total losses
Conservative	–	62	119	181
Labour	20	–	48	68
Liberal Democrat	32	28	–	60
Total Gains	52	90	167	
Net gains/losses	−129	+22	+107	

Note: A party's gains should be read vertically while its losses are organised horizontally.

1987 general election confirmed what local by-elections over the previous four years had indicated. Labour's recovery from the débâcle of the 1983 election was far from complete and the Alliance was proving the more potent threat to the Conservatives in their heartlands.

The 1987–92 parliament witnessed the breakup of the Alliance and the uncertain beginnings of the Liberal Democrats together with an intense period of anti-government feeling associated with the introduction of the poll tax. These events are reflected in the transfer of seat figures between 1987 and 1992. Although the Conservative deficit was considerably less than in the previous parliament we should allow for the overall decline in the number of by-elections in Conservative seats. The most interesting feature, however, is the shift in Labour's favour, largely brought about not by a far better performance against the Conservatives but rather a more successful resistance to the Liberal Democrats compared with the Alliance parties. Between 1983 and 1987 Labour incurred net losses of 47 seats against Liberal/SDP candidates. Against Liberal Democrat candidates from 1987 to 1992 Labour had net gains of 6 seats. Once again local government by-elections proved to be a good guide to the likely pattern of party competition at the 1992 general election. Labour's ability to withstand the attack from the Liberal Democrats allowed it to make inroads into the more vulnerable of Conservative seats. The ability of the Liberal Democrats still to win more seats than it lost throughout this period underlined the strength of the party's local government base regardless of the difficulties it was facing nationally.

Since 1992 the pattern has been closer to that found during the 1983–87 parliament than between 1987 and 1992. The Liberal Democrats have re-established their position as major players in local government by-elections and the depth of Conservative unpopularity has been reflected in an increase in both the number and proportion of seats being lost in these contests. Labour continues to gain only a few more seats than it loses, but again, since Blair became leader its record looks much better. In the 2 years between April 1992 and June 1994 the party registered a net loss of 8 seats over 297 contests; in the period between June 1994 and May 1996 it made net gains of 30 in half the number of elections. This too may prove a pointer to the next general election.

While a party's decision to stand and its success in defending and winning seats provide important measures of political strength a more comprehensive picture can be gleaned from examining its share of the by-election vote. By restricting the analysis only to those contests featuring each of the three major party groups we can show the ebb and flow of support and how this might be a reflection of the national political scene. Because the number of by-elections in certain individual months can be quite small, Figure 11.1 displays the vote share in three-party by-elections for each quarter over a ten-year period. The graph demonstrates the sensitivity of vote share in local by-elections to the wider political environment. While the Conservatives have witnessed several electoral lows – for example, the mid-term unpopularity of the 1983–87 parliament, the controversy surrounding the introduction of the poll tax in 1989–90 and the rapid end of their honeymoon following withdrawal from the ERM in 1992 – their local vote has each time clearly recovered in advance of their calling a general election. The level of Labour's support in local by-elections has been less than impressive for most of the period – until 1994 the party's vote share rose above 40 per cent only when it benefited from widespread public disapproval of the poll tax in 1990.

The Liberal Democrats, and before them the Liberal/SDP Alliance, have experienced the greatest fluctuation in vote share, but also enjoyed some periods of being the most successful of all the parties. Their peak level of support came in the first quarter of 1986 when Alliance candidates obtained a 40 per cent share of the vote. The Conservatives were dogged by the split over Westland while Labour support was undoubtedly affected by the dispute with the print unions at Wapping and the adverse publicity surrounding Labour councillors in Liverpool and Lambeth. The ending of the Alliance after the 1987 general election contributed to a considerable dip in share of the vote received by centre party

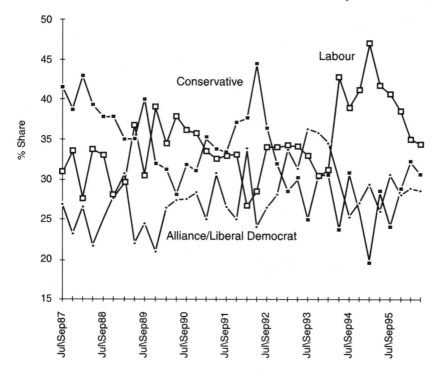

Figure 11.1 Quarterly vote share in 3-party by-elections 1987–1996

candidates in the third quarter of 1987. Periodically, both the Alliance and the Liberal Democrats have witnessed rapid and considerable falls in their vote share, indicating political support which is extremely volatile. In the two-year period beginning in January 1986 the Alliance saw its vote share fall 21 percentage points while in the six-month period from the beginning of January 1992 the Liberal Democrat share fell from 34 per cent to just 20 per cent. Figure 11.2 provides us with a graphic illustration of this phenomenon. Throughout the period the Alliance/Liberal Democrat share in by-elections has been at least 5 per cent higher than their opinion poll rating. This pattern revealed a party which was expert at exploiting the by-election protest vote and a natural reservoir of Conservative supporters disenchanted with their party during its parliamentary mid-term. At crucial points in the graph, however, the by-election vote drops rapidly. Prior to the 1987 general election the by-election collapse was matched by a similar drop in poll ratings. Before the last election the two measures actually moved closer together. Such volatility points to a party which is able to attract wide support but much of which consists of a 'protest vote' – departing as quickly as it arrived.

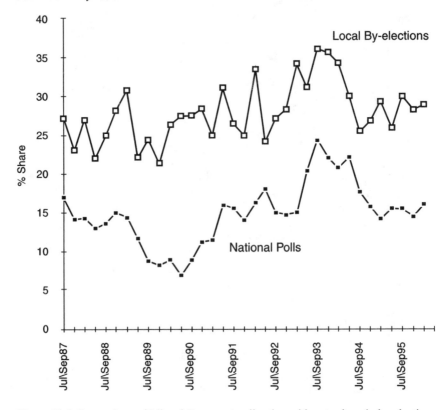

Figure 11.2 Comparison of Liberal Democrat poll rating with vote share in by-elections 1987–1996

It can be shown, therefore, that the overall level of party competition is high in local by-elections. Moreover, if a sufficient number of cases are aggregated together, a party's share of the vote in these contests at any one time can be related to its standing nationally. The question now remains one of sensitivity. To what extent are by-elections capable of picking up slight movements of public opinion and how far can they be used as barometers of electoral change?

BY-ELECTIONS AS A BASIS FOR ELECTORAL FORECASTING

Local by-elections, like their parliamentary counterparts, will sometimes be seized upon as indicators of significant political moments. In 1985, for example, Labour lost two seats to the SDP in the Nottinghamshire area which were viewed as crucial tests of the party's appeal in the light of tensions within the National Union of Mineworkers. The losses appeared to act as a catalyst for confrontation over the miners at that year's Labour conference and shortly afterwards the formation in Nottinghamshire of the breakaway Union of Democratic Mineworkers. Clearly, the loss of these seats did not cause the ensuing events but there can be little doubt that Labour's by-election defeats were an important factor in creating and sustaining media interest in the issue. Similarly, following a MORI poll which suggested that Dr Owen's SDP was more popular with the electorate than the Social and Liberal Democrats under Paddy Ashdown, interest in local by-elections featuring the two parties competing against one another attracted increasing attention. Despite the SDP's superior performance in the Richmond parliamentary by-election in February 1989 local by-elections continually suggested that the reverse was true: the Liberal Democrats were better organised and more effective at the local level than were the SDP. In time the markedly different performances of the parties in local elections removed any doubt in the electorate's mind about which party could legitimately claim to be the successor to the Alliance (Rallings and Thrasher 1989).

Clues to the fate of another major political figure, Margaret Thatcher, were also to be found by the media during the summer of 1990. In June the Conservatives lost a seat to the Greens in Glanford – an historic occasion in more ways than one – and over the ensuing months local by-elections were again used to test the state of electoral opinion and provide the basis of speculation about the fate awaiting the prime minister. The latest by-election to trigger a disproportionate amount of analysis occurred in Tower Hamlets in September 1993 when the British National party gained its first election victory by winning a former Labour seat in the Millwall ward. The result prompted an internal investigation by the Liberal Democrats into the activities of its local party which ran the council, sparked off anti-fascist rallies in London, and generally renewed public interest in the role of such parties as the BNP within the British political system.

Is there any evidence, however, to suggest that local by-elections can be used systematically, rather than sporadically, as indicators of national political mood? Prior to the last general election we were asked by the *Sunday Times* to report on what local by-elections might tell us about the state of electoral opinion throughout the country. Interest had been prompted by the claim in some political quarters, especially among Liberal Democrats, that opinion polls were not successful in capturing the true level of political support and that actual votes, rather than people's perhaps off-the-cuff responses to questions asked by pollsters, were a more reliable indicator. We began from the premise that local by-elections might capture underlying political allegiances better than either the polls or their frenetic parliamentary counterparts and developed a way of measuring swing between the parties since the last general election based on the results in local by-elections.

Although the concept of swing has had its critics, largely because it is more relevant for a political system dominated by two parties, it has the virtue of being relatively easy to explain and provides a simple mechanism for charting the rise and fall of party support (Curtice and Steed 1988; Butler and Van Beek 1990;

Rose 1991; Gibson 1992). We also decided that mapping by-election swing against that implied by an average of recent opinion polls would offer readers a reference point for the purposes of comparison. Beginning a monthly analysis in January 1990, all those contests which featured candidates from the main parties at both the by-election and the 1987 May elections were aggregated and an overall measure of swing calculated. The 1987 elections had covered almost 13,000 seats in the shire and metropolitan districts and the voting had proved to be a highly reliable indicator of political fortunes at the general election a month later. There were, however, some drawbacks to this particular method. First, the base date of 1987 meant by-elections in London and Scotland could not be included because the comparison elections had taken place the previous year. Second, a monthly analysis could be undermined by any imbalance in the type of by-elections which happened to occur – for example, too many in safe Labour seats or too few in rural England. Nevertheless, given that our purpose was merely to illustrate the broad drift of electoral support in much the same way as the opinion polls sought, we believed such weaknesses to be tolerable.

To put the findings in context it is necessary to remind ourselves of some of the electoral arithmetic which dominated media attention in the run-up to the 1992 general election (McKie (ed.) 1992). Following its 1987 defeat Labour had a number of swing targets. The Conservative's House of Commons majority would disappear on a uniform swing to Labour of some 4 per cent. In order to replace the Conservatives as the largest party Labour required a swing of 6 per cent. For Labour to win an overall majority it needed an 8 per cent swing. Whatever the outcome of the general election one electoral record was likely to be broken. If the Conservatives won, then they would have bounced back from a set of poll ratings which saw Margaret Thatcher as the most unpopular Prime Minister since polling began and her party similarly reviled. For Labour to win, a swing of post-war record breaking proportions would be required. Figure 11.3 shows the complete picture from 1990 to the beginning of April 1992 when the general election was fought. Swings of 4, 6 and 8 per cent are marked and since at no point during this period was there a swing from Conservative to Labour the lines do not dip below the zero point.

For a short period the two measures of swing, those shown by both the monthly average of the opinion polls and as found in local by-elections, were remarkably consistent. The controversy surrounding the poll tax is captured on both measures with polls and by-elections alike indicating a likely swing of some 17 per cent. Thereafter, however, the swing in by-elections fell quite steeply while that in the polls showed a more shallow decline. The challenge to Mrs Thatcher and her subsequent replacement by John Major in November 1990 marks the beginning of the Conservative recovery. That month's by-elections actually showed a much lower swing to Labour than was being recorded by the polls. During the following spring the polls and by-elections began to move apart. Mrs Thatcher's previous two general election victories in 1983 and again in 1987 had been achieved on the back of successful local elections. As the

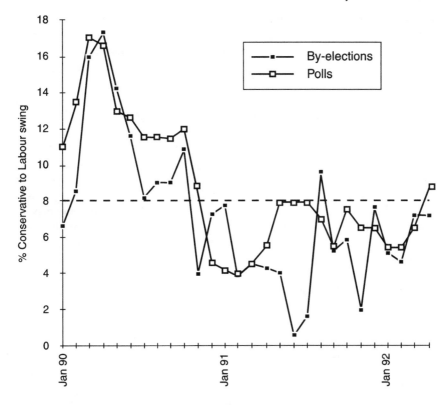

Figure 11.3 Percentage swing from Conservative to Labour in opinion polls and local by-elections 1990–1992

swing against them fell in by-elections, however, so it also rose in the opinion polls. John Major appeared less and less attracted to the idea of a summer election. In the event the outcome of the May 1991 elections saw the Conservatives sustain heavy losses in terms of seats but national projections of the vote put them only just behind Labour, implying a pro-Labour swing of about 6 per cent since 1987: a figure roughly in the middle of the gap between the figures suggested by the polls and local by-elections. Whether the calling of a general election at this time would have also brought a Conservative victory is, of course, a matter of pure conjecture. What is significant is that with one exception the swing against the Conservatives stayed below the 8 per cent level once John Major became Prime Minister. That exception came in August 1991 when a weakness in our method of tracking public opinion was exposed. By using a month as the period of study we became victims of the fact that August was the least popular month for by-elections. The smaller the number of by-elections, therefore, the more chance the overall swing figure could become distorted. This duly happened and the swing leapt from less than 2 per cent in July to 9 per cent the following month, with the polls actually showing a small swing back to the Conservatives over this period. Despite this blip both the polls and by-elections continued to hint at the prospect of a tight general election which proved to be correct in terms of the distribution of seats but not in that of vote share. In actual fact the swing from Conservative to Labour was little more than 2 per cent – certainly not the 4 per cent plus suggested by polls and by-elections alike. Much time and energy has been spent investigating the reasons why the polls seemed to be so inaccurate in 1992 (Market Research Society 1994). It is interesting to note that in tracking local by-elections, where we were analysing real votes rather than stated intentions and where voters had the secrecy of the ballot box, considerable dissatisfaction with the Conservatives was still being expressed in the weeks leading to the election itself. Our analysis, therefore, offers some comfort to those who believe the reason the polls 'got it wrong' was not so much a problem of technique but rather of a volatile electorate that in the final week of the campaign moved strongly back towards the Conservatives.

The main problem with the swing model is that it focuses necessarily on a two-party struggle in what is clearly a three-party system. Following the general election we decided to abandon this approach in favour of a model which could generate a national equivalent vote share for each of the Conservative, Labour and Liberal Democrat parties. Our purpose was two-fold. First, we required a means for producing reasonably accurate forecasts for the likely transfer of seats between the parties at each main diet of local elections held in May each year. Second, we wished to continue to supply a nationally relevant estimate of the current state of party popularity that did not require data from opinion surveys. Below, we provide a brief description of the model developed for this purpose.

The model relies on estimating what each individual local by-election result implies for the national standing of the parties. The first step in this process is to record vote share obtained by the three major parties both at the by-election and on the last occasion the ward was fought in the May contests. Only elections which feature Conservative, Labour and Liberal Democrat candidates are used. Next, the year in which those May elections occurred and the national equivalent vote share published at the time are noted. Then, the change in each party's share of the vote between the by-election and the relevant May elections is calculated and those change figures applied to the appropriate national equivalent vote. Naturally, as when a party's local election share increases or decreases by a factor greater than its national equivalent level of support, some of the results produced by this model will be nonsensical. However, it has become clear that by taking the mean change in all those by-elections which occur over the period of either a fixed quarter or any period of three consecutive months, extreme results are smoothed out and an accurate gauge of each party's national level of support implied by its local election performance can be produced.

How successful has this model proved, first in terms of forecasting the results of the May elections and second in describing the ebb and flow of national public opinion? The model has been used to forecast May election results since 1993. As Table 11.7 makes clear, the largest forecast error produced by the model for any party at any of the elections has been the 2 per cent overestimate of the Labour vote in 1993. This contrasts sharply with some of the opinion poll projections published close to the election which have over- or underestimated party shares of the vote by up to 10 per cent. Overall, this method of using by-elections to estimate the likely national equivalent vote share for the respective parties has thus far proved reliable. The issue of forecasting seat gains and losses still remains, and on this point we have been much less successful.

In principle forecasting the distribution of seats at any given election should be relatively straightforward given knowledge of how the votes were shared the last time the seats were fought and a robust measure for predicting how an impending election might develop. Taking the differences in vote share for the main parties and applying those figures to each ward should give an indication of whether party control would be altered. Using this method alone, however, proved unsatisfactory, as the figures for 1993 in Table 11.8 indicate. Although the model had, in fact, overestimated the eventual Labour vote the more significant error in the seat prediction lay with the Conservative/Liberal Democrat split. Quite simply, the Liberal Democrats had overperformed, winning many more seats than its vote share and a uniform swing derived from it would have suggested. We have explored this problem in more detail elsewhere (Rallings and Thrasher 1996a) and subsequently have moved away from an assumption that seats will be determined on the basis of uniform swing.

Forecasting vote shares and seat redistributions for the local elections is, however, only part of the model's purpose. Its other primary function is to provide an alternative measure for recording the ebb and flow in electoral support for the three main political parties. At the time of writing the model awaits its most critical test, a general election. As Figure 11.4 shows, there have been considerable differences between the model's estimate of electoral support and that provided by the national opinion polls. Consistently, local by-elections register much higher voter support for the third party than that picked up by the pollsters. Moreover, the gap between Labour and the Conservatives on the two

Table 11.7 Projected and actual national equivalent shares of the vote at local elections

	1993		1994		1995	
	Projected	*Actual*	*Projected*	*Actual*	*Projected*	*Actual*
Conservative	32	31	29	28	26	25
Labour	43	41	41	40	47	47
Liberal Democrat	23	24	27	27	23	24

Note: All figures as published in the *Sunday Times* before and after elections.

Table 11.8 Projected and actual seat gains and losses

	1993		1994		1995	
	Projected	*Actual*	*Projected*	*Actual*	*Projected*	*Actual*
Conservative	−100	−470	−300	−450	−1,750	−2,100
Labour	–	+90	+50	+110	+1,150	+1,800
Liberal Democrat	+150	+380	+250	+380	+600	+500

Note: All projection figures as published in the *Sunday Times*. Actual figures from C. Rallings and M. Thrasher, *Local Elections Handbook* (Plymouth: Local Government Chronicle Elections Centre, various years).

measures has varied by up to 12 points, with Labour's national support being much less according to the by-election model. As the general election approaches these differences may disappear, but if they do not it will be interesting to see which of the two methods proves the more accurate in projecting the actual share of the votes cast. Should our method prove superior then we might legitimately claim to have developed a useful, simple and relatively inexpensive method of election forecasting.

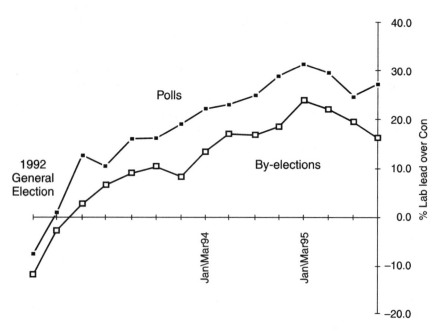

Figure 11.4 Labour's percentage lead over the Conservatives according to opinion polls and by-election model

CONCLUSIONS

The results of local government by-elections form a significant body of data, capable of offering insights into the nature of party competition and the fluctuating levels of electoral support. In some cases they can be used as instant litmus tests of political events, as happened with the poll tax and the ousting of Margaret Thatcher as Prime Minister. Over a longer time period their votes can be aggregated to give a sense of the rise and decline in the support for particular parties. The movement of this support and its relation to the national electoral cycle provides a useful addition to other devices such as the opinion polls for charting the general state of electoral intentions. Both the nature and frequency of local by-elections permits their use in this way, whereas parliamentary by-elections have become less relevant as political indicators the more campaigns and electors alike are driven by the media circus. For their part, the various parties have recognised the value of contesting and campaigning in local by-elections. The outcome has been a consistently high level of three-party competition and a desire to make the maximum political capital out of the seemingly most trivial result. Over the past decade local by-elections have thus become ever more closely-observed gauges of the nation's political temperature.

12 Local elections and representation

INTRODUCTION

When Michael Heseltine, as Secretary of State for the Environment, set out the terms of reference of the Local Government Commission for England there was no mention of electoral reform. The Commission was charged with making local government more accountable but it was not allowed to consider the part played by the electoral system itself in frustrating accountability. This is not altogether surprising, of course, since the Conservative party at the time was a prime beneficiary of Britain's use of 'first past the post'. In the 1992 general election, for example, the party won 54 per cent of the seats with 43 per cent of the vote. A month later Conservative candidates polled 45 per cent in the shire district elections and received 51 per cent of seats. Looked at through Conservative eyes the electoral system was not broken so there appeared to be no need to fix it. Neither was the Labour party about to shout from the rooftops about the perverse way in which local votes were translated into council representation. In those same 1992 local elections Labour won 54 per cent of seats in the metropolitan boroughs with just 39 per cent of the vote. As we noted in an earlier chapter the Liberal Democrats, although campaigning for reform of the electoral system, have learnt to work within its constraints. By targeting winnable seats and leaving the remainder either uncontested or with little more than 'paper' candidates, the party has steadily reduced the disadvantage usually suffered by third parties under our electoral system.

None of this, of course, removes the inequities which do exist and which arguably should have been part of the brief given to the Local Government Commission. An important aim in this chapter is to highlight the extent of the bias produced by the 'first past the post' system. In the first section, therefore, we will produce some of the more glaring examples of the inequality between votes and seats. Lest we be accused of exaggerating this bias we provide, in the second section, a broader analysis which looks in detail at an entire category of local authority, the county councils, responsible for the bulk of expenditure in the shires. In a third section some other electoral systems will be considered in terms of their applicability to British local government.

One perceived advantage of our electoral system is that it is supposed to produce clear-cut outcomes. The system may be unfair, the argument runs, but at least the outcome is generally a party with an overall majority. In the case of local government this argument now has much less force. The number of councils where no single party enjoys an overall majority has increased rapidly in recent years. These 'hung' councils (or 'balanced' if we accept the Liberal Democrats' preferred term) now comprise more than a third of all local authorities in Britain. The second objective of this chapter, therefore, is to examine how local election results have translated into council control, noting particularly the rise in the series of hung councils in the decade to 1995. Since 1985 we have conducted a series of surveys of these hung councils in an attempt to show how political life evolves under these new circumstances. Our primary concern has been to describe how the various local political parties have reacted to being in a situation where the normal conventions of government and opposition have been overturned by the electoral arithmetic. We report first on how attitudes to the policy and decision-making processes have altered as local politicians have had to come to terms with the fact that running a hung council has become an apparently permanent, not temporary, way of life. The section following examines the myriad of administrative arrangements on hung councils, noting how formal party coalitions have steadily increased in number. Finally, we consider the wider lessons to be learnt from studying political behaviour in hung councils. The combined vote for the Conservative and Labour parties has been eroded by minor parties in both local and parliamentary elections. The impact of this electoral change has been experienced first by local authorities and it is there that politicians have learned to adapt to those altered circumstances. To some observers it is but a matter of time, with or without electoral reform, before a parliamentary election fails to throw up a single party with an overall majority. What lessons may national politicians learn from their colleagues in local government in coping with such an outcome?

ELECTORAL UNFAIRNESS

Many councils in Britain are demonstrably unrepresentative of their local electorate. Such a fact sits uneasily with a system that was intended to be democratic in the sense of reflecting the wishes and needs of the population. Over the years there have been some spectacular instances of parties winning many more seats than their share of the poll could possibly justify. One of the principal reasons for an electoral imbalance arises when a single party achieves a sizeable share of the overall vote. Some of the worst examples of this occur amongst the metropolitan boroughs where the Labour party, particularly in recent years, has exercised a strong grip. Knowsley, for example, has become virtually a one-party authority through a combination of the operation of the electoral system followed by an understandable decline in party competition. In the mid-1970s a majority of wards were contested by the three main parties.

Although the Conservatives enjoyed a reasonable level of support this was rarely translated into seats. In 1978 the party won some 43 per cent of the vote across the borough but for that it was rewarded with just 2 seats out of a total of 14. Despite winning one in twelve votes cast the Liberals went away empty-handed in terms of seats. From that time onwards the opposition to Labour has all but evaporated within the borough. In 1990 Conservative candidates contested just 8 out of 21 wards; less than 40 per cent of Knowsley's electorate was able to vote for a Conservative if they so wished. The Liberal Democrats for their part had been reduced to fighting in just three wards. Most seats went to Labour without need of an election. This is, of course, not the fault of the Labour party but rather of an electoral system which rewards only winners. The collapse in Conservative local government support since 1992 has only served to exacerbate the problem. In 1995 the Conservatives won no seats at all in 17 metropolitan councils, including Tameside where their vote was in excess of 20 per cent.

Neither is the problem restricted to Labour strongholds amongst the metropolitan boroughs. In Bracknell Forest, for example, the Conservatives won 54 per cent of the vote at the 1987 local elections and took all 40 seats. The London borough elections of 1990 produced some similarly striking examples of electoral unfairness. In Islington, Labour polled 48.9 per cent of the vote and won all but 4 of that borough's wards. In Richmond on Thames, the Liberal Democrats, so often the victims of the present electoral system, won 92 per cent of the seats with 46.4 per cent of the vote.

Another problem with a 'first past the post' system has to do with the ward boundaries. Although we noted in Chapter 3 that responsibility for constructing these was the task of an independent Local Government Boundary Commission this process does not prevent anomalies from occurring. Part of the problem lies with population movements which proceed more quickly than do ward boundary revisions. Consequently within a single authority some wards will have falling electorates while in others population will be rising. In the West Midlands in 1991, we find wards in Solihull with electorates varying by a factor of 2, from 6,482 to 12,894. Comparisons across local authorities display even greater ranges in electorate size. In 1989 the average electorate in each single-member county council division was 7,589, with a range between 1,505 and 19,318. In London in 1986, the largest three-member ward had an electorate of 13,233, whereas the smallest had one of just 4,419 – less than the mean size of electorate in those wards with two members. In the shire districts, one rural ward has – as we noted earlier – as few as 190 electors, whereas ward electorates in some of the more densely populated districts are much larger – extending to a maximum of 6,191 electors in one single-member ward. It might be argued that this variation in size is necessary to ensure that the community of local interest is reflected in ward boundaries. However, such gross disparities do mean that some votes are more equal than others, and a common effect is to distort the relationship between seats and votes at the local authority level.

The effects of this are all too plain to see. In Crewe and Nantwich, for example, Labour, despite capturing 50 per cent of the vote at the 1987 elections, won three seats fewer than the Conservatives who polled just 40 per cent. In the same district in 1991 the Conservative and Labour parties each won nine seats, though Labour polled 12 per cent more of the vote. In Plymouth, the Conservatives won an absolute majority on the council in 1987 with just 38 per cent of the vote. In 1991, Labour won more than two-thirds of the seats on the city council with just 44 per cent of the vote. In the 1995 elections Labour won all but five of the council's sixty seats with a poll share of 61 per cent. Solihull's variation in ward sizes produces some interesting electoral outcomes. Labour's vote share of 23 per cent in 1991 was half that for the Conservatives but while Labour won five wards the Conservatives could only win seven. Since Labour's vote was concentrated in the borough's smallest wards it was able to gain a higher proportion of council seats than would normally be the case. In the London borough of Croydon in 1994 the distortion was sufficiently serious that the 'wrong' side won the election. The Conservatives' polled 42.3 per cent of the vote and won 30 out of the total 70 seats, with Labour winning 40 seats for its 39.2 per cent share. The mean councillor/elector ratio in Conservative wards was 3,580 and that in Labour wards 3,125. In 1995 in Bracknell Forest, the pendulum of electoral support having swung violently since the 1987 example above, Labour won twenty-two seats to the Conservatives' twelve despite polling just 1.3 per cent more of the vote than its rivals. In Broxbourne, where Labour won eight seats to the Conservatives' six with a smaller share of the vote, the mean councillor/elector ratio in wards where the Conservatives were successful (4,660) was 740 higher than in those where Labour was victorious (3,920).

PROPORTIONALITY

Ultimately, the purpose of an electoral system is to translate votes cast in the ballot box into seats in a legislature. Opinion differs, however, about the importance of equity between votes and seats thereafter. Proponents of proportional representation believe strongly that an electoral system should award seats to a party relative to votes cast in its favour. Under these conditions a perfect electoral system might be considered as one where the proportion of seats awarded was exactly equal to the proportion of votes received. Critics of proportional representation, however, claim that it leads to a multiplicity of parties and makes coalition government more likely. Whatever the respective merits of this debate we can agree that electoral systems can be assessed in terms of the proportionality of their results.

Various measures for identifying the degree of disproportionality produced by different electoral rules have been devised. What each measure sets out to do is to arrive at a single index which can be used to compare electoral systems and the extent to which they have an effect on proportionality (Gallagher 1991). One index, widely used in the literature, is termed, 'the Loosemore-Hanby index', after the two authors who first applied the statistic to electoral systems

(Loosemore and Hanby 1971). Below, we use this index to measure the extent of disproportionality in county council elections since 1985. These particular elections have been chosen because these authorities now use single-member divisions. Were we to use authorities with a mix of single and multiple-member wards the analysis would, necessarily, become extremely complex. Were we to examine authorities which have annual elections but for only part of the council we would be unable to treat the whole council as a single legislature. Our intention here is merely to give some insight into the extent of disproportionality sometimes produced under Britain's local electoral rules and the county councils provide a suitable case on which to base this analysis.

The Loosemore-Hanby index is derived as follows. First we calculate for each party both its vote and seat shares at a given election. Then, ignoring the signs, negative or positive, we simply sum the absolute values of the differences for all parties and divide the total by 2. Thus, if we assume three parties contest an election with party A obtaining 60 per cent of the vote and 75 per cent of seats, party B winning 30 per cent of votes and 20 per cent of seats while party C captures just 10 per cent of votes and 5 per cent of seats. The vote–seat differences for each party are as follows: party A $60 - 75 = -15$; party B $30 - 20 = 10$; party C $10 - 5 = 5$. Summing the absolute values gives $15 + 10 + 5$ for a total of 30. The final stage is to divide this total by 2 giving a Loosemore-Hanby index for our hypothetical election of 15. The critical question remains, how do we interpret this index? If we imagine an electoral system that rewarded parties with seats in the legislature *exactly* in line with vote shares then the differences between share of seats and votes would be zero in each case. Summing those zeros and dividing by 2 would still give us zero. A truly proportional electoral system will, therefore, produce a Loosemore-Hanby index score of zero. The more an election moves away from zero, therefore, the more disproportional the result. An index score of 60, for example, could indicate that one party had won all the seats with just 40 per cent of the vote.

We can now apply this index to county council elections to see how they rate. Table 12.1 shows for each of three election years, 1985, 1989 and 1993, the five counties with the highest and lowest Loosemore-Hanby index scores. Looking first at those with high scores and thus low proportionality we note that some counties appear more than once. The northern county of Durham appears three times while its near neighbours, Cleveland and Northumberland, appear twice. A closer examination of the voting data for these particular counties reveals that in Durham at least the explanation for electoral disproportionality is largely related to a high level of support for Labour. In each election Labour has polled above 50 per cent in six of the eight districts and one of the well-known characteristics of 'first past the post' is its propensity to over-reward large parties in terms of seats. The case of Northumberland is slightly different in that party support is more evenly spread, but whereas Labour dominates the larger districts of Blyth Valley and Wansbeck which have a greater number of county divisions, Conservative and Liberal Democrat votes in smaller districts like Berwick upon

Tweed and Tynedale are not translated into equivalent seats on the council. In Cleveland the Conservatives' respectable share of the vote of 36 per cent in Middlesbrough in 1993 only gave them four out of the twenty available seats because of its relatively even, but minority spread across the area. Their vote share was also boosted by the fact that turnout in strong Conservative divisions was often twice as high as in safe Labour ones. In Stockton on Tees, by contrast, the concentration of the Conservative vote in a relatively small number of divisions allowed them to win 30 per cent of the seats (seven out of twenty-four) with 30 per cent of the votes. Indeed the fact that the Conservatives polled as little as 6 per cent of the vote in some divisions was a help rather than a hindrance in their achieving such a proportional outcome.

Similarly, at the opposite end of the country two counties, Surrey and Buckinghamshire, also appear twice as authorities with disproportional election outcomes. In the case of Surrey, at least three factors have contributed to its appearing in the lists for the first two elections but not that for 1993. First, this is an area of substantial Conservative support. In 1985, for example, the party polled 45 per cent which the electoral system translated into 68 per cent of seats. By 1989 the party was receiving half of the vote and three-quarters of all seats. The Conservative decline in the 1993 county elections saw the party's vote fall to 41 per cent but its allocation of seats plummet to 45 per cent. That drop and our second explanation of electoral outcomes has to do with the behaviour of the Liberal Democrats. In 1985 the Alliance polled a respectable 34 per cent across the county but its return in seats (12 out of 76) was under half that proportion. Four years later the Liberal Democrats registered a very similar votes–seats relationship. By 1993, however, the party had embraced a more sophisticated campaigning strategy of targeting winnable seats. Their vote leapt to 38 per cent but instead of needlessly accumulating votes without reward, as in the past, the party's share of seats exactly matched its share of the poll. The third factor at work in Surrey has been the performance of Independent candidates. With their support concentrated in a handful of the county's divisions the seat share for such candidates has regularly exceeded the overall vote share. Buckingham-shire's double appearance in Table 12.1 mirrors that of Durham, with the strength of the Conservative party throughout the county being significant. In 1989, for example, the Conservatives won just under half the votes cast but received seven out of ten seats. In 1993, when the Conservative vote declined to 40 per cent, the bonus in seats was also reduced but remained sufficient to allow the party to retain an overall majority. Indeed the disparity in proportionality index scores between Buckinghamshire (14.8) and Surrey (6.8) in 1993 shows why it was the former that became the Conservatives' only remaining county council despite the fact that the party did better in terms of votes in the latter.

It is quite clear from Table 12.1, however, that 'first past the post' does not inevitably produce a disproportional result; it is capable of leading to an outcome as proportional as that produced by an electoral system regarded as fairer. Gallagher's (1991) analysis of the results of 82 general elections in 23

Table 12.1 Proportionality scores in English county councils 1985–1993

1985 – mean index score 12.0 (39 Counties)			
5 most proportional	Index	5 least proportional	Index
Cambridgeshire	3.4	Surrey	25.9
Wiltshire	3.7	Buckinghamshire	23.4
North Yorkshire	4.2	Cleveland	20.2
Somerset	4.4	Suffolk	19.7
Gloucestershire	5.5	Durham	18.7
1989 – mean index score 11.8 (39 Counties)			
5 most proportional	Index	5 least proportional	Index
North Yorkshire	3.6	Surrey	25.1
Wiltshire	3.7	Devon	21.7
Cumbria	4.8	Durham	21.2
Bedfordshire	5.4	Buckinghamshire	21.0
Hereford & Worcestershire	5.7	Northumberland	19.6
1993 – mean index score 11.1 (39 Counties)			
5 most proportional	Index	5 least proportional	Index
Cambridgeshire	2.8	Durham	22.7
Essex	4.0	Northumberland	21.7
Shropshire	4.1	Somerset	21.1
Lincolnshire	4.9	Isle of Wight	18.8
Kent	5.0	Cleveland	17.9

countries gives an average Loosemore-Hanby value of 8.1. At the top of his league table are countries such as Germany (index score 1.4), Austria (2.3) and Netherlands (2.7), all of which use some method of proportional representation. Ireland, which uses the single transferable vote system, averages 4.7 for five general elections. Cambridgeshire, North Yorkshire and Wiltshire all better that figure for two out of the three years listed in Table 12.1. On two occasions in the past twelve years Cambridgeshire has emerged as the county with the most proportional election result. A more detailed analysis of voting across the county reveals some explanation for this phenomenon. Unlike in many other counties electoral support for the main parties is not concentrated in one particular area. Both Conservative and Liberal Democrat parties have support relatively evenly spread across the county and at a high enough level for it to be reflected in seats won. Only the Labour party can be regarded as having its support concentrated, but its strength lies in Cambridge and Peterborough, two of the more populated districts within the county and the ones with the lowest elector–councillor ratio. The overall effect has been to give Cambridgeshire a council whose composition is generally a fair reflection of the county-wide electorate's party preferences.

One final county worthy of detailed comment is Somerset, which demonstrates the extent to which the relationship between a 'first past the post' system and proportionality has much more to do with happenstance than design. The county has the unique distinction of appearing as one of the five most proportional counties in 1985 and one of the five least proportional in 1993. The explanation for this, ironically, lies in the performance of the party most committed to changing the electoral system, the Liberal Democrats. In 1985 the Alliance challenged strongly across the South West of England and in Somerset succeeded in depriving the Conservatives of overall power. County-wide, Alliance candidates polled some 45 per cent of the vote but in some areas, notably Sedgemoor, Taunton Deane and West Somerset their seat/vote ratio was quite poor. Eight years later, however, two factors combined to alter the respective positions of the main parties and produce a disproportional electoral outcome. First, the Conservative vote declined with the Liberal Democrats gaining ground. Second, the Liberal Democrat vote itself was more efficiently distributed across the county. So successful was the party that it gained more than half of votes cast and received the normal bonus in seats received by large parties. In South Somerset, indeed, its 60 per cent share of the vote secured all 17 seats. In short, Somerset became similar to Buckinghamshire and Durham although unusually it was the Liberal Democrats which occupied the leading position.

What these examples show is that although simple plurality electoral systems can produce proportional results in terms of the seats/votes ratio they are not, in any sense, guaranteed. Movements of votes between parties can transform what had been a proportional outcome into something quite disproportional. A number of elements, particularly when combined together, can produce an important distorting effect. Problems of imbalance often occur when one party receives a significant share of the total poll across a local authority. Opposition groups may be able to challenge it if their vote can be concentrated in a relatively small number of wards, but where their minority support is itself widely dispersed, seats become harder to win and a distortion in outcomes is almost bound to arise. Even where support for the various parties is more even, the degree to which the composition of the local authority reflects the distribution of party support can vary enormously from election to election depending on exactly where each party draws its strength from. Two further factors which can distort results are, however, products of the system of fixing local electoral boundaries. First, when electorates become uneven across an authority, a party able to win seats in wards with small electorates can pile up its council representation for a relatively modest share of the total vote. Conversely, a party that wins in the larger wards or, worse, polls well but not well enough to win, will find that it is amassing votes which go unrewarded in terms of representation. Any dramatic variations in turnout in different types of seat often serve only to exacerbate the disparity. Second, this problem can be magnified where there are a small number of large, multiple-member wards. In the ten-member ward illustrated in Chapter 3, for example, eight Conservatives were elected and just one Labour councillor, even though the difference in the two parties' share of the total vote was just 10 per cent – 45 per cent to 35 per cent.

In the more usual three-member wards it is also often clear that opposition parties would have a much better chance of getting some tangible reward for their support if the same number of councillors were to be elected but from three separate geographical areas.

There is no suggestion in this evidence that the electoral system is biased for or against any particular party. A party whose support at one set of elections leads it to gain a disproportionate number of seats may find itself conversely damaged by the swing of opinion next time round. A classic example of this has affected the Conservative party in the English county elections. In the 1977 contests the party obtained 75 per cent of seats with 58 per cent of votes. In 1993 the Conservatives' 36 per cent share of the poll was rewarded with just 31 per cent of the seats. Although parties can and do take some steps to mitigate against such electoral effects, such as by adjusting their campaign strategy to minimise 'wasted' votes, in the final analysis arithmetical accident plays a crucial role in producing the local authorities which govern us.

A PROGRAMME OF REFORM?

The arguments for introducing some form of proportional representation for local government surely mirror those used in Northern Ireland, where protection of minorities is uppermost, rather than those adopted by proponents of PR for the UK parliament, where equality of representation is the driving force. The simple point is that in many parts of the country there are perpetual minorities unable either to vote their party into power locally or even to obtain a fair representation of their opinion on the council. Accountability currently fails by allowing too many local parties to believe they will enjoy a permanent majority on the council regardless of the quality of services they deliver. Such an atmosphere leads to complacency by the governing party, disillusion on the part of the hopelessly under-represented and outnumbered opposition, and encourages apathy amongst the electorate.

As we saw in Chapter 4 local electoral turnout in Britain is the lowest of any European Union nation. One characteristic which our better-participating partners share is a system of election enshrining a degree of proportionality. Local turnout among them can rival the 75 per cent plus level expected in British general elections. Such a figure in Britain is remarkable in individual wards and unheard of across an entire local authority. Even in the politically charged 'poll tax' election of 1990, average turnout across the country was just 48 per cent. Electors are more reluctant to turn out and vote in local elections the less they feel their vote has a chance of affecting the result in their own ward or local authority. Many electors in safe seats simply prefer to stay at home. A system which ensured that each vote was of equal worth in determining the outcome must surely encourage higher turnouts (Blais and Carty 1990).

Just as 'first past the post' under certain conditions dampens the electorate's enthusiasm it can also have an impact on political parties. This is shown to best effect in the campaigning tactics embraced by the Liberal Democrats, which have resulted in that party deliberately turning its back on some wards deemed as out of reach. As the costs of mounting local election campaigns rise, more local parties may feel the need to trim their presence and other parties' safe wards will be the first affected. Indeed, during their recent period of local electoral unpopularity, the Conservatives have also put forward fewer candidates in hopeless wards – contesting 30 fewer metropolitan and 300 fewer district wards in 1995 than in 1991. Such actions, of course, deprive electors of choice and depress turnout among committed supporters of the parties not represented.

One suggestion for increasing the accountability of councils to their electorates and perhaps encouraging greater participation is the introduction of annual elections for at least a third of each council. Certainly such a reform would concentrate elected members' minds on the likely electoral reaction to policies. But this system already exists in the metropolitan areas and across a large slice of the English shires, and whilst it may discourage excesses of policy, it does not in itself make local authorities any more representative. Indeed, it is frequently the case that although the electorate may wish to express displeasure with the ruling party, the party's numerical majority is larger than the number of seats it has to defend in any one year. In 1996, for example, the Labour majority on 24 of the 30 metropolitan boroughs which the party controlled was sufficient for the party to retain office even if it won no seats at all in the elections for those authorities. Unless councillors were to be made to seek re-election each year or wards with very large numbers of electors and councillors were to become the order of the day, annual elections would seem to imply a single-member being elected on each occasion. Under such circumstances only the alternative vote system would prove practical and even that would not guarantee a better degree of representativeness than at present (Bogdanor 1984).

A more proportional system would require multiple-member seats, such as already exist in London and many of the English and Welsh shire districts. Sacrificing annual elections on grounds of practicality, at least three compensating benefits might be reaped. First, voters might be encouraged to pick and choose among candidates from the same party to a greater extent than they do currently. Second, there is some evidence from other countries that the representation of women, who currently comprise just over a quarter of all councillors in Britain, and minority groups is improved wherever parties have the opportunity to field multiple candidates in the same seat. Third, and most important, the parties winning seats in say three-, four- or five-member wards would be a more accurate reflection of the way the votes had been cast.

Proportional representation, however, is a catch-all term and is used to described a wide variety of electoral systems. Since no electoral system yet devised could ever be described as perfect each has its advantages and disadvantages. Moreover, particular consideration ought to be given, when choosing an alternative system, that its purpose would be to elect local authorities and not a national legislature. In this regard electoral systems could be divided between those that accord considerable emphasis to choosing parties for a legislature compared with those that view individual candidates as most important. The former include so called 'party list' systems where the voter chooses from candidates arranged in an order determined by the political parties. Seats are allocated to candidates according to their place in the party list with those higher up the list having a better chance of being elected than those lower down. Although there are some important variations which allow voters to choose amongst candidates within or even across party lists the basic principle that parties present candidates holds true. A quite separate approach is to give voters freedom of choice in expressing a rank order amongst candidates. One example of a proportional system that adopts this approach is that of the single transferable vote. Under this system multiple-member constituencies are used and electors are allowed to cast a ballot which reflects their rank ordering of the different candidates. Crucially, the order of the ballot paper does not reflect a political party's own set of preferences other than the fact that candidates with a party label have presumably been selected at some prior meeting. The respective qualities of these different approaches have been extensively discussed elsewhere (Rae 1971; Taylor and Johnston 1979; Balinski and Young 1982; Lijphart and Grofman (eds), 1984; Grofman and Lijphart (eds), 1986; Taagepera and Shugart 1989), but from the viewpoint of local government elections we believe STV to be the preferred choice. Quite simply this method best allows for non-party candidates to challenge alongside party candidates, thereby preserving one of the traditions of the British system of local election.

In the local authority as a whole such a system of single transferable votes would almost guarantee that the composition of the council would accurately reflect the pattern and current of opinions in the locality. It is true that more 'hung' councils might result. However, now they would indicate the division of party choice among the electorate rather than be the product of unpredictable electoral quirks and it would be that much harder for any central government to accuse the local authorities of being 'unaccountable'. Of course, opponents of proportional representation use the spectre of 'coalition government' as one of their principal arguments. However, as we shall discuss in the next section, Britain already has a considerable number of hung councils despite using an electoral system which is supposed to encourage single-party government. We can also show that it is not inherently the case that situations where no single party has an overall council majority result in administrative chaos and lack of clear policy direction.

HUNG COUNCILS

Growing party politicisation in local government coupled with a strong third party presence has meant that more local authorities than ever before are now classified as 'hung' councils. When no single party has an overall council majority the pattern of day-to-day politics and administration has to change. For some officers and councillors, used to the predictability of one-party rule, this development is seen as a disruption to the normal way of conducting local authority business. Others, and they are a growing number, believe that party politics has to adapt to these new circumstances. Below, we ask three basic questions about hung councils. First, have the attitudes of those with primary responsibility for running local authorities, namely chief executives and party leaders, shown any signs of learning to cope with their new environment? Second, in what ways have local parties tried to accommodate to life in hung councils? Third, what relevance, if any, does the experience of coalition in local government have for British political life generally?

Hung councils – attitudes to policy and decision making

Following the 1985 county elections the number of hung English shires doubled overnight. The Alliance's success meant that county administrations which had grown used to single-party rule now faced a period of uncertainty. Later that year we conducted the first of our three major surveys of councils leaders and chief executives on hung councils. That survey, not surprisingly, found that many chief executives felt frustrated by their inability to engage in long-term planning given the new climate of political uncertainty. Amongst politicians similar views were voiced by both Conservative and Labour party leaders, many of whom preferred the certainty of opposition to the unknown of sharing political power with another party. Labour local party leaders, moreover, were under strong pressure from the national leadership to shun political pacts and in some authorities this instruction led directly to confrontation between the different levels of the party. Nevertheless, in some key authorities, notably Devon, Gloucestershire, Somerset and Wiltshire, Labour cast crucial votes which enabled the Alliance to wrest control away from the traditional Conservative rulers (Rallings and Thrasher 1986a).

The county elections prompted wider interest in hung councils (Leach and Stewart 1986), but there were still scarcely 50 of them nation-wide – less than 10 per cent of all local authorities. By 1988 their number had doubled, caused largely by the continuing success of Alliance candidates in a series of local elections, and we again undertook a survey of those involved in their operation. One significant difference between this and the earlier survey was evidence of a greater willingness amongst politicians and officers to adapt to life without a majority administration. Instead of turning their backs on the situation a number had begun to create new methods for consulting more widely on policy decisions. This was particularly true with regard to the budget making process where parties now discussed their preferences at an earlier stage and in more detail than hitherto. Some officers remained sceptical, however, with one grudgingly admitting that decisions had become better because information was more widely shared but that policies had deteriorated because coherence was missing. Most significant of all, there were signs that the experience of being a

202 Local elections and representation

hung council was beginning to shift the balance of power. For this particular survey we established a control group of non-hung authorities and compared responses between the two. The contrast in opinion about where power lay was significant. On councils where a single party ran the administration chief executives and party leaders agreed that power resided principally in the hands of elected party élites and chief officers. Amongst those respondents from hung councils, however, power was seen as fragmented with the role of committees accorded a far greater prominence (Rallings *et al.* 1988).

Our third survey was conducted in 1993 when approximately 161 authorities, around a third of the total and triple the number surveyed in the mid-1980s, were hung councils. Again, questions were asked of chief executives and party leaders about the quality of both decision making and policy making. Overall, chief executives showed signs of becoming more positive in their attitude towards working within a hung council. Amongst politicians, however, party affiliation appeared to make a large difference to whether the situation was viewed positively or negatively. Labour and Liberal Democrat leaders, for example, were more positive, believing both the quality of decision making and policy output had improved. For the first time among Labour party leaders a majority reported that in their opinion decision making had improved under the hung council. Liberal Democrats, as might be expected, were the most enthusiastic grouping of all. Two in three thought decision making had improved and no less than seven in ten believed that policy was better than before. However, these views were diametrically opposed to those of the majority of Conservative group leaders who generally still took a negative view of the idea of political co-operation. More than three-quarters felt decision making had suffered as a consequence of becoming a hung authority while two-thirds thought policy had deteriorated. Interestingly, on the question of where power was perceived to reside, there was near unanimity amongst party leaders and officials. The triangle of power covering party leaders, chief executives and committees was again identified by our respondents (Rallings *et al.* 1995). In terms of decision making and the policy process, therefore, those most closely involved with administration in hung councils were agreed that, once the initial period of uncertainty had passed, politicians and officials alike could embrace new methods and procedures. Below, we show how that more positive attitude was manifested in the changing types of administration found amongst hung councils.

Hung councils and types of administration

Perhaps because of the belief that 'first past the post' would deliver political majorities, coalition government has been regarded as something negative and to be avoided. It was noticeable in our surveys that although the number of hung councils had steadily begun to increase there was still a pervasive attitude that the condition was only temporary and normal service would (fortunately) soon be resumed. Political life on the ground reflected this innate hostility towards co-operation with other parties. Our first survey of hung councils in 1985, for example, encountered a problem that would feature in future surveys, although thankfully not to the same degree. Comparing responses from party leaders in the same authority would often reveal that while one believed there was a coalition running the administration, another was adamant that different administrative arrangements were in place. It was only through extensive cross-checking that we were able to verify the position for ourselves. We concluded that of the hung local authorities surveyed at this time some 68 per cent were administered by a minority party, 15 per cent had no formal party administration while just 17 per cent exhibited all the characteristics of power-sharing or of a coalition between two or more parties (Rallings and Thrasher 1986a). These findings were not altogether surprising given the deep-rooted distrust of coalitions and a widespread belief, particularly in the counties, that once the next elections were due then the 'natural' party of government would resume control. Certainly, this research appeared at odds with mainstream coalition studies leading to the conclusion that, 'the office-seeking approach that underlies many existing coalition theories does not work at all well in British local politics' (Laver *et al.* 1987).

In later surveys the picture had changed considerably. The percentage of hung local authorities with some form of power sharing or coalition arrangements had leapt to more than 45 per cent by 1988, more than double the 1985 figure. The development of coalitions in local government has been dramatic. Leach and Game (1989) found minority administrations to be the commonest system in hung councils, findings further supported by Leach and Stewart (1992). A more recent analysis of coalition behaviour, however, found that one in ten authorities had a formal coalition in place while a further four in ten had some form of power-sharing arrangement (Rallings *et al.* 1995). This growth had come largely at the expense of authorities where a single party had attempted to govern alone. The most recent analysis of hung councils collected detailed information for a total of 142 authorities and discovered that in just 41 per cent of these minority administrations were in place (Laver *et al.* forthcoming). Interestingly, this proportion was close to that reported by Laver and Schofield (1990) in their major study of European legislatures, suggesting that Britain's experience of hung legislatures was gradually converging with that of countries more versed in the arts of coalition government. Closer analysis of some of these minority administrations showed the Liberal Democrats to be the 'pivotal' party, more likely than any other party to support a Conservative or Labour administration in power (Rallings *et al.* 1995).

Indeed, the Liberal Democrats have proved the key to understanding a great deal of the dynamics of local government coalition building in Britain. In common with coalition theory emphasising the value to a party of having such a pivotal position in the ideological spectrum (Laver and Schofield 1990), the Liberal Democrats have proved extremely successful in either forming or supporting minority administrations, or in becoming coalition partners. Temple (1995) has calculated that in local authorities whose elected members could be arranged on an ideological scale the Liberal Democrats were a member of all existing coalitions and had proved highly successful in achieving policy aims. It is, perhaps, reasonable to speculate that the Liberal Democrats are acutely aware of their pivotal position in hung councils and that this forms an extension of the party's overall electoral strategy. While undoubtedly the party will seek to gain majority control for itself in any local authority, it also acknowledges that in some cases the most it can currently hope for is to wield influence as a power broker in a hung council. The implications of this for national politics will be discussed in the next section.

Hung councils and a hung parliament

Following the 1992 general election representatives of no fewer than nine political parties were to be found sitting on the benches of the House of Commons. While all but three of these parties had just a handful of MPs, their presence contributes to the statistical possibility of no one party having an overall majority in the House. Even when a single party does govern, the experience of the Conservatives after 1992 in seeing their majority progressively undermined by by-election defeats should warn against complacently expecting the status quo to be maintained. Indeed our calculation of the electoral arithmetic following the most recent alteration of parliamentary constituency boundaries suggests that a hung parliament is the likely outcome of any general election in which the Conservatives are ahead of Labour by fewer than 6 percentage points or Labour ahead of the Conservatives by less than 1 per cent (Rallings and Thrasher 1995a). With or without electoral reform, therefore, the prospect of a hung parliament cannot be summarily dismissed.

Hung councils provide a rich source of information on the likely responses by national politicians and civil servants to such an important change in circumstance. Local politicians embrace the same political culture and many of the attitudes of national counterparts. Some believe the Liberal Democrats are closer nationally to Labour than to the Conservatives (Dent 1993). At the local level, however, Liberal Democrat parties have demonstrated a willingness to co-operate with both Labour and Conservatives in different circumstances. Though public announcements by the party leadership appear to favour future co-operation with Labour such statements must be taken as temporary rather than permanent. Certainly, any parliamentary coalition between Labour and Liberal Democrat would have to learn from mistakes made in forming administrative pacts in local government (Temple 1993).

Whatever the institutional and behavioural differences, a permanently hung House of Commons could not continue to run in its present élitist and adversarial way. Local authorities show that inevitably a learning process commences and that a more sophisticated coalition politics will emerge. Local politicians have learnt that there is an alternative to the tradition of adversarial politics. Confronted with the same electoral impasse national politicians would doubtless adapt in similar vein. Once again, local government would lead the way for national government.

CONCLUSIONS

We have shown in this chapter how the outcomes produced by the British local electoral system often bear little resemblance to the distribution of support for the various candidates throughout the local authority area. Such outcomes are not, however, the product of the operation of systematic bias, rather they reflect the imperfect and unpredictable way in which 'first past the post' represents the expressed preferences of voters. Some observers believe that the almost random relationship between votes and seats and the existence of many local authorities where minority voices are condemned to a perpetual wilderness has damaged local accountability and can account in good part for the poor level of participation in local elections. Advocates of reform, though disagreeing on the detail of the changes required, share a commitment to equalising the value of each vote and thereby helping to convince electors that their choices will influence the aggregate result.

Opponents of more proportional electoral systems have long focused their arguments on the consequences for governance, particularly the growth in the number of legislatures where a single party is unable to form an administration. Ironically, British local government has already experienced a sharp increase in 'hung' councils under the present electoral system. Survey studies suggest that both councillors and officers have been willing to adapt to such a situation over time and to put in place more co-operative methods for policy review and decision. Indeed, so many local authorities now expect elections to produce a 'balanced' council that more formal power-sharing arrangements between parties are in place, accompanied by a growth in more positive evaluations of the outputs of such administrations.

13 Conclusions

INTRODUCTION

We make no claim that this book is definitive, but for the time being at least it is unique. Our objective in writing it has been to provide an overview of local elections in Britain since local government reorganisation in the 1970s and, thereby, to identify some of the most important trends and themes which have characterised their development. The difficulties in collecting and collating electoral data have prevented such a broadly based study in the past, a fact reflected in the research literature. Previously, research has tended to concentrate either on a small range of authorities (Sharpe (ed.) 1967; Bristow 1984), or on one particular electoral cycle (Clark 1977; Curtice *et al.* 1983; Game 1981; Rallings and Thrasher 1991a; Gibson and Stewart 1992). The creation of the British Local Elections Database has removed such constraints. With information available for every ward in Great Britain over a period of more than two decades we have been able for the first time to describe local electoral developments in relation to voters, candidates, parties and outcomes.

Our analyses can now be summarised under three broad themes, each of which contains the seeds of a paradox which may have important consequences for the future conduct and significance of local elections in Britain. The first of these themes explores the relationship between voters and parties. The second looks at the way in which observers, particularly those in the media, report and interpret local elections and their outcomes. The third considers the democratic credentials of local government and the electorate's role in the legitimation process and in ensuring accountability. Finally, we will set out some thoughts about a future research agenda for the study of local elections as well as outline possible policy changes which may help to remedy some of the problems with the local electoral process that we have identified.

VOTERS AND PARTIES

Survey evidence shows that since the 1960s voters in Britain have identified less strongly with the established parties. Paradoxically, however, as the electorate has become less partisan, so the choice in local elections has become dominated by candidates chosen and sponsored by the political parties. The party politicisation of local government elections has had other effects too. Fewer councillors are now returned unopposed and there is greater overall competition for seats. Campaigns are better organised and local elections more widely publicised as a result. Local party manifestos shape the issue agenda and allow voters to choose among clearly defined alternatives. Parties provide the organisational structure through which elected members are allocated roles and make decisions. Indeed the existence of party groups brings a stability and certainty to the administrative process of local authorities on which councils have come to rely.

Yet, despite its pervasiveness, local party politics still has its critics. Councillors should be free, it is said, to exercise individual judgement, unconstrained by the needs of party discipline. Currently they, like backbench MPs, are perceived as little more than lobby fodder, simply required to vote as instructed at committee and full council meetings. Only Independents will decide an issue on its merits and with the interests of their ward electorate uppermost in their minds. Such views call up a mythical 'golden age' of local democracy. In fact many of the more celebrated municipal administrations of the past were less the product of open democracy than of dominant, even autocratic individuals effectively responsible to no one but themselves. Those Independent councillors who have survived have done so largely because of a 'personal' vote, and as they retire or die it is largely party candidates who will succeed them.

That process is just one of many leading to a growing homogenisation of local politics. Increasingly local election campaigns exist within a framework and are conducted to a timetable orchestrated by national party headquarters. Once one party calls a national press conference to launch its local election campaign, the others must follow suit or risk losing media coverage. Campaign slogans such as 'Conservative councils cost you less' (Conservatives 1995 and 1996) or 'Pay More, Get Less' (Labour 1996) are designed for universal use and appeal. Local parties and media organisations do try to transfer the focus back to the 'local', and the Liberal Democrats do not exercise the same degree of central control as their rivals, but for many uncommitted electors the campaign as determined by party apparatchiks in Westminster is the only one visible.

For party candidates this, too, produces a paradox. Unlikely to be elected unless formally associated with a political party, they know only too well that the label they sport could also bring about their defeat through no fault of their own. Indeed several Conservative councillors, accurately fearing the worst for their party in the 1995 and 1996 local elections, attempted to save their own skins by standing as Independents. The tactic was rarely successful. Long-serving and well-known local councillors do often enjoy a degree of personal support over and above their 'party' vote, but even that cannot withstand the tidal waves of voter antipathy against particular parties witnessed in local elections over recent years.

It would be a mistake, however, to think that national politics now determines all local election results. Partisan dealignment also means that many voters claim to be influenced by local issues when making their choice. We found evidence of considerable variations in outcome between authorities and over time. In the London boroughs, for example, there were instances in both the 1990 and 1994 elections of each party's fortunes falling and rising in different locations. At the 1993 county elections and again at the district level in 1995 the swing against the Conservatives favoured Labour in some parts and the Liberal Democrats elsewhere. Such 'tactical' voting patterns, encouraged by differential campaigning by the parties themselves, appeared designed to inflict the maximum damage on Conservative incumbents. They are the product of an electorate more certain of what they do not want than what they do, but they have the added effect of bringing a new dimension of 'localness' into local election outcomes.

NATIONAL IMPORTANCE – LOCAL IMPOTENCE?

Football clubs attract more support, from the general public and financial sponsors alike, when the team wins trophies. Success fuels further success when the well-managed club re-invests additional gate-receipts and sponsorship money into buying better players and providing better facilities for spectators. The majority of clubs, despite empty trophy cabinets, still attract support, but this seldom extends beyond the immediate area. National interest focuses on the successful teams whose activities are reported by the media, anxious to satisfy the public's appetite. Judged on such terms, local government has all the hallmarks of a successful football club. National media coverage of local elections has grown considerably since the 1970s. Both print and broadcasting organisations cover the campaign, attend press conferences, and even commission 'experts' to assess the major issues and to speculate about the outcome. Cameras film activity around polling stations, while politicians and commentators assemble in studios to give their version of events as the results are announced. For some parties and leaders the results will be considered a triumph; for others a disaster. Discussion soon turns to the political consequences of the election – long-term prospects, policy changes, even leadership contests and resignations. But an examination of local government's trophy cabinet reveals something strange. Far from a display of silverware it contains only empty spaces where trophies once stood. Local authorities once exercised considerable power over our lives but a succession of legislative changes, restricting local scope and autonomy, has reduced the administrative importance of local government. The paradox here is that media interest in local government has risen at the same time as its powers of independence have diminished.

This second paradox, like the first, owes much to the development and extension of party politics. Media interest in local elections reflects the fact that the national parties themselves regard the number of council seats and councils under their control as measures of success. In this way local elections become elevated into national events. Indeed, the increase in party candidates has had the consequence that local electoral competition more closely resembles that found at the parliamentary level. Chapter 11 revealed that local elections, including the more frequent by-elections, can be used as surrogate indicators of the state of national opinion. Acknowledging this each of the main parties devote more care and attention both to contesting such elections and to providing the media with their own interpretations of the overall outcome. These processes feed off one another and media interest in local elections shows no sign of abating.

Faced with such a development voters could legitimately ask what it is that they are voting for. The more local authorities have their powers restricted, the less it matters in policy terms which political party has control of the council. Central government now provides directly more than 80 per cent of the money councils require to run statutory services, with the ability of local authorities to make up any perceived shortfalls severely restricted by the capping by law of the sole local tax, council tax. The cumulative effect is that local government's freedom of manoeuvre has almost vanished. It is difficult to know with confidence how voters perceive local elections, but there is evidence of the pervasive effect of national issues and there are concerns over the continuing low level of turnout. Should voters decide that the local effect of their actions will be limited they might instead use the election solely as an opportunity to express feelings about national politics. Alternatively, if the impact of local voting is seen as negligible the rational individual might decide that the costs of voting outweigh the benefits and therefore abstain. Both reactions will have a profound consequence for local democracy. Steadily declining turnout, and the evidence of the very recent past is disturbing, will give local government's critics more reason to argue that services administered by local authorities could be transferred to more efficient bodies, particularly in the private sector. Should those voters who do bother to go to the polls increasingly treat local elections as a national political contest, then their actions will merely endorse media preconceptions which already follow a similar premise. The plaintive claims by elected local politicians that they have received a mandate from local voters will then be open to even greater dispute.

LOCAL DEMOCRACY AND ELECTORAL COMPLEXITY

Opinions differ over the most appropriate model for local government but there is widespread agreement that councillors should be democratically elected and fully accountable. Indeed, the logic behind the community charge legislation was that the relationship between voting rights and local taxation had grown tenuous and that a per capita tax could re-establish that link. We would argue, however, that the local government electoral system itself operates as a barrier to public awareness and, by implication, reduces the chances of a system of strong local democracy developing. The wholesale reorganisation of local government in the 1970s was a lost opportunity in that although the number of authorities was reduced, no attempt was made to streamline the electoral process. Indeed different systems were allowed to operate alongside one another. In London, where reorganisation preceded that in the rest of Britain by a decade, the practice was to hold whole borough council elections once every four years using a mix of single- and multiple-member wards. The new metropolitan boroughs had three-member wards, with one councillor from each being elected annually to a sort of rolling council. Among the shire districts in England and Wales authorities with identical functional responsibilities were allowed to operate different electoral systems and timetables.

Far from recognising and remedying this situation, the decision to implement structural changes in English local government piecemeal will exacerbate confusion. In 1995, for example, elections were held for 14 new all-purpose unitary councils established as replacements for the two-tier structure in the administrative counties of Avon, Cleveland, Humberside and the Isle of Wight. In some cases the boundaries of the new authorities were coterminous with those of former district councils. The district council of Bristol, for example, was replaced by a new unitary authority bearing the same name and boundaries. In other cases amalgamations of former district authorities have been made. The former districts of Bath and Wansdyke were merged to form a new unitary authority called Bath and North East Somerset, and Kingswood and Northavon together became South Gloucestershire. Despite their names, and doubtless confusingly for the public, neither authority falls within the boundaries of the continuing counties whose names they appear to bear and of which they were not even a part prior to this reorganisation. In May 1996 elections for a further 13 unitary authorities took place. Whereas the first set of unitary councils had wholly replaced the previous county and district structure in those areas, the second set of authorities were effectively districts removed from counties which would otherwise continue to exist as a two-tier rump without them. For example, both Portsmouth and Southampton have become unitary authorities but Hampshire, the county where those two councils were formerly located, will survive along with its remaining ten constituent district councils. The final tranche of new unitary authorities will have their inaugural elections in May 1997, and they – like their predecessors – will be allowed to opt for either whole or partial council elections. Indeed Bristol is to retain its former system of having both two-member wards and annual elections which means, of course, that different wards – and never the whole city – have elections each year – see Chapter 3.

If the local electoral process tends on occasion to be too complex for the general public to understand, the same may be said about the electoral outcomes it produces. The 'first past the post' system is designed to reward only winners and help produce legislative majorities by giving the largest party a bonus of seats. In Chapter 12 we described election results where the largest party defined by vote share did not receive the biggest payoff in seats. General elections can produce similar results but in local elections, where ward populations are small and where parties concentrate their vote, such outcomes are more frequent. On other occasions the most widely supported party does receive the winner's seat bonus, but sometimes it is so large that the opposition parties are obliterated. At the 1995 district elections in Plymouth, for example, the Labour party won 61 per cent of the vote but 92 per cent of seats on the 60-member council. In both 1983 and 1987 the Conservatives won all the seats on Bracknell Forest council with little over 50 per cent of the total vote each time. In 1996 Labour did the same in the first elections for the Stoke on Trent unitary authority with a 65 per cent share of the vote. No one has asked the citizens of Stoke on Trent what they make of such an electoral outcome, but should a similar result occur at a general election it is certain that the public outcry would be immense. At the other extreme, the votes are often cast so that no one party can claim a legislative majority and the different parties are obliged to work together in the council in a way which was never put before the electorate for their endorsement at the time of the election.

Our third paradox, therefore, is that the electorate, on whom so much reliance is placed in terms of legitimising the system of local democracy, understandably find it very difficult to comprehend both how the electoral process operates and how their choices are translated into electoral outcomes.

A RESEARCH AGENDA

Each of these themes raises more questions than it provides answers. To a large extent our choice of topic in this book was determined by the available data and our approach has been to eschew complex statistical methods for fear of deterring a wider readership. When considering the nature of a future research agenda, however, such constraints are less relevant. Instead, we can approach the topic from a different direction by asking not what can be done but rather what should be done?

Parties are clearly a key factor in understanding the development of local elections in Britain and a more substantive analysis of their activities is long overdue. A survey of local party activists, for example, would identify how local election campaigns are organised, and particularly the process whereby campaigns target key wards in a locality. Some local parties have been more successful than others in this regard and it would be interesting to discover the reasons for that success. In an analysis of Liberal Democrat performance in local elections, for example, we have already identified an interesting phenomenon in that there appears to be a spatial pattern to the party's expansion. Wards adjacent to those already controlled by the Liberal Democrats have a greater chance of falling to the party than have those where no Liberal Democrat incumbents are nearby (Dorling *et al.* forthcoming). Whether there is a conscious strategy to target such wards or whether the logic of organising an election means it is easier to campaign in adjacent wards has yet to be discovered.

Such research would lead to a more refined analysis of whether and how far tactical campaigning is a necessary prerequisite to tactical voting in local elections. Our analysis of changes in party support was largely concerned with the aggregate picture. Closer examination of voting data within regions and counties, for example, might reveal correlations with variations in the strength and vitality of local party organisations. Such a relationship has already been noted among parliamentary constituencies (Denver and Hands 1993). Variations in party change within individual local authorities could also be analysed in the light of the relative strength of ward organisations and deliberate party campaign strategies. Party campaigning can influence levels of turnout and it is important to discover whether that effect extends to the specific direction of voters' choices. The success of parties in maximising their vote can readily be seen by examining voting in multiple-member wards. Our analysis of voting in such situations was largely restricted to the question of whether voters discriminated amongst candidates on grounds of gender and incumbency (with ethnicity being another characteristic on which more data are badly needed) but that approach could easily be extended to include variations within parties. Our initial research in this area has shown that some voters do not use their full quota of votes (Rallings and Thrasher 1996b) and the next stage of that inquiry is to identify the circumstances where such behaviour operates.

We still know relatively little about the behaviour of voters in local elections. Survey studies have been few and far between, but aggregate local election data, especially when matched with ward level census information, do provide the opportunity for some valuable insights into the patterns and correlates of party support. Wards are the lowest level of aggregation at which electoral data are available in Britain and their size means that they have a number of advantages over parliamentary constituencies as the base unit for ecological analyses. Individual wards are likely to be both more homogeneous and also more subject to rapid changes in their overall composition than constituencies, and thus can provide evidence on such issues as the political impact of the increase in home ownership, the loyalties of ethnic groups, the social base of party support, especially that of the Liberal Democrats and minor parties, and the existence of intra-regional and intra-cluster variations in behaviour (see Rallings and Thrasher 1995b).

The availability of data on local elections in Britain makes it possible for the first time to conduct comparative analysis with their counterparts in other countries. We have already examined the surprising degree of similarity in the explanations of intra-country variations in turnout in Britain and France (Hoffmann-Martinot *et al.* 1996), and this approach could be used more widely in the exploration of a number of research questions about the interplay between electoral systems and party systems. First, although we know that electoral participation is generally higher at local elections in countries using proportional electoral systems than in Britain, we do not yet understand precisely how far turnout varies and what other factors affect that relationship other than the operation of electoral rules. We have not, for example, encountered any research which controls for the powers administered by local authorities in different countries to see how far voters are influenced by the strength or weakness of the institutions for which they are asked to vote.

A second approach which might prove fruitful would be to explore in greater detail those factors which appear to produce proportionality of electoral outcome. How far, for example, does the size of the council to be elected affect the chances of a proportional outcome in terms of relative equity between a party's vote and seat share? If, as we saw in Chapter 12, proportionality is affected by the size and distribution of a party's vote can we codify that relationship to any significant extent? Clearly, how seats are allocated within an authority will have a direct bearing on the degree of success achieved by parties whose support is geographically concentrated. Past election results demonstrate that in certain authorities a particular party appears disadvantaged by the way in which ward boundaries have been drawn. A programme of local ward boundary revisions will proceed in England over the next few years offering a unique opportunity to discover whether that apparent electoral bias operates in a systematic or random fashion.

A third line of inquiry for comparative analysis would be into the development of party systems at the sub-national level of government. The relationship between electoral and party systems is undoubtedly complex but local elections offer opportunities for new parties to develop and compete successfully which are not always available at the national level. In a sense local government elections can operate as a nursery for parties with wide ambitions but few resources. Most of these parties will not succeed but a few will flourish and an analysis of the role of different electoral and party systems in that process would enhance our understanding of party development.

The prime function of local elections is, of course, to choose members of the council. Those councillors then become responsible for the implementation of policy and accountable to the electorate at a later stage for what they have done. There has in fact been a considerable amount of research into the impact of party on policy outputs in local government but much of it, it has recently been claimed, suffers from the use of mis-specified or inaccurate political variables (Boyne 1996). The existence of the local elections database not only provides an improvement in the raw material for such research, but also enables additional questions to be asked. Are local authorities characterised by political stability better at providing services than those where electoral changes are more frequent? Do policy differences have a demonstrable effect on election outcomes, both across a range of authorities and over time?

The answer to many of these questions about the character and impact of local elections involves a qualitative dimension. We have already noted in Chapter 4 the difficulty in explaining patterns of turnout wholly by reference to statistical correlations, and the 'localness' of local elections similarly defies systematic analysis. The dilemma is a familiar one in social science. On the one hand only case studies can provide the flavour and subtlety of explanation required to interpret atypical events and trends. On the other, they cannot be used as the basis for generalisations about other places and other times. The study of local elections and their outcomes must remain an eclectic one, but at least now the data exist against which individual circumstances and idiosyncrasies may be compared.

A POLICY AGENDA

One clear conclusion that has emerged from our analysis of local elections in Britain, and which strongly reinforces the view of earlier studies (Bogdanor 1986; Widdicombe 1986a; Game 1991; Rallings and Thrasher 1992b), is that the current system is in need of reform. It is too confusing and convoluted for many electors to understand. It provides no guarantee that each individual vote will be of equal value in the determination of the outcome. It discourages turnout, not only because of those factors but through a set of regulations which seem increasingly inappropriate to the modern world. Each of these issues could easily be addressed by a review of policy, but currently there is no political consensus on whether anything, let alone what, should be done.

The simplification of electoral arrangements was strongly supported by the Widdicombe Committee a decade ago when it recommended the universal adoption of single-member wards and whole council elections. Notwithstanding the pros and cons of those particular arrangements, it is difficult to dispute its observation that, 'Citizens have a reasonable expectation that the electoral arrangements should be simple, and that, when they move from one area to another, the arrangements should be the same' (Widdicombe 1986a: 167). Scottish local voters have enjoyed the luxury of such clear uniformity since 1974 and have usually boasted higher local election turnouts than their English counterparts. A much simpler system was introduced to Wales with the unitary council elections in 1995, although the mix of single and multimember wards remains. The Local Government Commission-inspired structural reforms in England have been accompanied by no such electoral streamlining, though voters in new unitary authorities should now be clearer who is responsible for the provision of services even if the pattern of elections remains confusing in some places.

Political parties in government have been even more reluctant to grasp the nettle of electoral reform. We have demonstrated previously how local voters are poorly served by existing methods of electing councils in the sense of having their views properly reflected in the composition of the legislature (Rallings and Thrasher 1991b). Arguably this facet of democracy is more important at local than national level where the emphasis is less on the need for strong and stable one-party government than the desirability of giving proper expression to local needs and aspirations and providing representation to the different communities of interest. However, whilst it is widely accepted that a 'first past the post' system of election produces distortions in election results, there is much less agreement on what, if any, other method would be better. The single transferable vote is already used in local elections in Northern Ireland and its supporters point to the greater choice it would offer voters and the relative ease with which it could be introduced. Of the main political parties only the Liberal Democrats are at the time of writing clearly committed to proportional representation for local government. The Labour party, which has promised a referendum on the subject of electoral reform for parliamentary elections, would doubtless feel obliged to funnel down any reform introduced at Westminster, but the report of the party's own internal enquiry showed no enthusiasm for the introduction of a properly proportional system (Labour party 1993). While any change in the electoral system would be likely to improve the fit between voter choice and legislative representation, most methods would require a wholesale review of ward boundaries – and thus of councillors' fiefdoms – and for that reason alone would be something which most governments would be unwilling to tackle in isolation from broader constitutional innovation.

Although structural and electoral system reforms of this type would be likely to increase turnout, more modest measures to facilitate registration and participation also suggest themselves. In recent years a range of organisations including the Local Government Management Board (Game 1991; Wahlberg *et al.* 1995), the Commission for Local Democracy (Commission for Local Democracy 1995) and the Joseph Rowntree Foundation (Rallings *et al.* 1996) have sponsored research which has come out in favour of innovations such as weekend voting; easier entitlement to absent voting; a constantly updated rather than an annually fixed register; the siting of polling stations in town centres and other places where people gather. The official Home Office response to such representations has been extremely cautious (Home Office 1994a and 1994b), but the report of the Labour party's working party on electoral systems holds out the prospect that Labour in government may be prepared to act. Modernisation of the electoral process in this way would certainly have more impact at local than at general elections (where turnout remains respectably high), but the narrowing of the gap between the two is precisely what local government requires. Turnout levels are such a potent symbol of democratic health and legitimacy that, unless something is done to reinvigorate participation, local authorities will find it still harder to get governments of any party to accept that they have a mandate to represent their electorate. We make no apology for ending a book on local elections in Britain on such a note.

Bibliography

Acland, C. (1882) 'County Boards', in J. W. Probyn (ed.) *Local Government and Taxation*, London: Cobden Club Essays.

Atkinson, S. and Braunholtz, S. (1996) 'What Can We Learn From June', in C. Rallings, D. Farrell, D. Denver and D. Broughton (eds) *British Elections and Parties Yearbook 1995*, London: Frank Cass.

Balinski, M. and Young, H. (1982) *Fair Representation: Meeting the Ideal of One Man, One Vote*, New Haven and London: Yale University Press.

Barron, J., Crawley, G. and Wood, T. (1991) *Councillors in Crisis*, London: Macmillan.

Bartley, J. and Gordon, I. (1982) 'London at the Polls: A Review of the 1981 GLC Election Results', *The London Journal* 8: 1.

Bealey, F. and Bartholomew, D. (1962) 'The Local Elections in Newcastle under Lyme: May 1958', *British Journal of Sociology* 13: 273–85, 350–68.

Bealey, F., Blondel, J. and McCann, W. (1965) *Constituency Politics*, London: Faber.

Bentham, J. (1843) 'The Constitutional Code', in J. Bowring (ed.) *The Works of Jeremy Bentham*, Edinburgh: Tait, 11 volumes.

Birch, A. H. (1959) *Small Town Politics*, London: Oxford University Press.

Blais, A. and Carty, R. (1990) 'Does Proportional Representation Foster Voter Turnout?', *European Journal of Political Research* 18 (2): 167–81.

Bloch, A. and John, P. (1991) *Attitudes to Local Government*, York: Joseph Rowntree Foundation.

Blydenburgh, J. (1971) 'A Controlled Experiment to Measure the Effects of Personal Contact Campaigning', *Midwest Journal of Political Science* 15: 365–81.

Bochel, J. and Denver, D. (1971) 'Canvassing, Turnout and Party Support: An Experiment', *British Journal of Political Science* 1: 257–69.

—— (1972) 'The Impact of the Campaign on the Results of the Local Elections', *British Journal of Political Science* 2: 239–42.

—— (1974 on) *Scottish Local Election Results*, Dundee: Election Studies.

—— (1994) *Scottish Regional Election Result*, Dundee: Election Studies.

—— (1995) *Scottish Unitary Election Results*, Dundee: Election Studies.

Bogdanor, V. (1984) *What is Proportional Representation?*, Oxford: Martin Robertson.

—— (1986) *Electoral Systems in Local Government*, Study Paper no. 4. Birmingham: Institute of Local Government Studies.

Boyle, C. (1888) 'The Local Government Bill', *Quarterly Review* 167: 258–9.

Boyne, G. (1996) 'Assessing Party Effects on Local Policies', *Political Studies* 44 (2): 232–52.

Bristow, S. (1978) 'Local Politics After Reorganisation: The Homogenisation of Local Government in England and Wales', *Public Administration Bulletin* 28: 17–38.

—— (1981) 'County Council Elections: What the Trends Show', *Municipal Journal* 89, 22, 29 May.

—— (1982) 'Rates and Votes: The 1980 District Council Elections', *Policy and Politics* 10 (2): 163–80.

—— (1984) 'The Results', in S. Bristow, D. Kermode and M. Mannin (eds) *The Redundant Counties?*, Ormskirk: G. W. and A. Hesketh.

Brodrick, G. (1883) 'The Reform of Local Government in the Counties', *Fortnightly Review* 33, January–June.

Brown, J. (1958) 'Local Party Efficiency as a Factor in the Outcome of British Elections', *Political Studies* 6: 174–8.

Bruce, A. and Lee, G. (1982) 'Local Election Campaigns', *Political Studies* 30: 247–61.

Buckley, J. K. (1926) *Joseph Parkes of Birmingham*, London: Methuen.

Budge, I. (1965) 'Electors' Attitudes to Local Government', *Political Studies* 13: 386–92.

Budge, I., Brand, J., Margolis, M. and Smith, A. (1972) *Political Stratification and Democracy*, London: Macmillan.

Bulpitt, J. (1967) *Party Politics in English Local Government*, London: Longman.

Burnham, J. (1990) 'District Councils in the South of England – Is Labour Doing Well?', *Local Government Studies* 16 (5): 9–16.

Butler, D. (1973) 'By-Elections and their Interpretation', in C. Cook and J. Ramsden (eds) *By-Elections in British Politics*, London: Macmillan.

—— (1992) 'The Redrawing of Parliamentary Boundaries in Britain', in P. Norris, I. Crewe, D. Denver and D. Broughton (eds) *British Elections and Parties Yearbook 1992*, Hemel Hempstead: Harvester Wheatsheaf.

Butler, D. and Stokes, D. (1971) *Political Change in Britain*, Harmondsworth: Penguin.

Butler, D. and Van Beek, S. (1990) 'Why Not Swing? Measuring Electoral Change', *Political Science and Politics* 23: 178–83.

Butler, D. and Waller, R. (1983) 'Labour and Alliance have Mountains to Scale', in *Times Guide to the House of Commons June 1983*, London: Times Books.

Butler, D., Adonis, A. and Travers, T. (1994) *Failure in British Government*, Oxford: Oxford University Press.

Byrne, T. (1985) *Local Government in Britain* (third edition), London: Penguin.

Cain, B., Ferejohn, J. and Fiorina, M. (1987) *The Personal Vote*, Cambridge, MA: Harvard University Press.

Capron, H. and Kruseman, J.-L. (1988) 'Is Political Rivalry an Incentive to Vote?', *Public Choice* 56: 31–43.

Clark, D. (1973) *Greater Manchester Votes*, Manchester: Redrose Publications.

—— (1977) *Battle for the Counties*, Manchester: Redrose Publications.

Cole, G. D. H. and Postgate, R. (1961) *The British Common People*, London: Methuen.

Cole, P., Harrison, L., Rallings, C. and Thrasher, M. (forthcoming) *Sub-National Electoral Systems within the European Union*, Plymouth: Local Government Chronicle Elections Centre.

Commission for Local Democracy (1995) *Taking Charge: The Rebirth of Local Democracy*, London: Municipal Journal.

Connolly, M. and Knox, C. (1986) 'A review of the 1985 Local Government Election in Northern Ireland', *Local Government Studies* 12 (2): 15–29.

Cook, C. (1975) *The Age of Enlightenment: Electoral Politics in Britain 1922–29*, London: Macmillan.

Cover, A. (1977) 'One Good Term Deserves Another: The Advantages of Incumbency in Congressional Elections', *American Journal of Political Science* 26: 523–42.

Cox, W. H. and Laver, M. (1979) 'Local and National Voting in British Elections: Lessons From The Synchro-polls of 1979', *Parliamentary Affairs* 32 (4): 383–93.

Craig, F. W. S. (1989) *British Electoral Facts 1832–1987*, Aldershot: Dartmouth.

Crewe, I. (1983) 'Why Labour Lost the Election', *Public Opinion*, June/July.

Crewe, I., Alt, J. and Fox, A. (1977) 'Non-voting in British General Elections 1966–

October 1974', in C. Crouch (ed.) *British Political Sociology Yearbook*, volume 3, *Participation in Politics*, London: Croom Helm.

Curtice, J. (1996) 'What Future For The Opinion Polls? The Lessons From The MRS Enquiry', in C. Rallings, D. Farrell, D. Denver and D. Broughton (eds) *British Elections and Parties Yearbook 1995*, London: Frank Cass.

Curtice, J. and Payne, C. (1991) 'Local Elections as National Referendums in Great Britain', *Electoral Studies* 10: 3–17.

Curtice, J. and Steed, M. (1984) 'The Results Analysed', in D. Butler and D. Kavanagh (eds) *The British General Election of 1983*, London: Macmillan.

—— (1988) 'The Results Analysed', in D. Butler and D. Kavanagh (eds) *The British General Election of 1987*, London: Macmillan.

—— (1992) 'The Results Analysed', in D. Butler and D. Kavanagh (eds) *The British General Election of 1992*, London: Macmillan.

Curtice, J., Payne, C. and Waller, R. (1983) 'The Alliance's First Nationwide Test', *Electoral Studies* 2 (1): 3–22.

Cutright, P. and Rossi, P. (1958) 'Party Organization in Primary Elections', *American Journal of Sociology* 64: 262–9.

Dearlove, J. (1979) *The Reorganisation of British Local Government*, Cambridge: Cambridge University Press.

Dent, M. (1993) 'The case for an electoral pact between Labour and the Liberal Democrats', *Political Quarterly* 64 (2): 243–51.

Denver, D. (1993) 'Trends in Scottish Local Elections 1974–1992', in C. Rallings and M. Thrasher (eds) *Local Elections in Britain: a Statistical Digest*, Plymouth: Local Government Chronicle Elections Centre.

—— (1994) *Elections and Voting Behaviour in Britain*, Hemel Hempstead: Prentice Hall.

Denver, D. and Hands, G. (1975) 'Differential Party Votes in Multi-Member Electoral Divisions', *Political Studies* 23 (4): 486–90.

—— (1977) 'Politics' in J. D. Marshall (ed.) *The History of Lancashire County Council 1889–1974*, London: Martin Robertson.

—— (1985) 'Marginality and Turnout in General Elections in the 1970s', *British Journal of Political Science* 15: 381–98.

—— (1993) 'Measuring the Intensity and Effectiveness of Constituency Campaigning in the 1992 General Election', in D. Denver, P. Norris, D. Broughton and C. Rallings (eds) *British Elections and Parties Yearbook 1993*, Hemel Hempstead: Harvester Wheatsheaf.

Department of the Environment, *Paying for Local Government*, Cmnd 9714, 1986.

Dorling, D., Rallings, C. and Thrasher, M. (forthcoming) 'The Epidemiology of the Liberal Democrat Vote', *Political Geography*.

Dunleavy, P. (1990) 'Mass Political Behaviour: Is There More To Learn?', *Political Studies* 38 (3): 453–69.

Dyer, M. and Jordan, G. (1985) 'Who Votes in Aberdeen? Marked Electoral Registers as a Data Source', *Strathclyde Papers in Government*, no. 42, Glasgow: University of Strathclyde.

Eagles, M. and Erfle, S. (1989) 'Community Cohesion and Voter Turnout in English Parliamentary Constituencies', *British Journal of Political Science* 19: 115–25.

Economist (1980) 10 May.

—— (1990) 12 May.

Eldersveld, S. (1956) 'Experimental Propaganda Techniques and Voting Behavior', *American Political Science Review* 50: 154–65.

Everett, C. (1966) *Jeremy Bentham*, London: Weidenfeld & Nicolson.

Ferry, J. (1979) 'Rates and Elections', *Centre for Environmental Studies Review*, vol. 5.

Fitzmaurice, E. (1882) 'Areas of Local Government', in J. W. Probyn (ed.) *Local Government and Taxation*, London: Cobden Club Essays.

Fletcher, P. (1967) 'The Results Analysed', in J. Sharpe (ed.) *Voting in Cities*, London: Macmillan.

Fothergill, S. and Vincent, J. (1985) *The State of The Nation*, London: Pan.

Franklin, M. and Curtice, J. (1995) 'Britain: Opening Pandora's Box', in C. van de Eijk and M. Franklin (eds) *The European Electorate on the Eve of Union*, Ann Arbor: University of Michigan Press.

Fraser, D. (1976) *Urban Politics in Victorian England*, Leicester: Leicester University Press.

Freeman, E. (1888) 'The House of Lords and County Councils', *Fortnightly Review* 43.

Gallagher, M. (1991) 'Proportionality, Disproportionality and Electoral Systems', *Electoral Studies* 10 (1): 33–51.

Gallagher, M., Laver, M. and Mair, P. (1995) *Representative Government in Modern Europe*, New York: McGraw Hill.

Gallup (1988) Political Index 332, April.

—— (1989) Political Index 344, April.

Game, C. (1981) 'Local Elections', *Local Government Studies* 7 (2): 63–8.

—— (1991) 'Local Elections' in J. Stewart and C. Game (eds) *Local Democracy – Representation and Elections*, Belgrave Papers No. 1, London: Local Government Management Board.

Game, C., Leach, S. and Williams, G. (1993) *Councillor Recruitment and Turnover*, Luton: Local Government Management Board.

Gibson, J. (1988) 'Rate Increases and Local Elections: A Different Approach and a Different Conclusion', *Policy and Politics* 16 (3): 197–208.

—— (1992) 'Measuring Electoral Change: Look Before You Abandon Swing', *Political Science and Politics* 25 (2): 195–8.

Gibson, J. and Stewart, J. (1992) 'Poll Tax, Rates and Local Elections', *Political Studies* 40 (3): 516–31.

Goschen, G. J. (1872) *Reports and Speeches on Local Taxation*, London: Macmillan.

Greaves, T. (1982) *How to Fight Local Elections and Win*, Hebden Bridge: ALC Campaign Booklet No. 8, 3rd revised edition.

Green, G. (1972) 'National, City and Ward Components of Local Voting', *Policy and Politics* 1 (1): 45–54.

Gregory, R. (1969) 'Local Elections and the "Rule of Anticipated Reactions"', *Political Studies* 17: 31–47.

Grofman, B. and Lijphart, A. (eds) (1986) *Electoral Laws and their Political Consequences*, New York: Agathon.

Gunter, C., Rallings, C. and Thrasher, M. (1996a) 'Calculating Total Vote Where District Magnitude is Greater Than One', Plymouth: Local Government Chronicle Elections Centre, *mimeo*.

Gyford, J. (1985) *The Politics of Local Socialism*, London: Allen and Unwin.

Gyford, J. and James, M. (1983) *National Parties and Local Politics*, London: Allen and Unwin.

Gyford, J., Leach, S. and Game, C. (1989) *The Changing Politics of Local Government*, London: Unwin Hyman.

Hampton, W. (1970) *Democracy and Community*, Oxford: Oxford University Press.

Hansard (1888) *Parliamentary Proceedings*, 3rd series, volumes 324 and 326.

Hennock, E. P. (1973) *Fit and Proper Persons*, London: Edward Arnold.

Hill, D. (1967) 'Leeds', in J. Sharpe (ed.) *Voting in Cities*, London: Macmillan.

Hoffmann-Martinot, V., Rallings, C. and Thrasher, M. (1996) 'Comparing Local Electoral Turnout in Britain and France', *European Journal of Political Research* 30: 4.

Home Office (1994a) *Report of the Working Group on Electoral Registration*, London: Home Office.

—— (1994b) *Report of the Working Group on Absent Voting*, London: Home Office.
ICM (1994) Results of a Poll Conducted after the European Elections, London: ICM Research.
Inter-Parliamentary Union (1992) *Women and Political Power*, Reports and Documents No. 19, Geneva.
Jackson, J. (1994) 'Incumbency in the United States' in A. Somit *et al.*, *The Victorious Incumbent: A Threat to Democracy?*, Aldershot: Dartmouth.
Jackson, K. (1994) 'Stability and Renewal: Incumbency and Parliamentary Composition' in A. Somit *et al.*, *The Victorious Incumbent: A Threat to Democracy?*, Aldershot: Dartmouth.
Jacobson, G. (1992) *The Politics of Congressional Elections*, Boston, MA: Little, Brown and Co.
Johnston, R. (1986) 'The Neighbourhood Effect Revisited', *Environment and Planning* 4.
Jones, G. W. (1969) *Borough Politics*, London: Macmillan.
Jones, G.W. and Stewart, J. (1983) *The Case for Local Government*, London: Allen and Unwin.
Keith-Lucas, B. (1952) *The English Local Government Franchise*, Oxford: Basil Blackwell.
—— (1978) *A History of Local Government in the Twentieth Century*, London: Allen and Unwin.
Kelley, J. and McAllister, I. (1984) 'Ballot Paper Cues and the Vote in Australia and Britain: Alphabetic Voting, Sex and Title', *Public Opinion Quarterly* 48: 452–66.
Kirkpatrick, J. (1974) *Political Women*, New York: Basic Books.
Kramer, G. (1970) 'The Effects of Precinct-Level Canvassing on Voter Behavior', *Public Opinion Quarterly* 34 (4): 560–72.
Labour Party (1993) *Report of the National Executive Committee Working Party on Electoral Systems*, London: Labour Party.
Lakeman, E. (1974) *How Democracies Vote: A Study of Electoral Systems*, London: Faber.
Lansley, S., Goss, S. and Wolmar, C. (1989) *Councils in Conflict*, London: Macmillan.
Lasham, C. and Smith, G. (eds) (1992) *The Electoral Administrator's Handbook*, London: Shaw and Son.
Laver, M. and Schofield, N. (1990) *Multiparty Government: The Politics of Coalition in Europe*, Oxford: Oxford University Press.
Laver M., Rallings, C. and Thrasher, M. (1987) 'Coalition Theory and Local Government Coalition Payoffs in Britain', *British Journal of Political Science* 17: 501–9.
—— (forthcoming) 'Policy Payoffs in Local Government', *British Journal of Political Science*.
Leach, A. (1888) 'What the Local Government Bill Should Be', *Westminster Review* 129: 279–80.
Leach, S. and Game, C. (1989) *Co-operation and Conflict: Politics in the Hung Counties*, London: Common Voice Research Paper No. 1.
Leach, S. and Stewart, J. (1986) 'Hung County Councils', *New Society*, 4 April.
—— (1992) *The Politics of Hung Authorities*, London: Macmillan.
Lijphart, A. (1984) *Democracies: Patterns of Majoritarian and Consensus Government in Twenty-one Countries*, New Haven and London: Yale University Press.
Lijphart, A. and Grofman, B. (eds) (1986) *Choosing an Electoral System: Issues and Alternatives*, New York: Praeger.
Local Government Commission for England (1996) *Periodic Electoral Reviews*, London: HMSO.
Loosemore, J. and Hanby, V. (1971) 'The Theoretical Limits of Maximum Distortion: Some Analytic Expressions for Electoral Systems', *British Journal of Political Science* 1: 467–77.

Lucy, G. (1994) *Northern Ireland: Local Government Election Results, 1993*, Armagh: Ulster Society Publications.
Lynn, P. (1992) *Public Perceptions of Local Government: Its Finances and Services*, London: HMSO.
MacDonagh, O. (1977) *Early Victorian Government 1830–1870*, London: Weidenfeld & Nicolson.
McKie, D. (ed.) (1992) *The Election: A Voter's Guide*, London: Fourth Estate.
McLean, I. and Mortimore, R. (1992) 'Apportionment and the Boundary Commission for England', *Electoral Studies* 11: 293–309.
McLean, I. and Smith, J. (1995) 'The Poll Tax, The Electoral Register, and the 1991 Census', in D. Broughton, D. Denver, D. Farrell and C. Rallings (eds) *British Elections and Parties Yearbook 1994*, London: Frank Cass.
McLean, I., Heath, A. and Taylor, B. (1995) 'Were the 1994 Euro- and Local Elections in Britain really Second-Order?' Paper delivered at Elections, Parties and Public Opinion conference, London.
Mann, T. (1977) *Unsafe at Any Margin: Interpreting Congressional Elections*, Washington DC: American Enterprise Institute.
Market Research Society (1994) *The Opinion Polls and the 1992 General Election*, London: Market Research Society.
Masterson, R. and Masterson, E. (1980) 'The Scottish Community Elections: The Second Round', *Local Government Studies* 6: 63–82.
Maud Report on the Management of Local Government (1967) volume 3, *The Local Government Elector*, London: HMSO.
Mill, J. S. (1968) *Utilitarianism, Liberty and Representative Government*, London: Dent.
Miller, W. (1986) 'Local Electoral Behaviour' in Widdicombe Committee of Inquiry into the Conduct of Local Authority Business Research, volume 3, *The Local Government Elector*, London: HMSO.
Miller, W. (1988) *Irrelevant Elections?*, Oxford: Oxford University Press.
Miller, W., Clarke, H., Harrop, M., LeDuc, L. and Whiteley, P. (1990) *'How Voters Change: The 1987 British Election Campaign in Perspective'*, Oxford: Clarendon Press.
Minors, M. and Grenham, D. (1994) *London Borough Council Election Results 1994*, London: London Research Centre.
Muller-Rommel, F. and Pridham, G. (1991) (eds), *Small Parties in Western Europe*, London: Sage.
Municipal Corporations Commission (1835) Report of the Municipal Corporations Commission, *House of Commons Papers*, volume XXIII.
Newton, K. (1972) 'Turnout and Marginality in Local Elections', *British Journal of Political Science* 2: 251– 5.
—— (1976) *Second City Politics*, Oxford: Oxford University Press.
Norris, P. (1990) *British By-Elections*, Oxford: Clarendon Press.
Norris, P. and Lovenduski, J. (1994) *Political Recruitment*, Cambridge: Cambridge University Press.
O'Loughlin, J. (1981) 'The Neighbourhood Effect in Urban Voting Surfaces: A Cross National Analysis', in A. Burnett and P. Taylor (eds) *Political Studies from Spatial Perspectives*, New York: Wiles.
Parker, G. (1980) 'The Advantages of Incumbency in House Elections', *Legislative Studies Quarterly* 6: 219–34.
Parkes, J. (1835) 'Corporation Reform', *British and Foreign Review* 1: July–October.
Parry, G., Moyser, G. and Day, N. (1992) *Political Participation and Democracy in Britain*, Cambridge: Cambridge University Press.
Peardon, T. (1951) 'Bentham's Ideal Republic', *Canadian Journal of Economics and*

Political Science 17, 2: 19–51, reprinted in B. Parekh (ed.) *Jeremy Bentham: Ten Critical Essays*, London: Frank Cass, 1974.

Petrie, C. (1936) *Walter Long and his Times*, London: Hutchinson.

Pimlott, B. (1972) 'Does Local Party Organisation Matter?', *British Journal of Political Science* 2: 381–3.

—— (1973) 'Local Party Organisation, Turnout and Marginality', *British Journal of Political Science* 3: 252–5.

Pinto-Duschinsky, M. and Pinto-Duschinsky, S. (1987) *Voter Registration: Problems and Solutions*, London: Constitutional Reform Centre.

Powell, G. B. (1980) 'Voting Turnout in Thirty Democracies: Partisan, Legal and Socio-Economic Influences', in R. Rose (ed.) *Electoral Participation: A Comparative Analysis*, Beverly Hills: Sage.

Rae, D. (1971) *The Political Consequences of Electoral Laws*, New Haven and London: Yale University Press, 2nd edition.

Rallings, C. and Thrasher, M. (1985) *The 1985 County Council Election Results in England*, Plymouth: Centre for the Study of Local Elections, 2 volumes.

—— (1986a) 'Parties Divided on Hung Councils', *Local Government Chronicle* 6185: 12–13.

—— (1986b) *The 1986 Metropolitan Borough Council Election Results*, Plymouth: Centre for the Study of Local Elections.

—— (1986c) 'Assessing the Electoral Performance of the Alliance', *Local Government Studies* 12: 31–6.

—— (1988 and annually) *Local Elections Handbook*, Plymouth: Local Government Chronicle Elections Centre.

—— (1989) 'Richmond Panicked Ashdown into Offering Needless Truce', *Guardian*, 11 March.

—— (1990) 'Turnout in Local Elections: An Aggregate Analysis with Electoral and Contextual Data', *Electoral Studies* 9: 79–90.

—— (1991a) 'Community Charge and the 1990 Local Elections', *Parliamentary Affairs* 44 (2): 172–84.

—— (1991b) *Electoral Reform for Local Government*, London: Electoral Reform Society.

—— (1992a) 'The Electoral Impact of the Poll Tax: Evidence from the 1990 Local Elections in England and Wales', in I. Crewe, P. Norris, D. Denver and D. Broughton (eds) *British Elections and Parties Yearbook 1991*, Hemel Hempstead: Harvester Wheatsheaf.

—— (1992b) 'The Impact of Local Electoral Systems', *Local Government Studies* 18 (2): 1–8.

—— (1993a) 'Exploring Uniformity and Variability in Local Electoral Outcomes', *Electoral Studies* 12 (4): 366–84.

—— (1993b) 'Opinion Polling and the Aftermath of the 1992 General Election', *Contemporary Record* 7 (1): 187–97.

—— (eds) (1993c) *Local Elections in Britain: A Statistical Digest*, Plymouth: Local Government Chronicle Elections Centre.

—— (1994) *Explaining Election Turnout: A Secondary Analysis of Local Election Statistics*, London: HMSO.

—— (1995a) *The Media Guide to the New Parliamentary Constituencies*, Plymouth: Local Government Chronicle Elections Centre.

—— (1995b) 'Explaining the Local Electoral Performance of the Liberal Democrats', Paper presented to Political Studies Association conference, York.

—— (1996a) 'Forecasting Vote and Seat Shares in Local Elections' in D. Farrell, D. Broughton, D. Denver and J. Fisher (eds) *British Elections and Parties Yearbook 1996*, Ilford: Cass.

—— (1996b) 'Patterns of Voting Choice in Multimember Seats', Paper delivered at American Political Science Association conference, San Francisco.

Rallings, C., Temple, M. and Thrasher, M. (1994) *Community Identity and Participation in Local Democracy*, London: Commission for Local Democracy.

—— (1995) 'Coalitions in Britain: Administrative Formation in Hung Councils', *Policy and Politics* 23 (3): 223–32.

Rallings, C., Thrasher, M. and Downe, J. (1996) *Enhancing Local Electoral Turnout*, York: Joseph Rowntree Foundation.

Rallings, C., Thrasher, M. and Temple, M. (1988) 'Governing With A Fragile Balance of Power', *Local Government Chronicle* 6334: 18–19.

Ranney, A. (1962) 'The Utility and Limitations of Aggregate Data in the Study of Electoral Behavior', in A. Ranney (ed.) *Essays on the Behavioral Study of Politics*, Urbana: University of Illinois Press.

Rasmussen, J. (1983) 'The Electoral Costs of Being a Woman in the 1979 British General Election', *Comparative Politics* 15: 462–75.

Rathbone, W., Pell, A. and Montague, F. C. (eds) (1885) *Local Administration*, London: Sonnenschien.

Redcliffe-Maud, J. and Wood, B. (1974) *English Local Government Reformed*, London: Oxford University Press.

Redlich, J. and Hirst, F. W. (1970) *The History of Local Government in England*, London, Macmillan, 2nd edition.

Reed, S. (1994) 'The Incumbency Advantage in Japan', in A. Somit *et al.*, *The Victorious Incumbent: A Threat to Democracy?*, Aldershot: Dartmouth.

Reif, K. (ed.) (1985) *Ten European Elections*, Aldershot: Gower.

Rennard, C. (1988) *Winning Local Elections*, Hebden Bridge: ALDC.

Representation of the People Act (1918) 7 & 8 Geo. 5 c.64.

—— (1928) 18 & 19 Geo. 5 c.12.

Rhodes, E. (1938) 'Voting at Municipal Elections', *Political Quarterly* 9 (2): 271–80.

Roebuck, J. A. (1835) 'Municipal Corporation Reform', *The London Review* 1 (1) April.

Rose, R. (1991) 'The Ups and Downs of Elections, or Look Before You Swing', *Political Science and Politics* 24 (1): 29–33.

Rossiter, D., Johnston, R. and Pattie, C. (1996) 'New Boundaries, Old Inequalities: the Evolution and Partisan Impact of the Celtic Preference in British Redistricting' in I. Hampshire-Monk and J. Stanyer (eds) *Contemporary Political Studies 1996*, Exeter: Political Studies Association.

Rowley, G. (1971) 'The Greater London Council Elections of 1964 and 1967: A Study in Electoral Geography', *Transactions, Institute of British Geographers* 53: 117–32.

Schofield, M. (1977) 'The "Nationalisation" of Local Politics', *New Society*, 28 April.

Self, P. and 'Administrator' (1947) 'Local Government and the Community', *Fabian Quarterly* 53, March: 15–22.

Seymour, C. (1970) *Electoral Reform in England and Wales*, Newton Abbot: David and Charles Reprints.

Sharpe, J. (ed.) (1967) *Voting in Cities*, London: Macmillan.

Spiers, M. and Le Lohé, M. (1964) 'Pakistanis in the Bradford Municipal Election of 1963', *Political Studies* 12.

Stanyer, J. (1976) *Understanding Local Government*, London: Fontana.

Steed, M. (1979) 'The Liberal Party', in H. Drucker (ed.) *Multi-Party Britain*, London: Macmillan.

Studlar, D. and Welch, S. (1987) 'Understanding the Iron Law of Andrarchy: Effects of Candidate Gender on Voting in Scotland', *Comparative Political Studies* 20: 174–91.

—— (1988) 'The Effects of Candidate Gender on Voting for Local Office in England', *British Journal of Political Science* 18: 271–81.

—— (1991) 'Does District Magnitude Matter? Women Candidates in London Local Elections', *Western Political Quarterly* 44 (2): 457–66.

—— (1993) 'A Giant Step For Womankind?' in D. Denver, P. Norris, D. Broughton and C. Rallings (eds) *British Elections and Parties Yearbook 1993*, London: Harvester Wheatsheaf.

Swaddle, K. and Heath, A. (1989) 'Official and Reported Turnout in the British General Election of 1987', *British Journal of Political Science* 19: 537–71.

Taagepera, R. and Shugart, M. (1989) *Seats and Votes: The Effects and Determinants of Electoral Systems*, New Haven and London: Yale University Press.

Taylor, A. (1973) 'Journey Time, Perceived Distance, and Electoral Turnout: Victoria Ward, Swansea', *Area* 5: 59–63.

Taylor, P. and Johnston, R. (1979) *Geography of Elections*, Harmondsworth: Penguin.

Temple, M. (1993) 'Devon County Council: a Case Study of a Hung Council', *Public Administration* 71 (4): 507–33.

—— (1995) 'The relevance of ideological position and policy closeness to English local coalition pay-offs', *Local Government Studies* 21 (1): 65–81.

Thompson, P. (1967) *Socialists, Liberals and Labour: The Struggle for London 1885–1924*, London: Routledge & Kegan Paul.

Todd, J. and Dodd, P. (1982) *The Electoral Registration Process in the UK*, OPCS, Social Survey Division, SS1711, London: HMSO.

Todd, J. and Eldridge, J. (1987) *Improving Electoral Registration*, London: HMSO.

Toulmin-Smith, J. (1851) *Local Self-Government and Centralisation*, London: Chapman.

Upton, G. and Brook, D. (1974) 'The Importance of Positional Voting Bias in British Elections', *Political Studies* 22: 178–90.

Verba, S. and Nie, N. (1972) *Participation in America: Political Democracy and Social Equality*, New York: Harper & Row.

Wadsworth, J. and Morley, D. (1989) 'Compiling a Register for the Poll Tax', *Public Finance and Accountancy*, 24 February.

Wahlberg, M., Taylor, K. and Geddes, M. (1995) *Enhancing Local Democracy*, London: Local Government Management Board.

Wallace, W. (1983) 'Survival and Revival' in V. Bogdanor (ed.) *Liberal Party Politics*, Oxford: Oxford University Press.

Waller, R. (1980) 'The 1979 Local and General Elections in England and Wales', *Political Studies* 28 (3): 443–50.

Warde, A., Savage, M., Longhurst, B. and Martin, A. (1988) 'Class, Consumption and Voting: An Ecological Analysis of Wards and Towns in the 1980 Local Elections in England', *Political Geography Quarterly* 7 (1): 339–51.

Webb, S. and Webb, B. (1963) *English Local Government*, London: Cass, 11 volumes.

Welch, S. and Studlar, D. (1986) 'British Public Opinion toward Women in Politics: a Comparative Perspective', *Western Political Quarterly* 39: 138–52.

—— (1988) 'The Effects of Candidate Gender on Voting for Local Office in England', *British Journal of Political Science* 18: 273–86.

—— (1990) 'Multi-Member Districts and the Representation of Women: Evidence from Britain and the United States', *Journal of Politics* 52 (2): 391–412.

Widdicombe Committee of Inquiry into the Conduct of Local Authority Business (1986a) *Report of the Committee of Inquiry*, London: HMSO.

—— (1986b) Research volume II, *The Local Government Councillor*, London: HMSO.

—— (1986c) Research volume III, *The Local Government Elector*, London: HMSO.

Wolfinger, R. and Rosenstone, S. (1980) *Who Votes?*, New Haven: Yale University Press.

Young, K. (1975) *Local Politics and the Rise of Party*, Leicester: Leicester University Press.

Index